Yochanan's Gamble

University of Nebraska Press
Lincoln

YOCHANAN'S GAMBLE

Judaism's Pragmatic Approach to Life

RABBI MARC KATZ

The Jewish Publication Society
Philadelphia

© 2024 by Rabbi Marc Katz

All rights reserved. Published by the University of Nebraska Press as a Jewish Publication Society book.

Library of Congress Cataloging-in-Publication Data
Names: Katz, Marc, author.
Title: Yochanan's gamble: Judaism's
pragmatic approach to life / Marc Katz.
Description: Lincoln: University of Nebraska Press; Philadelphia: The Jewish Publication Society, [2024] | Includes bibliographical references and index.
Identifiers: LCCN 2024011351
ISBN 9780827615564 (paperback)
ISBN 9780827619272 (pdf)
ISBN 9780827619265 (epub)
Subjects: LCSH: Rabbis—Office. | Rabbinical literature—Criticism and interpretation. | Jewish ethics. | Jewish way of life. | BISAC: RELIGION / Judaism / Rituals & Practice | RELIGION / Ethics
Classification: LCC BM652 .K38 2024 |
DDC 296.6/1—dc23/eng/20240805
LC record available at https://lccn.loc.gov/2024011351

Designed and set in Adobe Text Pro by L. Welch.

To Jack, whose keen observations
were the catalyst for this book.

CONTENTS

Acknowledgments		ix
Preface		xi
Prologue: Yochanan's Gamble		1
1. Recalibrating Truth		13
2. Upholding Compromise		35
3. Not Leading Too Far Out in Front		53
4. Abiding by the Wisdom of the Masses		75
5. Keeping the Peace with Neighbors		91
6. Avoiding Infighting		111
7. Employing Tools to Transform Law		127
8. Sinning for the Greater Good		153
9. Hedging Against the Misuse of Pragmatism		171
Final Thoughts: Yochanan's Uncertainty		191
Notes		195
Bibliography		233
Subjects Index		237
Biblical Sources Index		241

ACKNOWLEDGMENTS

This book took shape over the course of a many-year process but began in a New York City coffee shop with Rabbi Barry Schwartz, then director of The Jewish Publication Society (JPS), who kindly met with me after the publishing house of my first book was sold. I had noticed on the JPS website that he was looking for someone to write a book on "Judaism and integrity," and asked him for the opportunity to try it. Through patience and multiple book proposals he stayed with me, even after I admitted that I could not adequately define integrity, and he helped me shift my approach toward *Yochanan's Gamble*.

Early conversations with Rabbis Joe Schwartz, Leon Morris, and Neil Hirsch proved invaluable and set me off on the right course. Later in the process, I gained valuable feedback from Rabbi Sam Lebens. A special thanks go to my father-in-law, Jack Nelson, to whom this book is dedicated. Jack was the first to hear my idea and remind me of Rabban Yochanan ben Zakkai's story. The book blossomed from there.

Thanks go to Joy Weinberg, managing editor of JPS, whose careful reading and line-by-line editing turned my amalgam of loosely connected observations about the Rabbinic world into a cohesive whole. Gratitude also goes to Dr. Elias Sacks, whose attention to detail and endnote suggestions benefited the work immensely. I also want to thank the University of Nebraska Press team for bringing this book to fruition.

I owe everything I know about Talmud to my amazing teachers at the Hebrew Union College–Jewish Institute of Religion. These include Drs. Alyssa Gray, Michael Chernick, Aaron Panken, and Norman Cohen. I also feel such gratitude for the time I got to spend learning from Rabbi David Ellenson, my thesis advisor, with whom I first studied and wrote about the concept of *lo titgodedu*. In my last year of rabbinical school I audited a class on the academic study of Talmud with Dr. Jeffrey Rubinstein. One after-class conversation helped me understand that my approach to Talmud need not fall neatly into either a religious or academic framework. This book is my attempt to marry the two.

I have been blessed to work with two amazing congregations in my career: Congregation Beth Elohim in Brooklyn, New York, and Temple Ner Tamid in Bloomfield, New Jersey. The beginning ideas of this book began to take shape in Brooklyn but found their real footing in Jersey. My "Lunch with the Rabbi" class at Temple Ner Tamid allowed me to try out many of the ideas presented here. I deeply thank every one of the class participants.

My parents, Jerry and Leslie Katz, were my first teachers, and they instilled in me a real sense of practical ethics as I watched them navigate the world. My hope is that I can carry it forward with my own children, Lev and Amalia, who have already shown they have both the head and the heart to be moral exemplars in their own right.

Every day I feel lucky to be married to Ayelet Nelson. Understanding how important this book is to me, she has been a constant source of support and input along the way. Like the Rabbis, she is masterful at navigating competing needs, desires, and obligations, and arriving at exemplary balance in all she does.

PREFACE

We live in an age of stridency. Instead of valuing disagreement and seeking subtle points of connection with others, we often stand firm in our resolve, vilifying our disputants and believing we alone occupy the moral high ground. Since society values those with the most conviction, we aim to shout the loudest. Instead of seeing the world as complex, with competing values and needed concessions, we simplify and "neaten" it. Absolutist, inviolable moral certainty makes us largely unable to view the world through any eyes but our own.

Yet as Jews entrusted to heal our fragmented society, we need to model other ways of being in the world. We can lift up countervailing virtues that balance our assuredness: humility, self-reflection, openness to ideas, willingness to compromise. We can stretch ourselves to see another person's conflicting view as possessing integrity—integrity like our own. We can then reconsider deeply held opinions in this light.

We can also build up our appreciation for nuance. Ethical choices are rarely simple calculations between right and wrong. A host of pragmatic concerns heighten the difficulties of moral decision-making. Which course of action is more likely to succeed? Which gets me to a desired outcome faster? What will preserve my social capital so I can do more good in the future? What choice might adversely affect other people? If I have to prioritize one value over another, which value matters more and why? How, you might ask, can we possibly accomplish all this? Thankfully, I believe we have just the right paragons to guide us.

The Rabbis: Our Pragmatic Paragons

Two thousand years ago, Judaism made a turn toward pragmatism. By its simplest definition, pragmatism means doing what works. As the quip goes, the optimist says the glass is half full, the pessimist says it is half empty, and the pragmatist says, "Will it quench my thirst?" The pragmatist has an objective and a will to engage with the real world to achieve it.

In the years before 70 CE, our ancestors were living in their own fragmented world. Many Jews resided in Judea under Roman rule. Some were comfortable with this, especially the Sadducees, the priestly class that maintained good relations with the empire. Others were strongly opposed to Roman hegemony. Jewish groups of religious zealots roamed the streets, attempting to foment rebellion and murdering any Jews who disagreed with them. A splinter group called the Essenes, who viewed the reigning priesthood as illegitimate, abandoned society altogether, fleeing to the desert to observe their own practices by themselves.[1] Yet, amid a world of moral absolutism and stridency, a small group of leaders known as the "Rabbis" forged a new path.

Understanding the Rabbis

The Rabbis were a group of sages who lived and wrote in the first five centuries CE. Especially after the destruction of the Second Temple in Jerusalem in 70 CE, these thinkers reinvented Judaism, reimagining its rituals and practices once Temple sacrifice was no longer possible. Much of what we take for granted in Jewish living today came from them, from the schedule and liturgy of prayer to how to fast on Yom Kippur, from the lighting of candles on Hanukkah to the definition of what constitutes "work" on Shabbat. Though scholars believe they were in fact a minority religious voice at their time, their legacy has been the single greatest factor in shaping and preserving the Jewish people after the Temple's destruction till today.[2]

Rabbis who lived in the decades before the Temple's destruction, until the start of the third century, are known as *tanaaim*. Those who lived after the year 200 until around the year 500 are called *amoraim*. Some of these sages lived in Palestine and others in Babylonia, where an enclave of Jews had been flourishing after having been exiled there after the first Temple's destruction in 586 BCE.

Each era and every geographic locale had its own character and outlook. Tanaaim tended to study in disciple circles; later Amoraim, especially in Babylonia, learned in academies.[3] Palestinian Rabbis were immersed in Roman culture and had to deal with a nascent and growing Christian movement, while Babylonian Rabbis in the Amoraic era were products of the Sasanian Persian culture around them. Because of these cultural factors, along with many others, scholars can trace philosophical differences between the different schools. Yale professor Christine Hayes, for example, sees Rabbis from Palestine as more willing to entertain legal fictions in their writings and to ignore facts in pursuit of more fanciful judgment, as compared to Babylonian Rabbis, who were much more realistic in their outlook and conservative in their methodology.[4]

Despite their differences, the Rabbis shared certain key beliefs. All held that the written Torah was not God's only source of revelation. According to tradition, God also gave an oral Torah on top of Mount Sinai to Moses, who passed it down to Aaron, and so on and so on, until this oral Torah was bequeathed to the Rabbis in their day.[5] As a result, the Rabbis understood their work in writing law was directly tied to a chain of tradition dating back to the days after the Exodus from Egypt. For them revelation was an unfolding process. As new generations arose with new insights, their opinions became part of the corpus of oral Torah.

Today we study this oral Torah through the works of these Rabbis. At the turn of the third century Judah the Prince compiled the Mishnah, a collection of the oral laws, philosophy, and stories of these early Rabbis that categorized their teachings and preserved both majority and minority opinions. Later, two other seminal works would be produced from discussions rooted in the Mishnah: the Jerusalem Talmud, compiled in the fourth century, and the Babylonian Talmud, assembled in the fifth and sixth centuries.

Contemporaneous with these major collections was a body of work called Midrash. This literature aimed to derive law (halakhah) and legend/lore (*aggadah*) from the nuances of the biblical text, deriving from a line, a word, or even a letter "piles and piles of law."[6] Regardless of the form—line-by-line commentaries, sermons, even complete rewritings of the source material—midrashic teachings were also seen as an authentic representations of God's true intent at Sinai. In essence, God gave the Torah, but it becomes the Rabbis' task to make the text speak to them in their day.

The Rabbis' Pragmatic Approach to Morality

Although there are philosophies in Rabbinic literature, the tanaaim and amoraim were not philosophers as we have come to define them. Philosophers tend to live in the world of big ideas and then apply those precepts to the world, whereas the Rabbis generally began with the trials and troubles in the world and found doctrines to guide them through it. Chaim Saiman, chair of Jewish Law at Villanova University, explains:

> For all the focus on themes of justice, holiness, and faith, nowhere in the Talmud's two million words is there a sustained discussion on topics such as "What is Justice?" or "What is holiness" or "What is faith?" In fact, the Talmud seems preternaturally suspicious of such philosophical abstractions. Moreover, generally foreign to the talmudic mind are such central legal, political, and scientific categories as logic, rhetoric, ethics, philosophy, theory, universalism, particularism, and even theology. . . . What is beauty? What is truth? What is the best

political ordering? The Talmud anchors such macro questions in the context of a specific mitzvah and its obligations.[7]

In large part, the Rabbis turned toward practical applications of law because they themselves were of this world. Some were blacksmiths (e.g., Rabbi Joshua), others were tanners (e.g., Rabbi Yosi). Some made sandals (Rabbi Yochanan the shoemaker) and others were shepherds (Rabbi Akiva). Some ran businesses (Rabbi Chiya b. Yosef) and others owned property (Rav Huna). Many were communal leaders. Almost all of them married and sought to fulfill the command to have children.[8] Almost all paid taxes. As they determined what acts were obligatory, allowed, disfavored, or prohibited, they knew their legislation would likely affect themselves, if not now then someday. Acts of lawmaking had to be tempered by the real-world implications of the legislation.

Perhaps the most important of these real-world pressures was living under foreign rule. In the century after the Temple's destruction, the Jews realized: whenever the Jewish community rebelled against foreign rulers in the past, the community had been decimated.[9] Thus, Judaism's survival necessitated pragmatic acquiescence and political acumen. Both the Palestinian and Babylonian Jewish leaders made numerous concessions aimed at helping the Jews live peacefully with their neighbors, including, as we will see, accepting certain idolatry in their midst, sometimes obeying a Roman or Persian law even when it disagreed with Jewish law, and sometimes amending their own laws proactively to be in tune with the laws or practices where they lived.

The Rabbis came to view moral decision-making as an imperfect dance. Ethical decisions were to be tempered by practical constraints. Law would not only embody the Rabbinic understanding of God's truth, but at times yield to the people's needs and thereby encourage the masses to follow it. In hopes of making the wisest decision at any given moment, the Rabbis discerned truth in the workings of the wider world and then weighed competing values, relationships, and outcomes. Sometimes they would ignore or change a law. Oftentimes they risked an uncertain approach called for in the moment. At times they stretched the biblical text to its limit, interpreting it to say nearly the opposite of its seemingly intended meaning.

In effect, our ancestors had to be pragmatic in difficult times, and their creative approach to law is one of the reasons we can look to them today as exemplars of moral discourse. As they worked imaginatively at solving the hardest moral questions of their day, they became spiritual and moral guides for us in adapting innovatively to our own labyrinthine world.

Understanding This Book

Few popular works have been devoted to the pragmatic, practical spirit of the Rabbis.[10] Those that are tend to give more weight to the stories of the Talmud, and for good reason: these tales are more accessible and inviting. Nonetheless, narrative alone falls short in capturing the many nuances of Rabbinic thought. In order to see a fuller picture of the Rabbis' thinking, one needs to marry narrative with law.

This volume presents a novel framework for understanding Rabbinic teachings. It examines our forebears' embrace of pragmatism in their lawmaking as well as their stories. It uplifts pragmatism as *the* creative Rabbinic strategy that saved Judaism from Emperor Vespasian's siege of Jerusalem. It brings to life episodes in which the Rabbis privileged compromise and subtlety over intransigence and stridency. It models not only what these key Jewish legalists thought but *how* they thought—how they endeavored to apply halakhah to be faithful both to their received tradition and to the people and circumstances before them. Ultimately it recasts the pragmatic strain of Rabbinic thought as an authentic Jewish strategy we too can employ to add nuance to our moral decision-making.

The prologue relates the central framing story of the volume: Rabban Yochanan ben Zakkai's meeting with the soon-to-be Roman Emperor Vespasian, where he makes one of the most controversial requests in Jewish history. Rather than beg Vespasian to spare Jerusalem, Yochanan asks for a plot of land in the town of Yavne to rebuild Judaism after the Roman legions destroy the Temple.

After this foundation, the book examines thematic permutations of Yochanan's pragmatic spirit. Chapter 1 explores the unique, intermittently pragmatic way in which the Rabbis define truth. Chapter 2 drills down on Rabbinic compromises—when they backtrack, when they flip positions, when they find middle ground—as well as the Rabbis' nuanced view of integrity.

The next two chapters examine how the Rabbis lead while listening to the population around them. In chapter 3 we see the Rabbis take care not to lead too far in front of the people, aware that if they ask too much, they may lose peoples' trust and patience. Chapter 4 looks at how the Rabbis gain knowledge of the people. By studying the behavior of the *amei haaretz* (unlearned populous), through listening to rumors, and heeding folk sayings, the Rabbis can tailor their messages to their audience more sensitively and effectively. Chapters 5 and 6 investigate the extremes to which the Rabbis will go to avoid conflict. In chapter 5 we watch the Rabbis bend the law to keep peace with foreign sovereigns and kingdoms; in chapter 6 we follow their legal innovations aimed at avoiding infighting within the Jewish community. Chapter 7 analyzes tools the Rabbis employ to enact change: reapproaching scripture, playing with logic, opting for loopholes. Chapters 8 and 9 are foils of one another. In chapter 8 the Rabbinic idea of "sins for the sake of heaven" grounds a survey of times when the Rabbis permit murder and torture for pragmatic purposes—a presumably greater good. Chapter 9 is a moderating force for many previously examined innovations. Recognizing that pragmatic solutions can also be misused, the Rabbis create certain hedges around their own pragmatic thinking. For example, even if a law mandates nominal action to assist someone else, we should strive to do "what is right and good" (Deut. 6:18), which may mean going above and beyond what the law requires. "Final Thoughts" returns to Rabban Yochanan ben Zakkai on his deathbed, asking an important question: How can we ever know whether our own pragmatic "gambles" are right?

Readers who wish to use *Yochanan's Gamble* to teach in both informal and classroom settings will benefit from downloading the volume's complementary study and discussion guide at https://jps.org/study-guides/. Questions grounded in the important texts and ideas in each chapter are designed to deepen readers' engagement with the material and help them think about how the ancient themes explored in these pages inform their lives.

Disclaimers

I must give disclaimers. As a rabbi I read the Talmud with a religious, not academic mindset. A university scholar covering this material might highlight the significant disagreements between early scholars (*Tannaim*) and later scholars (*Amoraim*) or between Rabbis living in Palestine under Roman rule and those in Sasanian Persia. They might parse out what stories in this volume are true and which are myths. I rarely do. To my way of thinking, whether an anecdote happened as the Rabbis say it did or is a fabrication is not the salient point, because either way, Jews and Judaism look the way they do now because Jews have been informed, shaped, and guided by truths in the Talmud as they understand them. The Talmud's stories and laws "work" for us whether or not they are true.

Whenever I mention that a given understanding is according to halakhah or Jewish law, I mean it as "traditional" or "classical" Jewish law, understood as the law in the Shulkan Aruch, the widely accepted Jewish law code from the sixteenth century to which almost all discussions of law turn. In the text whenever I discuss an issue using my Reform approach, I indicate this specifically.

Additionally, when I say "the Talmud" I mean the Babylonian Talmud, which stands apart as the emblematic text of the Rabbinic period. When I cite other Rabbinic works like the Jerusalem Talmud or collections of Midrash, I either cite them by name or refer broadly to them as "Rabbinic texts," with needed clarifications given in the notes. There may well be parallels, or slight variations, in other Rabbinic works that are not cited.

In making my case for Rabbinic pragmatism, I naturally choose examples from the Rabbinic literature that bolster my view. At the same time, knowledgeable readers may be able to point to counterexamples—Rabbinic literature is too vast and varied for this not to be so. I try to report on contradictions and tensions when I see them, most often in the notes.

In the final analysis, this book presents my conclusions after having engaged in a decades-long process of studying these texts, living with them, and allowing certain key ideas to rise to the top amid the noise. You may do the same and come to your own conclusion about the ethos of the Talmud. As you read this book, I invite your critique.

To me, even harsh critiques can be compliments. I have always been struck by the scene in the Israeli film *Footnote* when Eliezer, an older scholar of Rabbinics, chooses to take aim at his son Uziel's style of popular scholarship. In an interview about the different approaches father and son have to Jewish text, Eliezer proclaims:

> Say we both deal with potsherds. Yes? Broken pottery? One of us examines these potsherds, cleans them meticulously, catalogs them, measures them scientifically and precisely, tries to decipher which period they are from, and who made them. And if he succeeds, he has done his work properly, and it has scientific value for generations. The other looks at the potsherds for a few seconds, sees they are more or less the same color, and immediately makes a pot out of them. The potsherds may be from different periods, they may not exactly match, main

thing is, he has a pot! The pot is very nice, very attractive, but it has nothing to do with scientific truth. It is an empty vessel. An illusion. A tower with no foundation. There is no pot! That is the point! It is fiction.[11]

Though Eliezer tries to minimize his son's scholarship, I have never viewed his critique as that biting. When Eliezer calls his son's "pot" fiction, he may be critiquing him in the academic sense, but to at least this religious Jew it is a compliment. To my way of thinking, our goal as Jews is not to catalog shards of unusable pottery, relegating them to cabinets with the tags still on. Our task is to use them, albeit imperfectly, in our quest to create a productive and effective story for living our lives today. We may choose to emphasize some details over others. Like all narratives, there may be holes. But in the collective fiction that is Jewish memory, Jewish texts—and hopefully this book—will help you grow.

Great care was taken in choosing the title: *Yochanan's Gamble: Judaism's Pragmatic Approach to Life*. One can of course read it as an overstatement. As a three-thousand-year-old tradition, Judaism has many approaches to life. The philosophy of the biblical prophets differs radically from the worldview found in the book of Ecclesiastes which looks far different from that of the mystics and Kabbalists. Even the Talmud contains minority and majority opinions that feel absolutist and idealistic, anything but pragmatic. Yet it is not my intention to claim that Judaism's approach to life is inherently pragmatic. Rather, the title is meant to convey that Yochanan's gamble gave birth to Judaism's pragmatic strand and is one particularly useful way to help us walk through this world.

Leaps of Faith

The American pragmatist William James famously wrote in his book *The Will to Believe*: "Moral questions immediately present themselves as questions whose solution cannot wait for sensible proof. A moral question is a question not of what sensibly exists, but of what is good, or would be good if it did exist."¹² In a way, James's observation is the essence of this book. The world does not always afford us the luxury to wait until we know that a certain moral path is correct in some ultimate sense. We must act, doing what we can with the information we have at hand. Moral living inevitably involves taking leaps of faith.

This book is filled with Rabbinic personalities who took such leaps and now provide a model for how we can act similarly in our lives. My hope is that when you face similar choices, you will recall the ideas in this book and know you are in good company. Judaism was forged through a series of pragmatic risks. Some worked, others did not, but all have something to teach us. We begin with the birth of Rabbinic pragmatism forged by the revolutionary character of Rabban Yochanan ben Zakkai.

Notes on Sources, Language, and Style

Unless otherwise noted, all biblical references are from the Revised Jewish Publication Society translation of the TANAKH, perhaps better known as THE JPS TANAKH: Gender-Sensitive Edition. Many of the Rabbinic texts are available for public use on Sefaria.org. The far majority of Rabbinic texts are taken from the Koren edition of the Babylonian Talmud, referenced in each case.

This volume adheres to the JPS Style Guide for all words that are not proper names. For names, familiar transliterations are often used to make the text as accessible as possible to all readers, even when these transliterations do not follow JPS style.

Yochanan's Gamble

Prologue

Yochanan's Gamble

The year is 70 CE. Jerusalem and its inhabitants find themselves surrounded by a Roman army ready to raze both the city and its holiest site, the Second Temple. For years the Romans have been struggling against a Jewish rebellion. Yet, in spite of Rome's decorated army, those dwelling within Jerusalem's walls are certain they have the upper hand. The walls are secure. Their hilltop positions in the Jerusalem mountains makes defense relatively easy. As long as they have food, they can outlast any foe.

Knowing that ample supplies will mean a prolonged engagement, a group of zealots burn the food stores. Now the people will be hungry. They will have to open the gates and ignite the simmering war.

The Talmud is full of heart-wrenching accounts of the aftermath of these zealots' decisions. In one story a wealthy maiden named Marta bat Baitos sends her servant out to buy a particular food. He leaves to do her bidding, only to return quickly with the news that the requested item is gone. She sends him out with a new item to buy and he fails again. As this continues for many rounds, her increasing hunger leads her to abandon refined requests for anything he might find and, eventually, to venture out barefoot into the chaos on her own. Seeing the filth caused by the mayhem around her she dies of shame. In one tradition she empties her pockets of her gold and silver, proclaiming in defeat, "Why do I need this [anymore]?"[1]

It is against this backdrop that we meet Rabban Yochanan Ben Zakai, one of the key leaders of the Rabbis. Witnessing the chaos around him, Yochanan sends a message to his nephew Abba Sikkara, the leader of the zealots. In a secret meeting Yochanan implores him to stop the uprising. Abba Sikkara confides that he too is ready to end the struggle, but if he says anything negative toward his fellow zealots, his minions will murder him.

Realizing he cannot change things in Jerusalem, Yochanan asks Abba Sikkara how he might escape the city. Maybe, if he is able to break free from the siege, he can achieve at least a modicum of salvation (*hatzalah perutah*), extracting some good out of the impending disaster. Knowing that no one is allowed in or out of the city unless they are burying a loved one, his nephew tells him to fake his death. If he is lucky, this will allow him to pass through the gates unhindered. Then he can find freedom.

Yochanan pretends to grow sick and die. Gathering around him, his students carry his funeral bier to the edge of the city, asking the guards at the gate to let them leave to bury their teacher. But the sentries can sense that the students are hiding something. They demand proof that Yochanan is dead. To be certain of it, they propose piercing his casket or throwing it down a ravine. Yochanan is in danger.

His disciples respond that desecrating his corpse will only look bad in the eyes of the Roman legions beyond the gates. The argument works, and they are allowed to pass.

Clearing the border, Yochanan exits the casket and goes in search of Vespasian, the commanding Roman general. When he finally meets the enemy leader, Yochanan looks him in the face and says, "Greetings to you, King." Vespasian is confused. Why would Yochanan promote him to the rank of Caesar when the rabbi knows full well that at the time, Vitellius is the sitting emperor?

Yochanan responds with a prophecy. Recalling a passage from the book of Isaiah that the Temple will only fall by the hands of a king, Yochanan tells Vespasian that for the prophecy to come true, Vespasian, who is leading the siege against the city, must be promoted to emperor.[2] A great city like Jerusalem would never be delivered into the hands of a simple general, skilled or not. Vespasian will need to assume the throne before he can be successful. Vespasian listens, intrigued. If there is a chance Yochanan may be correct, he is worth engaging further.

Sensing that Yochanan will ask him to spare the city of Jerusalem, Vespasian draws an analogy. "Imagine there is a barrel of honey with a venomous snake coiled around it. Would one destroy the barrel in order to kill the snake?" Yochanan understands the parallel. Because the zealots have gotten too powerful and obstinate, the general is saying, both the city and the Temple need to be sacrificed, like the proverbial barrel, to root out the insurrection within. Yochanan chooses to remain silent. He knows his audience with Vespasian is tenuous. Should he push too hard, he might lose the trust he has built.

The Talmud takes a break from the story to note that later Rabbis will condemn Yochanan for not arguing with Vespasian in that moment. They quote a verse from Isaiah that implies that despite all of his Torah learning, Yochanan's decision not to advocate for his people made his knowledge "nonsense" and his "[wisdom] turned back."[3] Had Yochanan raised his moral voice, he might have convinced Vespasian to spare the city. "He should have said we take tongs, remove the snake, and kill it, and in this way we leave the barrel intact," meaning there is an imagined path where Vespasian can kill the rebels without completely leveling the city.[4]

Well, no sooner does Vespasian finish speaking than he learns Emperor Vitellius has died and Vespasian needs to leave immediately for Rome for his own coronation. Thankful and impressed with Yochanan's wisdom and foresight, he offers his new friend the opportunity to ask him for a favor.

Immediately the rabbi responds with three requests. First, he asks that Vespasian spare the town of Yavneh—a small settlement about 20 kilometers south of Jaffe and around 7 kilometers inland—and give him control of it. As Yochanan probably knows, it is being used to house a Roman garrison; thus it will be easy for Vespasian to hand it over.[5]

Second, he asks that the family of Rabban Gamliel be spared.

Finally he asks for Rabbi Tzadok's life. The aesthetic and wonder worker rabbi is currently undergoing a fast, credited with undermining Rome's success in the war. Evidently God, seeing Rabbi Tzadok's faith and willingness to starve himself half-to-death for his people, has been moved to act favorably toward the Jews.

Why did Yochanan gamble the fate of the Jewish people on these three seemingly minor asks? Later talmudic authorities take issue with his priorities. When Yochanan was standing in front of Vespasian, the emperor's welcoming ear before him, he should have asked Vespasian to end the siege and save the Temple. Why had he squandered his immense opportunity? Why had this wise man turned backward?

Interestingly, earlier in the story, when Yochanan fails to rebuke Vespasian for his metaphor of the snake and honey, the Talmud lets the critique stand, but this time it comes to his defense. The Talmud's anonymous editor and commentator (known as the *stam*) jumps in and affirms that Yochanan remained silent for good reason: "He thought: perhaps [Vespasian] might not do that much [for him] and there would not be even a small amount of salvation."[6]

Yochanan worried that if he pushed too hard against Vespasian, he would not get anything in return. In his own way Yochanan understood the old adage, "If we try to take too much, we take nothing at all."[7] For him, achieving something was better than falling short of nothing.

The story abruptly ends here. Yet we know the next chapter in talmudic history: Rabbis Gamliel and Tzadok make it out, Yochanan gets his plot of land in Yavneh, and slowly his students make their way to this new home. Once there, they join with their teacher to reenvision a new Judaism—one that does not rely on Jerusalem and the Temple as its basis, but one that (at least according to the story) lays the groundwork for the living, vibrant post-Temple Judaism of today.

Why Such a Strange Founding Myth?

The Rabbis consider Yochanan's story the foundational story of the Rabbinic period. It is the pivot point on which the Jewish story changes, setting the stage for everything that will come later. However, scholars have largely debunked the story as legend.[8] Rabbinic Judaism has a rich and complex history, but it was likely not founded through Yochanan's mythic escape from Jerusalem and secret rendezvous with a nascent Roman Caesar.[9]

However, just because it is not historically accurate does not mean Rabban Yochanan's story has nothing to teach us. Fiction is powerful because its imagined situations can expose key truths in deeper ways than those of everyday experience. In fact, we might say that it is precisely because of its questionable historicity that Yochanan's story takes on added significance. If Yochanan's famous gamble with Vespasian never happened, the Rabbis must have composed it for a reason.

In highlighting his gamble as the founding story of Rabbinic Judaism, our sages are making an important point about the practical, political, and realist worldview inherent in the Rabbinic spirit. As we will see, pragmatism embodies a multitude of teachings of many of the most important sages in Jewish history. Read as literature, the story makes many subtle points about the importance of taking a pragmatic stance when faced with tough choices.

Of course, the clearest examples of Yochanan's pragmatism are evidenced in his two aforementioned decisions to avoid asking Vespasian to end the siege on Jerusalem. First, Yochanan stays silent after Vespasian draws his famous metaphor of the venomous snake around the barrel of the honey. One can only imagine the strength it took him to be silent in the face of Vespasian's claim that the only way to destroy the zealots within the city was to burn his sacred city to the ground. Second, he chooses to make three requests of Vespasian rather than ask for Jerusalem's salvation.

Yochanan's first request for Yavneh is the most obvious example of pragmatic necessity. Yochanan knows that he and other survivors will need to recreate a post-Temple Judaism. For centuries Judaism had been geographically bound. Religious practice was centralized in Jerusalem; sacrifices at the Temple were the major means of communicating with God. Once the city is destroyed, Yochanan will need a space, away from the Temple ruins, to imagine what Judaism will be.

Yavneh, as the story goes, would birth Rabbinic Judaism. It would be the seat where Yochanan and his disciples would figure out how Judaism could survive without Jerusalem at its center. Through creativity and vision they would give us many of the most familiar aspects of Jewish practice we know today: our prayer service, calendar, and several of our most treasured holiday practices. Without the Rabbis we would not light Hanukkah candles,[10] fast on Yom Kippur,[11] or join in a Passover seder.[12] Also at Yavneh, generations of Yochanan's students would learn the hallmarks of his pragmatic thinking: to adopt a practical mindset that engages with the world, weighs competing values, privileges facts over desires, and consistently questions one's own assumptions. These characteristics would become embedded in every corner of Jewish law.

So, too, Yochanan's other two requests are no less practical and politically astute. If Yochanan is able to save someone (besides himself), Rabban Gamliel (along with his family) is a natural choice. He is the grandson of Gamliel the Elder, formerly the head of the great court in Jerusalem known as the Sanhedrin, the great-grandson of the famous Rabbi Hillel, and also a descendant of King David. Gamliel is esteemed as one of the great minds of his generation and Yochanan knows that he will be able to carry on the intellectual legacy of his forebears. If he survives the war, Gamliel will serve as the Nasi, the next political leader of the Jewish people, in a post-Temple era.

However important Gamliel is, though, Yochanan's attempt to save him does not come without risks. The Romans have already killed Rabban Gamliel's father, Rabbi Shimon Ben Gamliel, over his prowar stance, and it is well known that Gamliel retains ties to the zealots.[13] Personality-wise, too, Gamliel can be difficult. When he is promoted to Nasi, Yochanan may come to regret his choice.

Yet, for all the risks, Yochanan is smart to prioritize Gamliel in his requests to Vespasian. First, if he himself hopes to assert any influence over the zealots after the Roman purge, it will be wise to elevate to *nasi* someone the zealots likely respect. Beyond this, Gamliel has a worldliness about him which allows him to communicate with foreign powers. In one famous episode, he travels to Syria to be confirmed as a leader by their governor;[14] other stories find him in Rome or disputing with Romans over the political future of the Jews.[15] Gamliel can somehow talk to both occupier and rebel alike.

As for Yochanan's choice to help Rabbi Zadok, who foresaw the destruction of the Temple forty years prior and was fasting to keep it from being destroyed,[16] this wonder worker is descended from the priestly caste and even served in the Temple in that role.[17] By saving him, Yochanan is bringing in a person who can lend some authenticity to his nascent Rabbinic project. Both Jews who admire Zadok's miracles and those who feel a tie to the Temple priesthood will see Zadok among Yochanan's ranks and feel an immediate connection to Yochanan's project in Yavneh.

Here, too, Yochanan's decision to include Zadok in his request does not come without risks. There is tension between the Rabbinic forebearers, the Pharisees, and the Sadducees, a group more closely associated with the priestly class that serves in the Temple and rejects much of the way in which the Pharisees (and, later, Yochanan and other Rabbis) interpret the Torah (e.g., the Pharisees' beliefs in free will, the immortality of the soul, and the importance of retaining extra degrees of purity through hand-washing and ritual baths).[18] Yet Yochanan knows Zadok is different. Though Zadoks's name literally means "the Sadducee," he is anything but the quintessential priest. He actually has one foot in each world: proudly descended from priests but also strongly identifying as a Rabbi. Moreover, he is his own thinker. There are rival factions within the Rabbinic world as well: the school of Shammai and the school of Hillel. Though Zadok is a disciple of Shammai, he usually made decisions along with the school of Hillel.[19] If Yochanan is to save one exemplar of what a Rabbi might be, Zadok, the nonconformist and bridge-builder, is the natural choice.

Thus, in two requests Yochanan is able to speak to some of his greatest critics and political adversaries. Through Gamliel, Yochanan will at once keep his pulse on the zealots and the Romans and placate those who want David's progeny to remain in power. Through Zadok he will likely find allies among the soon-to-be defunct priesthood and win over pious Jews who look to the great miracle workers as guides.

Yochanan's Natural Pragmatism

It is not that surprising that Yochanan is able to make the quick decision to save these individuals. Pragmatic thinking is part and parcel of his nature. In fact, it is present in the earliest moment of his origin story in his conversation with his nephew Abba Sikkara, which leads him to flee Jerusalem in the first place.

Looking back on the myth it may seem odd that Yochanan has an open dialogue with the zealot leader, even one who is a close relation. Abba Sikkara is a dangerous foe. His brand of rebels are infamous for the curved knives they wield to secretly assassinate their political opponents.

By all accounts Yochanan should be a great adversary of these zealots. He opposes much of what they stand for. Famously he preaches capitulation to the Romans, admonishing:

> Be not in haste to pull down the high places of the Gentiles, lest you have to rebuild (them) with your own hand; lest you pull down those made of bricks and they order you: "Rebuild

them of stone!" or those made of stone and they enjoin you: "Rebuild them of wood."[20]

This teaching, which the famous Rabbinic scholar Ephraim Urbach dates to the Roman general Cestius Gallus's siege of Jerusalem in 66 CE, four years before the Temple's destruction, shows Yochanan's reluctance to engage in zealous tactics.[21] He knows that if the Jews seek to destroy the Roman culture around them, they may feel a brief sense of accomplishment, but Rome will return and make them suffer. It is better to remain in peace, even if it means having to stomach problematic aspects of Roman culture like idolatry. In the long-term, stability is best.

Yochanan has an uncanny ability to open channels of communication with the most important leaders around him, from the Romans to the zealots, from the Rabbis to the priests, from the followers of Hillel to those of Shammai. The reason he is able to open up so many channels of communication is that at his heart he is a peacemaker. He understands that ideology is a double-edged sword. Without it we become aimless—but if we are too married to it, our opinions can drive wedges between us. He preaches peaceful relations with all groups he encounters.

Stressing this point in a later Rabbinic discussion, after the dust has settled on Jerusalem's destruction, Yochanan looks back at the fact that the Temple altar, the place God ordained for the Jews to offer sacrifices to the Divine, was not made with iron tools, since iron is a symbol of war and violence:

> If now the stones of the altar, which neither see nor speak, yet, because they make peace between Israel and their Father in heaven, the Holy One blessed be He, said "Thou shalt lift up no iron tool upon them"; how much the more so shall one who makes peace between man and man, between man and his wife, between city and city, between nation and nation, between government and government, or between family and family, not suffer tribulation.[22]

Here, Yochanan is making an important point: if God cares so much about the symbolism of the Temple's sacrificial platform and the message it sends about peace, then the Divine cares all the more for humans, whose individual and communal stakes in peace are much more dire. And Yochanan does not stop there. In the same way that the Temple's altar brings salvation and merit to those who use it, those who seek peace will find the redemption. This is not only practical advice—the absence of discord does reduce suffering—but is good religious counsel as well: if you want God to lessen your trouble, seek harmony with your neighbor.

Rabban Yochanan Sets the Stage for Millenia of Jewish Thinking

Rabban Yochanan's gift to us was not just Yavneh. It was not just the saving of Rabbis Gamliel and Zadok. It was not even just the reimagining of a post-Temple Judaism. It was also the normalizing of a way of thinking that gives license to the generations after him to pursue the pragmatic course.

Yochanan set the tone for much of the ideology that has become a hallmark of Rabbinic thinking. His legacy can be found in every corner of the Talmud, from how we listen to public opinion when making legislative decisions (see chapter 3) to whether we permit Roman culture in our backyard even if it offends us (see chapter 5). It appears in how we view compromise (see chapter 2) and what legal loopholes we are willing to exploit to keep the peace with our neighbors (see chapter 6). This book examines the Rabbinic world Yochanan inspired. Subsequent Rabbis will make similar calculations to his that are equally audacious gambles, assessing not only what the law should be but how it should be received, compromising long-held ethical and legal principles for the sake of progress.

To be sure, Yochanan's legacy is not the only important one in the Talmud. Rabbi Akiva, who appears throughout the Talmud, is a zealot and iconoclast who chooses to martyr himself rather than turn his back on his religion. Shimon Bar Yochai insults the Roman government, flees for his life, and ends up spending more than a decade buried in the sand up to his neck, discussing philosophy with his son and eschewing the events of the outside world. However, these critical members of the talmudic cannon are memorable in part because their worldviews break the predominant mode. They stand as outliers from the realist, rational Rabbinic norm. In this sense we are all heirs to Yochanan's outlook.

Recalibrating Truth   1

One of the most tragic tales in all of Rabbinic literature involves the story of Eliezer, who is excommunicated over being right.[1] At issue is a minor technicality on the purity of an oven. Eliezer feels the oven is pure. His fellow Rabbis deem it impure and thus unusable.

Struggling to prove his point, Eliezer employs every argument he can come up with. None work; he cannot sway his contemporaries. Exasperated, Eliezer tries a different tactic. Pointing to a nearby tree, he says, "If I am right, let that carob tree prove it." Immediately the tree uproots itself and moves. Yet the Rabbis scoff at the miracle. One cannot prove the legal status of an oven from the actions of a tree!

Eliezer will not give up. Next he makes a stream flow backward. When that too does not work, he compels the walls of the study hall to collapse—thankfully one of his disputants stops them before they fall and anyone is hurt. Like before, his fellow Rabbis ignore the sign of the teetering walls. A rabbi who can command a building to crumble may be incredible, but that is not related to the issue at hand.

Finally Eliezer calls on God. If he is right, then the heavens will proclaim his Truth.

This is exactly what happens. God issues a heavenly voice that affirms Eliezer's position. Yet even with Divine verification, the other Rabbis are unswayed. Their response to God, articulated by a rabbi named Yehoshua, is swift and radical: when it comes to humanity's legal deliberations, God has no place anymore.

As we will see, Yehoshua understands something profound about Truth. Truth is not only about who or what is right, but also it has to attend to what works in real life. And Eliezer's position, though cosmically ordained, will never work.

To prove his point, Yehoshua employs two of God's own teachings against God. First he quotes the Torah's claim that the Torah "is not in the heavens" (Deut. 30:12). Rather than the property of God, the Torah is the heritage of humanity. Like all great authors, when God put the Torah out into the world, God gave up control about how it would be read. Many writers want to retain control of their work, to wrest it back from their readers. Mark Twain famously wrote that anyone attempting to find "a motive in this narrative will be prosecuted," only to have generations of overzealous academics do just that. Despite being the great Author, there is similar futility in God's quest to affirm a True reading. God may have written the Torah, but it is ours to make something of it.[2]

Though this argument alone might suffice, Yehoshua employs a second text, namely, a creative misreading of Torah that silences God. Although Exodus 23:2 literally reads that we should not "side with the mighty to do wrong," Yehoshua reads it in the opposite way: we should "incline after the majority."[3] In other words, the Torah instructs us not to legislate in a vacuum. In a court, if the majority of judges rule one way, that is the law. It is now Truth, or at the very least binding legal fact, whether or not God ordains it so.

Here Yehoshua is a philosophical pragmatist, an idea we encountered in the Introduction and will explore further in this chapter. Rather than ask whether something is inherently true, he asks: Will it work?

Yehoshua can imagine what would happen if God went around correcting us. No one would accept any legal ruling as valid. Instead everyone would hold out hope that a Divine voice might appear ready to course correct. Because all working legal systems are built on trust, Yehoshua cannot abide any action, even one from God, that might erode his community's faith in the law. It is more important that the law "work" than it correspond to God's will.

Yehoshua's Backstory

It is no surprise that Rabbi Yehoshua takes the pragmatic view. A star pupil of Yochanan ben Zakkai (see "Prologue"), he follows a great deal in his master's ways. One of the most famous stories about Yehoshua's pragmatic spirit surrounds a particular dispute with Rabban Gamliel, the chief Rabbinic authority of the time. The two Rabbis disagree over when the month of Tishrei starts, and, more to the point, over who has the authority to set the calendar.[4]

In the ancient world, there was no set time for a month to begin. Astronomy was too nascent to make accurate predictions. Witnesses had to look at the sky and notice the emergence of a tiniest sliver of a new moon. Then they would attest to its sighting in court, and that day would become the first day of the next month.

The Talmud relates that once Gamliel's witnesses get it wrong. They attest to seeing a moon that likely did not appear. Nonetheless, Gamliel is intransigent. Despite knowing that his witnesses may have erred, he proclaims that day the start of the month of Tishrei.

Yehoshua speaks up. The stakes are too high for him to remain quiet. If Gamliel is off by a day, as he himself holds, it means that every holiday in the month of Tishrei will be off as well. Everyone will be blowing shofar before Rosh Hashanah, eating on Yom Kippur, and blessing the sukkah before the holiday arrives.

Yet hard-headed Gamliel will not be challenged by his younger colleague. The elder sends a message to the younger, demanding that he appear to him on the 9th of Tishrei, *his* Yom Kippur, carrying a walking stick and money purse.

Faced with this bold request, Yehoshua has to choose carefully. Will he defy Gamliel but keep his integrity intact? Or will he show up, even if it means breaking the legal prohibition against traveling and carrying money on what he believes is Yom Kippur?

Thankfully, his colleague, Rabbi Akiva, appears on his doorstep to help him. Pointing to the Torah verse that established the process of setting months and festivals, Akiva emphasizes the pronoun God uses there, "These are the set times of GOD, the sacred occasions, which *you* shall celebrate each at its appointed time" (Lev. 23:4). By saying to the Jews, "you shall proclaim" rather than having God say "I will proclaim," Akiva intimates the Torah is making the radical claim that humanity has the sole task of setting time. Akiva implies that God does not proclaim the start of a holiday; we the Jews do. With this in mind, God will have no recourse to correct us if we mis-observe the moon and start a month on the wrong date. Akiva continues: "Whether [you have proclaimed festivals] at their [proper] time or whether [you have declared them] not at their [proper] time, I have only these Festivals."[5] In other words, the courts make and set the start of the holidays, and even if God were to disagree in theory, God will hold by humanity's decisions.

Here Akiva is gently coaxing Yehoshua toward acquiescing to Gamliel, as by virtue of Gamliel's position in the court, the elder sage has the authority to determine time. If not even God can overrule Gamliel's calendar, then certainly Yehoshua has no leg on which to stand.

Yehoshua does not seem convinced, because instead of going immediately to Gamliel, he instead turns to another colleague, Rabbi Dosa Ben Horkinas, for additional advice.

Dosa tries another tack. Rather than explore grand statements about the nature of Truth, as Akiva does, he instead makes a pragmatic, sociological argument:

> If we come to debate [and question the rulings of] the court of Rabban Gamliel, we must debate [and question the rulings of] every court that has stood from the days of Moses until now. As it is stated: "Then Moses went up, and Aaron, Nadav and Avihu, and seventy of the Elders of Israel" (Exodus 24:9). But why were the names of these [seventy] Elders not specified?

Rather, [this comes] to teach that every [set of] three [judges] that stands as a court over the Jewish people [has the same status] as the court of Moses.[6]

Here Dosa is claiming that society has invested Rabban Gamliel's court with the authority to set the calendar. Although the court might get things wrong sometimes, questioning the court is a dangerous enterprise. Casting doubt on a single ruling chips away at our trust in the court to deliver correct rulings in general. This "slippery slope" argument puts Yehoshua in his place, taking away his agency to question Gamliel.

To further his point, Dosa reads closely a scene from the Torah in which Moses, accompanied by seventy elders, ascends Mount Sinai to meet with God. One might think that the Torah should mention Moses' companions by name. There is no shortage of lists of leaders in other sections of the Torah, but here the text leaves out these sages' names, because, Dosa argues, every society must see its judges as if they are stand-ins for these original elders, drinking their wisdom right from the Divine source.[7] Dosa seems to believe that leaving these elders anonymous makes the claim that their collective identity supersedes that of any one individual. They are subsumed by the institution they stand for. The same is true for the courts; no one person matters compared with the integrity of the legal system.

Finally Yehoshua is swayed. Armed with the knowledge that God wants us to set the calendar, despite potential mistakes, and that society needs courts to function without intervention to uphold the integrity of the system, Yehoshua travels to see Rabban Gamliel as requested, on the very day he, Yehoshuah, believes to be Yom Kippur. Thankfully Gamliel is moved by his willingness to accede:

> [Yehoshua] took his staff and his money in his hand, and went to Yavne to Rabban Gamliel on the day on which Yom Kippur occurred according to his calculation. Rabban Gamliel stood up and kissed him on his head. He said to him: Come in peace,

my teacher and my student, "my teacher" in wisdom, and "my student," as you accepted my statement.[8]

The scene is touching on many levels. Gamliel seems not to expect Yehoshua's visit. Although he just showed himself to be dominant in their exchange, Gamliel makes an uncharacteristic gesture of submission; he rises, which in the Rabbinic world is reserved for showing honor to a greater person. Perhaps his deference is due to the lesson of Yehoshua's humility. Here Yehoshua is the greater of the two, willing to sacrifice his pride and self-respect for a higher societal good. In doing so, he is both the student and teacher, willing to accept Gamliel's position but at the same time modeling for his elder that being right is not always the ultimate end.

The story ends with their embrace. Gamliel has won the dispute, and if this does not sit well with you, it might be because the story depicts a radically different way of defining what is and is not True. And it is to this new way of seeing Truth that we turn to now.

Theories of Truth

For centuries people have struggled to define truth. Up until the late nineteenth century, there were two primary theories of truth: the correspondence theory and the coherence theory.[9]

THE CORRESPONDENCE THEORY OF TRUTH

The correspondence theory says that something is true if it "corresponds" to the facts at hand. If I want to know, for example, whether an animal is kosher, I can look at the way it was killed and handled and make a decision from there.

For most of this chapter, we have been defining truth using this lens. When Eliezer called on God to authenticate the oven, he was holding by this definition. He developed a theory about its purity and went looking for evidence that he was right. Because no evidence could (seemingly) be more definitive than God's own testimony, Eliezer felt he had conclusively proven his point. His theory corresponded to the will of the universe.

Eliezer is not alone in defining truth this way. Because the correspondence theory of truth is the way most of us think of truth, it appears on virtually every page of the Talmud and Jewish law. In fact, seeing the world through this lens comes so naturally to us that we likely do not realize there is an alternative. Truth is simply what happened, what is real.

However, in as much as the correspondence theory does a good job of defining "what is and is not," as we saw with Eliezer, this theory of truth often falls short of defining "what should be." And because much of the Rabbinic project is aimed at creating proscriptive law that aims at a future not yet envisioned, we need to add other theories of truth into the mix.

THE COHERENCE THEORY OF TRUTH

With this in mind, it is no accident that a second theory of truth, the coherence theory, took shape and gained popularity a few centuries ago. It says an idea is true if it holds together with other ideas we already know to be true. If we know nine things and a tenth appears that seems to work with our existing knowledge, we should be confident that it too is true. If it does not match what we already know, we should abandon it because it does not "cohere."

Though this theory is rarer in Jewish law, the thinking does arise in select circumstances. For example, one biblical test of whether someone is a false prophet is whether the purported prophet's prophecy is so novel, it contradicts existing norms:

> If there appears among you a prophet or a dream-diviner, who gives you a sign or a portent, saying, "Let us follow and worship another god"—whom you have not experienced even if the sign or portent named to you comes true, do not heed the words of that prophet or that dream-diviner. (Deut. 13:2–4)

Notice what the Torah is saying. If we hold to the first theory cited, the correspondence theory, we might follow this false prophet, as the prophesy actually did come true. However, by coherence theory standards, listening to such a false prophet is dangerous because when placed alongside the rest of the commandments, the prophesy contradicts the many prohibitions on the worship of other gods. Coaxing us to turn away from God, the false prophet contravenes and defies the established religious system. Such idolatrous words cannot stand.

In later generations the Rabbis expanded on this notion in an even more radical way:

> One who prophesies in the name of idol worship and says: This is what the idol said, even if he approximated the [correct] *halakha* [in the name of the idol] to deem ritually impure that which is ritually impure and to deem ritually pure that which is ritually pure [is executed by strangulation].[10]

To understand the Rabbinic innovation here, we must note the difference between it and its biblical forerunner. In the biblical example, the Torah seems concerned with a person showing up, predicting some miracle that somehow happens, and then using that marvel to inspire others to worship his God. Yet in the Talmud text just cited, the effect is much more subtle. The person shows up and states a law the Rabbis know to be true, though this individual's source is problematic. Unlike the biblical example, he is not imparting this information to lead people to idol worship. Yet, nonetheless, in crediting some idolatrous practice as his source of truth, he is sowing doubt in God's revelation as the sole source of legal authority. If his legal conclusion can be right, idol worship is liable to be misconstrued as viable to mainstream Jewish practice. For the Rabbis, even if a prophet gets the perfect answer, if that interpretations of law is done in the name of an idol, the message does not cohere to the many texts that condemn foreign worship, and thus it cannot be true. It is too dangerous to be true because it chips away at the core story of God's role in revelation and must be quashed by any means necessary.

THE PRAGMATIC OR UTILITY THEORY OF TRUTH

For centuries the correspondence and coherence theories of truth ruled the day. However, in the late nineteenth century, Western thought developed a third theory: the pragmatic or utility theory of truth.

Although technical and complicated, in essence this theory says that something is true if it is useful. In practice, this means that after we are presented with a new piece of information, we ask, "What will happen if I apply this?" If doing so helps us solve a problem—or, to use a definition by Rabbi Larry Hoffman, if it helps us "advance the human project of navigating life"—it is of utility and worthy of being called true.[11] As William James, one of the fathers of philosophical pragmatism, put it: "Any idea upon which we can ride . . . ; any idea that will carry us prosperously from any one part of our experience to any other part, linking things satisfactorily, working securely, saving labor; it is true for just so much, true in so far forth, true instrumentally."[12]

To say that the Rabbis are William James-type pragmatists would be a wild anachronism.[13] However, the Talmud is full of Rabbinic personalities who voice the pragmatic spirit: for one, Rabbi Yehoshua, with whom we began our chapter.

The Talmud (Largely) Agrees with Yehoshua

Yehoshua's approach to Truth is the predominant approach taken throughout the Talmud whenever questions are less straightforward than simply observing "what is." Throughout the Talmud, Truth is often supplanted for the sake of other more pressing concerns.

In a telling story, the Rabbis debate whether we should be praying during the first three hours of the day, while God is said to be judging humanity, or over the next three hours, while God is imagined to be studying Torah.[14] In which part of God's day is God be more likely to heed our prayerful calls? When might God be in a good mood and less apt to scrutinize us?

At first glance, it might seem as if we should ask God for what we want while God is studying (the second three hours) and not as God judges us (as the day begins). Because God is already investigating and analyzing everything we do during the Divine judgment period, God might find us unworthy and ignore our pleas. However, in a surprising twist, the Rabbis argue that we should choose to pray to God while God sits in judgment of us:

> [In the case of the] Torah, with regard to which it is written: Truth, as it is written: "Buy the truth, and sell it not" (Proverbs 23:23), the Holy One, Blessed be He, does not act in a manner that is beyond the letter of the law. [But with regard to] judgment, with regard to which it is not written: Truth, [but it is a process that involves mercy and compromise], the Holy One, Blessed be He, can act in a manner that is beyond the letter of the law.[15]

Here the Rabbis are making a distinction between two alternatives, truth and judgment, and between the two, judgment is more forgiving.

THE TRUTH ALTERNATIVE

Truth is what God does when God studies. According to the Rabbis, it is best found in the pages of Torah. A person who studies it taps directly into God's source of wisdom. As one develops ideas from Torah, the answers might seem untenable and sometimes farfetched, but if an answer is read authentically from the text, one can call it God's Truth.

We can relate to this phenomenon. We have all heard an academic (or two or three) propose outlandish solutions to the toughest economic and political challenges of the day—those that makes sense on paper, even if they are unlikely to ever work in the real world. Now imagine that God is that academic.

We do not want to approach God when God is engaged in scholarship, because the Divine answer may not be useful. It might be too harsh or too lenient because God is only accounting for the facts on the page, not the complicated reality of our lived experience.

THE JUDGMENT OPTION

Judgment, however, is something different. It is the act of taking the Truth and applying it to our world. Judges cannot work in a vacuum. They have to look at the tear-stained faces of their litigants, deal with the political blowback of their decisions, and assess if the next case might take today's precedent too far. Even if the answer of guilty/not guilty or liable/not liable seems straightforward, their sentences often have a degree of flexibility to them. When human beings have been convicted of a crime, judges often ask, "Will this punishment change them?" For civil suits, judges have to ask, "Will the payment I am asking them to make bankrupt them?" As opposed to scholarship, law is circumstantial, even if we might sometimes wish it were otherwise. To borrow a phrase from above, a judge cannot help but go "beyond the letter of the law."

Many of these concerns are pragmatic. Judges who are doing their jobs well have to weigh a myriad of factors, all of which mediate the question of "what should be" in the ideal with "what will work" in the moment. They need to be flexible, observant, open, even creative.

Knowing this, we can return to God. God may not be sitting in a courtroom, but in the Rabbinic imagination, God is capable of functioning like the wisest of judges, contemplating the many extra-legal factors that come with making fair rulings. We want to approach God when God's eyes are open and ready to place our pleas alongside the concerns of the world. We want God to burst open the vacuum that comes with intense study and take in all the complexities around us.[16]

To see this Talmudic observation in action, one need look no further than the opening Mishnah in the tractate most young students will encounter early in their Talmud study. The Rabbis wrestle with what to do if two people each demand ownership over the same garment, as both claim to have seen it first lying on the sidewalk:

> If two [people came to court] holding a garment, and this one, [the first litigant], says: I found it, and that one, [the second litigant], says: I found it; this one says: All of it is mine, and that one says: All of it is mine; [how does the court adjudicate this case?] This one takes an oath that he does not have ownership of less than half of it, and that one takes an oath that he does not have ownership of less than half of it, and they divide it.[17]

This Mishnah seems reasonable. If a judge cannot figure out who owns a garment, the claimants should split it. True, this solution is imperfect; likely, one of them did spy the garment first, even if only God knows which one. But the "Truth" of its ownership is less relevant than bringing an end to the dispute.

There are certainly cases in Rabbinic literature in which a decision is held off until a certain Truth is known. An occasional refrain in the Talmud when there is intractable disagreement is to put aside the answer until "Elijah comes." In other words, we should wait until the Messianic Era to settle it.[18] Elijah, knowing God's intent, can set us right if our courts and judges err.

Yet that is not what happens in the vast majority of cases, including the garment dispute. If a judge were to hold on to the garment in question until an answer actually emerged, it would create havoc. Not only would the courts need to build warehouses to hold all the items in dispute, but also the animosity and ill-will invoked by the judge's lack of action would pull at the delicate fabric of society. For this reason, the Rabbis do not wait for a definitive answer. Often, speed and finitude are privileged over the perfect resolution.[19]

Pragmatists Pick Sides

Truth, it can be said, is only partially dependent on fact. Knowing more than your opponent does not necessarily mean you are any closer to the truth. To understand this, we can look to the debates between Shammai and Hillel, two of the forefathers of Rabbinic thought and famous rivals. History agrees that Shammai was the smarter of the two.[20] On multiple occasions, when their students spar, Shammai's disciples humble Hillel's students with their intellectual prowess, causing the latter to change positions.[21] Yet when God finally comes to settle their arguments, he rules in favor of Hillel—not because Hillel is more right, but because God cares about deeper things than veracity and logic:

> For three years Beit Shammai and Beit Hillel disagreed. These said: The *halakha* is in accordance with our opinion, and these said: The *halakha* is in accordance with our opinion. [Ultimately], a Divine Voice emerged and proclaimed: Both these and those are the words of the living God. However, the *halakha* is in accordance with the opinion of Beit Hillel. Since both these and those are the words of the living God, why were Beit Hillel privileged to have the *halakha* established in accordance with their opinion? [The reason is] that they were agreeable and forbearing, [showing restraint when affronted, and when they taught the *halakha* they would] teach both their own statements and the statements of Beit Shammai. Moreover, [when they formulated their teachings and cited a dispute], they prioritized the statements of Beit Shammai to their own statements [in deference to Beit Shammai].[22]

Although this text seems to state that God prefers both the opinions of Hillel and Shammai, the Talmud is clear that this is an opinion *only* God can hold. Law must conform to one of these two views. For society to work, there must be limits to behavioral pluralism.[23] In theory, two contradictory contentions can both be right, but when one advocates for standing during prayer and the other for sitting,[24] or when one states that a *tallis* consists of three knotted strands of wool, whereas the other believes it should be four,[25] it becomes necessary to pick sides.

Living in a postmodern world, we might celebrate the multiple narratives, perspectives, and even truths around us, and the story of Hillel and Shammai seems to prefigure this. But in our world, as it was for theirs, we do not always have the radical flexibility to follow any given path, especially if we want to create cohesive communities.

With this in mind, it is no wonder the Talmud goes out of its way to imply that although Hillel and Shammai both have access to the truth, in practice we must act as if Hillel is its sole source. The reason Hillel wins is telling. It is not that he is smarter, sharper, or quicker than Shammai; he is chosen because he is kinder. The Rabbis know that society wins when our leaders practice humility and honor. By teaching Shammai's opinion alongside their own, even giving him top billing, Hillel and his disciples not only teach the law at hand but also model the way society should engage in discourse. For all we know Shammai may be more right, but Hillel, with his patience and constraint, gets closer to the true essence of Jewish ethical living, and for that, generations follow after him in his honor.

There is also something very pragmatic about God's ruling. If God is simply concerned with getting humanity as close to the Divine will as possible, either Hillel or Shammai's opinion would be on the table. But God is concerned with the workings of society as well. A world where multiple people hold conflicting opinions with equal conviction will often devolve into violence, which not incidentally is exactly what happens with the pair's students.

The disturbing story told about Hillel and Shammai's students appears in the Jerusalem Talmud.[26] One day, in the "loft of Hananiah ben Hezekiah ben Gurion," Shammai's students find themselves outnumbering those of Hillel.[27] Knowing this is not a standard occurrence and also how deeply everyone holds the mandate to follow the majority, they get busy ruling on as many laws as time will permit. What exactly happens is left to debate, but Rabbi Eliezer claims they "overflowed the measure," an opaque phrase that likely means one of two things. Either Shammai's students ruled on so many laws that everyone could not adequately capture them, and they were lost to history, thus overflowing the container of collective memory. Or as Richard Hidary of Yeshiva University thinks, in their rush to make their mark and cement a traditionally more conservative worldview than their contemporaries, Shammai's students made "stringencies [that were] overbearing and impossible for the masses to fulfill, thus causing them to violate the law."[28] Either way, the race to assert themselves led to waste.

The "loft of Hananiah" story is a cautionary tale. When rival factions lack clear guidance to decide differences in opinion, they will often take any available opening to assert their power. One need look no further than the way the U.S. Congress functions when majorities change. Representatives hurry to pass laws in accord with their positions before their authority is snatched away.

Yet the story does not end there. Shammai's students take things a frightening step further:

> The students of Beit Shammai stood at the bottom [of the stairs], and they killed the students of Beit Hillel. It was taught: Six of them went up [to the attic], and the rest of them attacked them with spears and swords.[29]

Shammai's students are not only certain their views are right, but also they will do whatever it takes to hold on to their majority and thus ensure that no one will stand in their way as they enact the law—regardless of the costs. It is no surprise that the Talmud proclaims, "That day was as difficult for Israel as the day the [golden] calf was made."[30]

In the Rabbinic timeline, the story of the "loft of Hananiah" takes place before God's proclamation that despite both Hillel and Shammai being rooted in the words of the "living God", the law must accord with Hillel. Realizing that only legal clarity will prevent further bloodshed, God appears to rule with Hillel, to guarantee that something like this never occurs again.

As it happens, even this is not the final word. Later in this book, we will see examples of Hillel changing his mind to rule with Shammai despite what God says. But this text puts a firm stake in the ground. For the good of society, God has to pick sides, and Hillel was the right side to be on.

We Cannot Always Rely on God:
Putting Our Faith in Human Reasoning

With it now firmly understood that the Talmud accepts Yehoshua's pragmatic truth over Eliezer's claim of objective or Divine truth— that the Rabbis prefer the laws that work over the seemingly correct answers— we might wonder: what is *so* wrong with Eliezer holding firm to his view? Why is he is excommunicated for it? After all, do not the stories in the Talmud itself demonstrate that both majority and minority viewpoints ought to be appreciated and recorded for future generations to recognize?

The Rabbis act harshly toward him for two reasons, one ontological and the other sociological. First, they imagine that their own pragmatic thinking bests God, and therefore they have God's divine stamp of approval on their approach. They imagine a scene where Rabbi Nathan meets the prophet Elijah and asks him, "What did the Holy One, Blessed be God, do in the hour [when the Rabbis essentially kicked God out of the study hall]?" Elijah answers, "God was laughing and saying, 'My children have defeated me, my children have defeated me.'"[31] In a way, this episode should be the feel-good capstone of the story. The Rabbis hold that even God wants human beings to follow their own earthly opinions. We have Divine license to own Torah and law—even to the point that God welcomes losing to us in a match of wits.

Having proven to their own satisfaction that God considers them right, the Rabbis then turn toward shoring up their power and ensuring that others will not question the status quo as Eliezer has done. No sooner does the story show us this wonderful image of God's mirth at the Divine defeat than it takes a dark turn with Rabbi Eliezer's excommunication:

> On that day, [the Sages] brought all the ritually pure items deemed pure by the ruling of Rabbi Eliezer [with regard to the oven] and burned them in fire, and [the Sages] reached a consensus in his regard and ostracized him.[32]

Ostracizing Eliezer is no easy decision for his contemporaries. Eliezer is not only an important voice in their community, but also he has the power to evoke miracles. Not only can he conjure trees and rivers to prove his legal points; he also can summon God.

Thus they have to be careful when telling him about his excommunication. In his anger, he might destroy the world.

Akiva is chosen to approach Eliezer. He succeeds in impeding the worst possible outcome but cannot stop the impending disaster. Even with Akiva's delicate framing, Eliezer cannot control his pain. It reverberates throughout the world, exploding the natural order:

> His eyes shed tears, [and as a result] the entire world was afflicted: One-third of its olives [were afflicted], and one-third of its wheat, and one-third of its barley. And some say that even dough kneaded in a woman's hands spoiled. [The Sages] taught: There was great anger on that day, as any place that Rabbi Eliezer fixed his gaze was burned.[33]

Eliezer soon turns his wrath on Rabban Gamliel, the leader of his generation of Rabbis who had signed his excommunication decree. In the Rabbinic imagination, core spiritual figures have the power to pray for a person's death, and God will grant it. As the story goes, Eliezer tries again and again to do just that to Gamliel, only to be intentionally interrupted by his own wife, Ima Shalom, who tries to save the leader's life. Eventually, Ima Shalom gets distracted, and Eliezer succeeds. Word quickly spreads of Gamliel's murder.

Knowing how the story tragically ends makes our original question all the more salient. The Rabbis could have avoided this calamity by accepting Eliezer's view, or, at the very least, by overruling him but honoring it. Why, then, do they put themselves at such risk by excommunicating him? What is the problem with Eliezer holding by God's given Truth?

Perhaps the best explanation comes from the writer and Holocaust survivor Elie Wiesel in his character study on Rabbi Eliezer. For Wiesel, Eliezer's problem is not that he disagrees with his colleagues but that he tries to change the rules on them. Rather than appeal to human notions of logic and reason, the way he is supposed to debate law, Eliezer cheats, invoking a Divine solution to a human problem:

> Rabbi Eliezer was a scholar of unparalleled erudition. Why then did he invoke God's opinion in a discussion with his colleagues? That was his mistake. They were not arguing about mysticism or poetry, or even an interpretation of the Aggadah; they were arguing over a point of law. Other sages disagreed with him? That was their privilege. He should have reasoned with them, drawing on his knowledge and experience. He should have used various and sundry tactics to win them over, seeking new evidence from different sources, formulating new interpretations, hoping to convince one colleague, and then another, and another. Isn't that what the Talmud is all about? Had the Tannaim relied on heavenly decrees, there would have been no room for debates, or study, or teaching, or any communal religious life. In short, there would have been no Talmud to begin with![34]

Wiesel then pronounces: "None is as fanatic as the one who claims to derive the truth from heaven."[35] By relying on magical maneuvers no one else can do, Eliezer exempts himself from the communal conversation. Debate has ended. Here the stakes are simply the purity of an oven. But what might happen in the future, when God's opinion might not be best for the community? Eliezer still would win, and society could be the worse for it.

In short, Eliezer has a right to be charismatic, in the religious sense, meaning he has a right to commune directly with God. But he has no right to impose that Divinely inspired will on the people. As dramatist Hyam Maccoby reminds us: "Not a single halakhic decision in the whole rabbinic corpus can be attributed to a claim of divine inspiration, and all attempts to solve halakhic problems by charismatic means were rejected."[36] No one, not even a sage of Eliezer's caliber, is to lay sole claim to the domain of truth.

The Power of Opacity

If this chapter has felt frustrating, you are not alone. One of the main critiques of the pragmatic way of thinking is that too often our most pragmatic leaders do what is easy, expeditious, even lazy, rather than pursuing what is right. Doing "what works" can feel slippery and opportunistic.

There is something very pragmatic, for example, about the biblical character of King Ahasuerus, who in the Purim story cares more about preserving his own power than in doing what is right. When Haman comes calling, looking for permission to wipe out the Jews, the king is all too happy to hand over the keys to the kingdom. Then, when the tides turn—Ahasuerus discovers that Haman and company are traitorous—the king is equally willing to give the power to the Jews so they can wreak vengeance on all of those who threaten him.

Ahasuerus, in his pragmatic self-interest, is his own kind of evil—one that arguably is as harmful, if not more, than evil purists like Haman. There have always been too many like him, willing to do what works for them and ignore what is required for others. This is pragmatism gone too far, and it should be fought at every turn.

Yet just because people like Ahasuerus exist does not mean that the pragmatic enterprise is tainted. Pragmatism is not an end but rather a tool. It is a framing set of questions to help us figure out how to get to an answer. If we seek to find a useful means to answer the question "How can I preserve my own power," that is a problem. If we instead search for a workable solution to enacting the ethical, fulfilling God's will, upholding the values of Torah—all the essence of the Rabbinic project—then pragmatism can help us navigate uncharted moral waters.

But how do we know we are doing the right thing? Like I imagine the Rabbis felt, it is hard to know the moral path when objective Truth is beyond our grasp. I yearn for a clear-cut Torah: my questions answered, my ethical knots swiftly untied. I want access to God's truth laid out before me—a road map to virtue. But is that actually good for me?

In the imagination of the Rabbis, the fact that the real, objective Truth cannot be defined is valuable. The flexibility of the Rabbinic system gives license for Jewish law to pivot to meet the needs of any era. "If the Torah was given in a clear cut manner," Rabbi Yanai proclaims in the Jerusalem Talmud, "no foot could stand firmly."[37] In other words, it is in the maddening, irksome unknown that law leaves us open to the possible.

To do this, the Rabbis envision that ideal leaders, studying the law, should become so adept at parsing its details that they can devise forty-eight reasons why a matter is impure while simultaneously developing forty-eight counter reasons for the purity of that same item:

> There was a student of R' Meir's named Sumchos, and he would give 48 reasons for anything that he declared impure and 48 reasons for anything that he declared pure.[38]

In essence, then, the best students must fully see the other side of any issue. They must understand that searching for Truth is not an easy enterprise and have the humility to know that they may be wrong.

As it happens, the use of the number forty-eight is not an accident. The Rabbis imagine that each of us can walk through "fifty gates of understanding" to reach God's truth. The more gates we walk through, the closer we get.[39] Even Moses, the Rabbis say, can only reach forty-nine. We humans will forever be a "little less than God."[40]

Because we cannot ever know what is right amid the melee of conflicting rationales, the best we can do is to rely on the majority to figure out the answer. As the Rabbis explain:

> Moses said to God, "Master of the Universe, when will we know the truth of the matter?" God said to him (Moses): "Go according to the majority: if the majority rules it is impure—it is impure, if the majority rules it is pure—it is pure."[41]

None of us are as smart as all of us. We need help to find the Truth. We may not all have perfect understanding, but collectively, listening to others will get us closer.

Yet even with the best counsel, as the story of the Oven of Akhnai teaches, we will sometimes get it wrong. But God is willing to live with these incorrect answers because we came to them with integrity, because we discovered them in a communal process.

It is in the opacity that possibility flourishes. The Rabbis love to debate the optimal metaphor for Torah. Is Torah strong and immovable like iron nails or branching and pliable like vegetation, well planted and swaying in the wind?[42] Though they entertain the first possibility, the Rabbis are clear: Torah, like Truth, is expansive and wild. Nothing is more adaptive than a vine, finding its way around obstacles, cutting many paths toward the light. In the Rabbinic imagination, the goal of Torah is to be that pliant as each of us forges many paths toward the light.

Upholding Compromise   2

As the Talmud story goes, Rabbi Yehudah HaNasi is about to host Rabbi Pinchas in a long-awaited dinner—the first time the two sages will dine together.[1] Walking toward his host's abode, Rabbi Pinchas is startled to observe the presence of white mules. Maybe it is because the mules are known to be dangerous. Perhaps he himself is superstitious—a white mule is commonly considered a bad omen. Then again, maybe, as Dov Zakheim notes in his magnificent study on Yehudah HaNasi's life, "R. Pichas, the austere pietist, disapproved of [Yehudah HaNasi's] lifestyle, which was marked by 'conspicuous affluence' as represented by the white mules."[2]

Whatever the reason, Pinchas questions the wisdom of sharing a meal with Yehudah HaNasi, saying to himself, "The Angel of Death is in this house, and I will eat with him?"[3] To Pinchas, HaNasi's choice to have these mules present at dinnertime has somehow tempted fate, symbolized by the Angel of Death. For his own good, Pinchas cannot break bread with him.

Hearing his guest's mumbling, Yehudah HaNasi offers any number of solutions to convince Pinchas to stay. First he suggests he himself sell the mules, but Pinchas demurs. If owning white mules is dangerous, then it is immoral to put a new buyer at risk. Next HaNasi proposes setting one of the animals loose and declaring it ownerless. Pinchas scoffs, "That will only increase the damage," as people who unknowingly encounter the beast will find themselves at risk. Third, HaNasi offers to "remove their hooves" so the mules cannot kick and destroy anything. That, Pinchas protests, will violate *tza'ar ba'alei ḥayim*, the prohibition against causing unnecessary harm to any of God's creatures. Trying a final time, Yehudah HaNasi offers to put the animals down. "No," says his guest, citing *ba'al tashḥit*, the injunction prohibiting wanton destruction. The mules have done nothing wrong. Killing them would violate this ethical principle.

Meanwhile, as Yehudah HaNasi begs Pinchas to come in for dinner and Pinchas rebuffs every attempt, a mountain rises between them. Suddenly the presence of the mules is no longer their most intractable problem. There is now a physical barrier between them, a manifestation of their inability to forge a compromise. There will be no more discourse, no more engagement. Seeing he can no longer speak with his guest, Yehudah HaNasi breaks into tears. A potential friendship has ended before it began. Unable to find a way to break bread, the two go their separate ways.

There is perhaps no more apt metaphor to describe the inability to compromise than that of a mountain dividing two people. Rabbinic literature is filled with individuals who stubbornly cling to their own beliefs and find themselves trapped behind a steep rock face they cannot traverse. Yet counter to these voices are individuals who take the opposite tack. People like Rabban Yochanan ben Zakai privilege the art of the compromise (see "Prologue"). People such as Yehoshua ben Hananiah show up to Gamliel with his staff and money purse (see chapter 1). People such as Hillel willingly engage with Shammai's harsh positions (see chapter 1).

This chapter will examine a number of the most important Rabbinic discussions on compromise. As we will see, compromise is not monolithic, and it is not called for universally. There are times to bend and times to stand firm in one's resolve. Yet more often than not, Rabbinic tradition honors, even celebrates, compromise. No relationship should end, as it did for Rabbis Yehudah and Pinchas, because the disputing parties cannot find a creative way forward.

"A Legitimate Partner for Negotiation"

When two people disagree, the most basic compromise they can muster is to agree that the other person is worthy of dialogue. Doing this, according to Israeli philosopher Avishai Margalit, is compromising not on the substance of a negotiation but on its "frame." As he explains, this type of negotiation "involves recognizing the other as a legitimate partner for negotiation."[4]

If we think about the many people with whom we disagree, Margalit's insight becomes all the more profound. Most of us have people in our lives with whom we will never have a thoughtful discussion. Perhaps we are incapable of hearing them, or they are too stubborn to give weight to our views. Maybe we fear repercussions—ad hominem attacks for even broaching an issue that is bothering us. Yet without the openness to allow in another's person's view, without the humility to really listen, and without the willingness to perceive cracks in our own collective armor, we will never find common ground.

While the Rabbis do not encourage us to engage with everyone with whom we disagree—in particular when they believe that the other person's point of view is beyond the pale—in general they do impel us to overcome personal pride and seek out compromise when we struggle to do just that.[5] Two tales in the Talmud spell out the costs of prideful intransigence and the opportunities of connection.

The Hezekiah-Isaiah Standoff

The Rabbis first imagine that King Hezekiah, who governed the Kingdom of Judah in the seventh century, and Isaiah, the chief prophet of his reign, desperately need to be in relationship, yet neither has the humility to visit the other.[6] Some background: In the ancient world, it matters that kings and prophets live side by side and in dialogue. Each needs the other. Kings need prophets like Isaiah to tell them the truth, hold them accountable, and help them see a future path forward. Prophets need kings because even when they themselves speak God's truth, they do not have armies or the power of decree to actualize the God's will.

As the Rabbis tell it, both King Hezekiah and the prophet Isaiah are students of history, yet they rely on differing examples. Hezekiah knows that in the past, when prophets like Elijah wanted an audience, they would present themselves at the king's doorstep. Thus Hezekiah expects that all seers, including Isaiah, will appear at his doorstep without summoning.[7] Isaiah, in turn, remembers another scene from history: when King Yehoram ben Ahab appeared at the prophet Elisha's abode to gain insight into a war the king was waging against the Moabite kingdom.[8] Because both Hezekiah and Isaiah have their own conflicting precedents of kings seeking prophets and prophets seeking kings, both are too proud to visit the other.

Someone has to be the bigger person; someone has to yield—but neither leader will. Knowing this, God brings sickness upon Hezekiah to force the two leaders together:

> What did the Holy One, Blessed be He, do [to effect compromise between Hezekiah and Isaiah?] He brought the suffering [of illness] upon Hezekiah and told Isaiah: Go and visit the sick. [Isaiah did as God instructed], as it is stated: "In those days Hezekiah became deathly ill, and Isaiah ben Amoz the prophet came and said to him: Thus says the Lord of Hosts: Set your house in order, for you will die and you will not live" (Isa. 38:1).[9]

Eventually Hezekiah and Isaiah do speak—and a miraculous conversation ensues.

Hezekiah tells Isaiah he is afraid to have children. Knowing that many in his lineage have turned to idolatry,[10] he worries that something inherent in his family will cause his progeny to turn away from God. But Isaiah tells Hezekiah it is not his choice to flout the Jewish mandate to procreate.[11] The king should not be questioning God's ways; if God blesses him with a child, it must be for a reason. An inspired Hezekiah prays for God's mercy. God hears his prayer and adds fifteen years to the king's life, a message that Isaiah delivers.[12] Soon Hezekiah has a son, Manasseh, who does turn to idolatry. Although their relationship is often rocky—in the biblical era, few kings and prophets avoided conflict—the two do engage for the rest of Hezekiah's life. Isaiah appears again on the king's doorstep to rebuke him for flaunting his wealth to the Babylonians.[13]

In using Hezekiah and Isaiah as unlikely archetypes of compromise, the Rabbis make important points. First, even a forced compromise, in this case due to God's intervention, can hold merit. Second, two people do not have to be close to arrive at compromise together. Third, compromise can open doors for growth: had Hezekiah not welcomed Isaiah, he never would have learned that he was erring in not producing an heir—and he never would have extended his life for fifteen years! More than anything, this story shows that failure to accommodate others may induce dire results. Even something as important as one's own life may be on the line when we let our ego get in the way of compromise.

The Pinchas-Jephthah Dispute

In the Rabbinic imagination, a similar dispute happens between Pinchas the High Priest and Jephthah, a chieftain in ancient Israel during the era of the biblical judges (1150–1225 BCE). According to the biblical story, Jephthah returns home after successful battle and vows in gratitude to sacrifice the first living being he sees to God. Expecting to spot a chicken or goat, Jephthah is shocked to discover that his (unnamed) daughter catches his eye first. Because vows must be upheld, he tells his daughter he is obligated to slaughter her. She agrees, asking only that she be granted two months to spend time with friends and mourn the life she could have led.[14] Eventually she returns home to face her fate.[15]

This tragic story is made all the more so because, as the Rabbis explain, Jephthah could have reversed his vow. They invent a midrash in which Phineas the High Priest has the ability to annul vows, but both men are too proud to forgo their pride to go to the other.

To understand this midrash, some background is needed. The Rabbis believe that almost any vow can be annulled. They invent hundreds of techniques to dissolve vows made in haste and later regretted. In one notable case, if the vower did not fully envision the results of a vow, a judge can dissolve it, grounded in the understanding that the vower's ignorance was a kind of duress.[16] Yet in the Jephthah and Phineas tale, Phineas asserts, "I am a High Priest, the son of a High Priest; shall I go there to help an ignoramus?" and Jephthah retorts, "I am the chief of Israel; shall I go to Phineas?"[17] As the two men bicker, the clock runs out on Jephthah's daughter.

Like the story of Hezekiah and Isaiah, the account of Pinchas and Jephthah serves as an extreme example of the cost of not compromising. One is supposed to leave this midrash with a feeling of disgust: an innocent girl had to die because neither leader would make the effort to approach the other.

Hillel and Shammai's Compromise on "Interschool" Marriage

When it comes to compromise, Occam's razor, the idea that the simplest solution is usually right, is often wrong. A garment can be torn in two (see chapter 1), but such a splitting is not always viable, as the Bible points out when two women come to King Solomon to dispute who is the baby's rightful mother.[18] A swift compromise may negate the feelings, agency, or integrity of one or more of the disputing parties. Sometimes the cleanest compromises need to be made messy to work.

One Hillel and Shammai story is a great example of this. Although the duo disagree about nearly everything (see chapter 1), in certain rare cases, they toy with dual compromises that acknowledge and address their opposing views. We see this in their decision to allow their daughters and sons to marry one another despite the two schools holding different standards for marriage:

> Beit Shammai did not refrain from marrying women from Beit Hillel, nor did Beit Hillel [refrain from marrying women] from

Beit Shammai. This serves to teach you that they practiced affection and camaraderie between them, to fulfill that which is stated: "Love truth and peace" (Zechariah 8:19).[19]

This ruling is audacious, in part because it comes with dire consequences. Because Hillel and Shammai have different criteria for marriage and divorce, situations will surely arise in which only one of the two schools considers a given couple's divorce valid, whereas the other school sees the couple as still married. If the woman then acts on her perceived singlehood and marries again, she will be an adulteress in the eyes of the other school. Adultery, a major sin in Jewish law, comes with steep penalties, including the labeling of the offspring as a *mamzer*, often mistranslated as a bastard but more correctly the product of a forbidden union. A *mamzer* is unable to marry anyone but another *mamzer*.[20] Shammai's ruling would have likely produced a significant number of questionable *mamzerim* from Hillel's point of view, and vice versa.

Seeing that they allowed their followers to violate a major prohibition for the sake of peace, there might seem to be no more perfect compromise in all of Rabbinic literature than this. The schools of Hillel and Shammai set aside differences even to the point of sacrificing the integrity of their own legal understandings to preserve their relationship. In both of their eyes, regardless of the other school's wrongheadedness in interpretation, pragmatism needs to be the priority value: society will work better if this major issue is bypassed. And yet, clean compromises rarely hold. No sooner does the Talmud laud Hillel and Shammai's heroic concession than it begins to chip away at it. The Talmud's editors interject a cryptic phrase by Rabbi Shimon: "They did refrain in the certain cases, but they did not refrain in the uncertain cases."[21]

As the reader soon learns, Rabbi Shimon is drawing a distinction between two marriages, that is, marriage with and without foreknowledge of problematic circumstances. If someone marries another person all the while knowing that the marriage violates a certain norm (perhaps, for example, a man marries someone whom he understands not to be sufficiently divorced), the union is forbidden. By contrast, if the man (or woman) is unaware of anything overtly wrong with the chosen partner in marriage (perhaps some time in the past, someone in the betrothed's line married in such a way that the untainted marrying partner would find abhorrent if known), then the union is acceptable. There is no need to worry, play it safe, and refrain from marriage altogether. Jews wishing to wed are not required to be purists. For the sake of peace and friendship, the two schools do not look too closely into any potential bride or bridegroom's past. The fences that could have been erected to keep Jews from unknowingly violating commandments are never built.

That said, after chipping away at the openness of the Hillel and Shammai relationship, Rabbi Shimon goes a step further. True, we do not need to do a heavy investigation into a person's family tree, but practicing "affection and camaraderie" requires couples to disclose any known information about their family unions both past and present. Each party must "notify" one another if entering into a marriage would violate a norm—even if it means you are not able to marry the person you want to.[22]

To summarize the logical twists and turns here, the Talmud waters down a simple compromise—Hillel and Shammai's students can marry one another despite holding different standards—in favor of a new standard that essentially meets this initial ruling halfway. Rather than permit or ban all unions outright, the Rabbis require each party to disclose any information the other might find offensive and only allow marriages in cases in which neither party suspects any issues.

This *suggiah* (extended section of legal talmudic discourse) demonstrates the moderate, pragmatic way of Rabbinic compromise. Instead of upholding Hillel and Shammai's willingness to marry into another's family as a paragon of openness and receptivity, the Rabbis hedge with nuance. For them, compromise does not mean surrendering all of one's ideals. It means holding fast to ideals you will never relinquish and moving on from those you are willing to cede. Furthermore, and equally importantly, compromise entails continuing to examine and question a decision's effects and making on-the-fly adjustments as needed.

Changing His Mind:
Hillel's Compromise on the Fate of a Slave

Because God famously appears to Hillel and Shammai's students to proclaim that the law will always follow Hillel (see chapter 1), one might assume that Shammai's position will never be victorious. Yet the Talmud tells of numerous instances in which Hillel decides Shammai's position is more meritorious than his own is and changes his view.[23]

In one telling example, the two sages disagree about the fate of a male slave jointly owned by two people.[24] When one frees him and the other does not, should he be considered free, slave, or some amalgam of the two?[25] According to Hillel, "One who is half-slave, half-freeman serves his master one day and works for himself one day."[26] In other words, a half-freed male slave vacillates between his two statuses. It is not his remaining owner's fault that the other acted independently to grant him his freedom.

Balking at Hillel's solution, Shammai retorts, "You have remedied [the situation of] his master, [who benefits fully from all his rights to the slave], but his own [situation] you have not remedied."[27] Shammai is protesting that a person who holds both free and slave status will be even worse off than having only slave status, in one specific respect: his ability to marry. Jewish law prohibits a slave from marrying a free woman. Likewise, a slave can only marry another slave living in the home. Because Jews are enjoined to marry and procreate, Hillel's quick-fix will leave the half-free slave in the lurch.[28] After weighing this, Hillel retracts his statement and rules with Shammai that if one owner frees a slave, the remaining owner must be forced to follow suit.

This story is one of many anecdotes in the Talmud demonstrating Hillel's willingness to change his mind.[29] In each case, Shammai reminds Hillel that the latter's position, though often the cleaner of the two, leaves some strand frayed, leading Hillel to closely weigh Shammai's competing logic. Because the most basic pragmatic requirement of law is that it must work, when Shammai's law works better, Hillel proceeds to adopt his adversary's beliefs. Thus, Hillel models integrity for us all.

Compromise at Last:
The Example of Akavya ben Mehalalel and His Son

Today, the idea of integrity is often misunderstood as being unwavering in one's views. Though grit often feels like a prerequisite to integrity, that simple definition can quickly devolve into stubbornness. Instead, people of integrity, like Hillel, will often vacillate between two "rights" as more information becomes available. They will question each belief's weight and the influence each view holds. They will grow in their views.

An interesting case study in both integrity and compromise appears in a short talmudic anecdote about a little mentioned figure named Akavya ben Mehalalel. According to the Rabbis, Akavya famously and consistently speaks out against the prevailing views of his fellow sages. The topics of these disputes are diverse and specific, ranging from how to diagnose the ancient skin disease *Tzaraat* to the color and purity of uterine blood, from the uses and misuses of blemished beasts to whom might be tried for adultery.[30] In every instance, Akavya holds opinions at odds with the leadership around him. Where his fellow Rabbis are stringent, he is lenient, and when he is permissive, they are strict.

One day, his contemporaries offer him a deal: if he rescinds his positions and conforms to majority opinion, he will be promoted to *av beit din*, the chief judge of the courts (the second most powerful position a Jewish leader can hold). Though this honor is enticing, Akavya does not waver, replying, "It is better for me to be called a fool all my days than to become a wicked person for even a moment before God."[31] Let people belittle me, he implies; God knows I am right. Upping the ante, Akavya then adds that in offering him the position contingent on his abandoning his beliefs, his fellow Rabbis are making it impossible for him ever to change his mind, lest others accuse him of "retracting his positions for the sake of [obtaining a position of] authority."[32]

Akavya ben Mehalalel pays a price for his principles. Though widely considered a brilliant legalist, he never rises to prominence. According to some accounts, he is excommunicated for offending two of his generation's most prominent Rabbis when standing up for his beliefs. Ostracized from his peers, Akavya grows old in solitude.

Finally when his time of death arrives, he gathers his son, Hananiah ben Akavya, to his bedside and implores him *not* to follow in his footsteps. Rule like the majority, he says, and retract my positions. Incredulous, his son asks him, "Did you not make a career out of iconoclasm? Why would you sacrifice so much for your ideals only to tell me to abandon them?"

Akavya proceeds to explain the talmudic principle of always ruling along with the majority while preserving minority opinions (see chapter 1). When he was younger, Akavya learned his opinions from teachers who then constituted the majority; then Akavya was ruling alongside the majority. But eventually another group of Rabbis holding opposing views came to power; then Akavya was ruling against the majority. He tells his son there is no way to know who is right. If both the earlier and the current generation of Rabbis believe they represent the authentic tradition, Akavya can lean on his received majority, and his fellow contemporary Rabbis can lean on theirs. Neither can be proven wrong.

That said, he tells his son, you do not have this luxury. I am an island of belief in a sea of discordant views. You need to heed mass opinion and follow the Rabbis, even though that means disagreeing with your father. His son says he is willing to change his position but asks a favor of his father in return. If he listens to Akavya and holds to the prevailing views of the time, will his father help him by making that known to his generation's leadership? Will he summon his colleagues to his bedside and endorse his son to them? Will he help his son get out from under his shadow? Without missing a beat, Akavya denies his request. He will not endorse his son in the presence of others.

Flabbergasted, his son wonders aloud why his father would act with such seeming callousness. "Why will you not stand up for me?" he protests. "Is it because you do not think me worthy of your kindness?" Realizing his son has taken this denial as a personal affront to his character, Akavya protests, "No! Your [own] actions will draw you near, or your [own] actions will distance you."[33]

In one last paternal act, Akavya assures his son, "If you succeed, it will be by your own merit and not by riding your father's coattails. You must make a name for yourself through your own conduct. You can find a way into the Rabbinic establishment without my help."

Hananiah does not respond—his silence is understood as tacit acceptance of his father's position—and the story ends here. Indeed, later in his life, Hananiah will heed Akavya's counsel. He will disagree with his fellow Rabbis and innovate, but he will not hold so firm to his opinions that he faces his colleagues' ire.[34] He will succeed on his own, just as Akavya predicts, because he marries the freethinking spirit of his father to sensitivity to social dynamics.

Commenting on Akavya's legacy a few generations after his death, Rabbi Judah, himself heralded as the compiler of the Mishnah, writes that few people are considered equal to Akavya in "wisdom, purity and fear of sin."[35] Akavya stands for his ideals and refuses to be bought by power. He understands the importance of earned merit and is willing to sacrifice his social standing for the pursuit of truth. He shows honor to the complex and sometimes contradictory rulings that dictate which traditions should be authoritative, and he deeply believes that while one path may be correct for him, his son may need to do the opposite to live an honorable and ethical life.

But is Akavya a person of integrity? In my view, this complex question boils down to whether he compromises his values when advocating a different path for his son. To me Akavya does not compromise his integrity when telling his son to switch sides. He factored in the value of honoring communal will as he made his decision. Although it did not sway him (though one could easily argue it should have), he could see the writing on the wall; society had moved on. Acknowledging, with humility, that he was on the wrong side of the next generation, he pushed his son to change his position.

The twentieth-century philosopher Bernard Williams's definition of integrity supports Akavya here. Teaching that integrity comes from the root "completeness or wholeness," Williams explains that living a life of integrity essentially means being able to see yourself as the same person before and after pursuing a course of action. Because our competing values, ideals, and traditions become the basis for our identity, before we compromise any of them, we should ask whether doing so keeps us whole. When we look in the mirror after taking action, will we be staring back at a recognizable picture of ourselves?[36] Williams adds that we are "specially responsible for what [we do], rather than for what other people do."[37] Akavya sees himself as having been consistent in upholding majority rule, and he holds himself to a higher standard than he does others, including his own son.

Upholding Compromise in Legal Disputes

How should compromise function in the Jewish courtroom? When a case is set to appear before a judge—or is even underway—should the plaintiffs be encouraged to figure out their own mutual solution? Or would that somehow undermine the authority and validity of Judaism's legal process? As we will see, the Rabbis uphold compromise even when they disagree on compromise!

COMPETING CAMPS ON COMPROMISE

In the most famous talmudic discussion on compromise, we find three competing camps:

1. Rabbi Eliezer: It is prohibited to mediate a dispute, and one who does is a sinner.
2. Rabbi Yehoshua ben Korcha: It is a mitzvah (commandment) to mediate a dispute.
3. Rabbi Shimon ben Menasya/Reish Lakish: One may mediate a dispute, but there are stipulations and timelines placed on when compromise can be employed (example: once a judge has heard the arguments from both litigants and made up his mind, he can no longer accept a compromise).

Rabbi Eliezer prohibits compromise out of the belief that compromise makes human needs and wants a priority over of God's Truth.[38] Reading a line from Psalms (in this author's view out of context), Eliezer condemns a person who engages in compromise as "[blessing] himself, though he despises Adonai" (Ps. 10:3).[39] Instead of truth being a human prerogative, he teaches, "The judgment is God's" (Deut. 1:17). It is a judge's job to figure out God's will. Doing right by God should not be easy. Jewish law is not about convenience; it is about meeting Divine standards. Human beings will fall short if they privilege expediency, harmony, and community over God's Truth.[40] Because the act of compromise elevates what works (pragmatic truth) over law in the ideal, it should never be employed. However, no sooner does the Talmud present this position than it undercuts it. The Rabbis bring in Aaron, Moses's brother and first Chief Priest of Israel, as a counter-example to Rabbi Eliezer's position.

In Rabbinic lore, Aaron is the emblematic pursuer of peace—he insists that making peace between people is the highest ideal, and he does whatever it takes to achieve it, as in this example from a famous Midrash:

When two people were fighting with one another, Aaron would go and sit next to one of them and say: My son, look at the anguish your friend is going through! His heart is ripped apart and he is tearing at his clothes. He is saying, How can I face my old friend? I am so ashamed, I betrayed his trust. Aaron would sit with him until his rage subsided. Then Aaron would go to the other person in the fight and say: My son, look at the anguish your friend is going through! His heart is ripped apart and he is tearing at his clothes. He is saying, How can I face my old friend? I am so ashamed, I betrayed his trust. Aaron would sit with him until his rage subsided. When the two people saw each other, they would embrace and kiss one another. And that is why it says (Numbers 20:20), "And the entire House of Israel wept for Aaron for thirty days" [after his death].[41]

Here, the Rabbis express admiration for Aaron's position on compromise. They imagine that Aaron's unending pursuit of peace leads the people to love him to the extent that every single Israelite mourns his death. It was rare for the Israelites to agree on anything. Their collective anguish—"the entire house of Israel wept for Aaron"—had to mean that Aaron must have been right.

Now, returning to the Rabbis' discussion of Rabbi Eliezer's position, they introduce Aaron into the conversation as "a lover of peace and a pursuer of peace."[42] That is all they have to say—it is presumed that anyone reading a page of Talmud has already read the rest of Rabbinic literature, so just by invoking Aaron, they have made their point.

The presence of the Aaron interjection waters down Rabbi Eliezer's position. True, the Rabbis are saying, compromise may erode the integrity of the law, but compromising will also uphold the integrity of society at large. Society works better when "rage subsides" and when friends "embrace and kiss one another."

To bolster this, the Rabbis end their discussion of Aaron by quoting the prophet Malachi: "The law of truth was in his mouth, and unrighteousness was not found in his lips; he walked with Me in peace and uprightness, and turned many away from iniquity" (Mal. 2:6).[43] The line they choose emphasizes not only Aaron's quest for "peace" but also his commitment to "truth." The two need not be in conflict. Truth is not solely in the Divine domain. Truth is also shaped by what works for us humans.

Ultimately Aaron's story opens the door for Rabbi Yehoshua ben Korcha to say regarding compromise, "It is a mitzvah to mediate a dispute."[44] His proof text is a verse that claims the compatibility of truth and peace: "Execute the judgment of truth and peace in your gates" (Zech. 8:16).[45] True, the two virtues of truth and peace can sometimes be in conflict; anyone who has ever lied to avoid conflict knows this. But to Yehoshua ben Korcha, compromise gets us closest to achieving both. A mediator strives to get both disputants as close as possible to a shared understanding of what is right and true for each.[46]

In the end, the Talmud is clear: "The halakha is in accordance with the opinion of Rabbi Yehoshua ben Korcha."[47] His belief in mediating compromise is the right solution. And yet, lest we think this concludes the matter, Yehoshua ben Korcha is not given the final word. Quoting later Rabbinic voices, specifically Rabbi Shimon ben Menasya/Reish Lakish, the Rabbis qualify Yehoshuah ben Korcha's ruling. We can advocate for compromise, but only early in a court case; it cannot be used after the judge has reached a conclusion or after the verdict has been announced. Furthermore, no judge can force a reconciliation. The judge must give the parties a choice, saying "Do you want [a strict] judgment, or do you want a compromise?"[48]

In doing this, the Talmud meets in the middle. The Rabbis understand that firm legal strictures must be in place to avoid the pursuit of compromise after a set legal judgment. Once the facts are known, and the judge who as been empowered to find Truth has come to determine that Truth, the matter rests. If we undercut that, we undercut society's reverence for the whole legal system. Thus it is that the Talmud both prioritizes the call to compromise and finds common cause with two of the three disputing positions on compromise. Yet again, compromise wins the day.

COMPROMISE WHEN FACED WITH INACCESSIBLE TRUTH: THE CASE OF STOLEN COINS

The Rabbis also uphold compromise in legal cases in which truth can never be known. Generally in Judaism, a judge's main task is to apply *God's law* to disputes. The judge is asked to discern what is right and true. If the judge applies the law correctly, the ruling should bring society closer to God's will.

But sometimes, the Rabbis realize, what is right and true is just not ascertainable. For example, the Rabbis imagine a thief who steals a coin worth 100 dinars from one person and a second coin worth 200 from another.[49] When caught and asked to return the coins, the thief no longer remembers whose was whose. If both parties claim the larger amount, the two must figure out the balance together:

> This one says: "The 200 belongs to me," and this one says: "The 200 belongs to me," [the judge] gives each one a maneh [100] and he does not give them the rest until they make a compromise between them.[50]

Both disputants are owed at least 100—which, the Rabbis say, is precisely what each of the two will get until they themselves figure out the remainder. The Rabbis put the onus back on the disputants because any judge presiding over this case will simply be assessing who seems more credible, not whose claim is right. To the Rabbis, a judge cannot determine an inaccessible truth. In this case, compromise gets closest to a smooth and fair outcome.

COMPROMISE EVEN IN BUILDING A GOLDEN CALF: AARON'S RISKY MEDIATION

According to a famous midrash, the Israelites are worried. Moses, their main connection to God, has been on Mount Sinai so long, he is liable never to return. Moses is their conduit to God, and they fear that without him, they will never gain access to the Divine. The people ask Aaron to build a Golden Calf through which they will approach God.

Aaron first demurs but then acquiesces. He understands: if he turns the people down, they are going to kill him. The Rabbis imagine that previously the people had asked Hur, another leader, to build the Golden Calf, and when Hur turned them down, they slaughtered him. Seeing Hur's murder, Aaron knows his fate if he too refuses. Furthermore, he reasons, if he is killed, the people are liable to face much direr consequences for murdering their own High Priest than they would for erecting an idol. So Aaron elects to compromise: "It is better for them to worship the calf, as it is possible they will have a remedy through repentance."[51]

Aaron proves to be right. By choosing the lesser of two evils, he preserves the people. God gets angry, but the people do repent, and legend says that on what eventually becomes Yom Kippur, God forgives the people. Nonetheless, for all of eternity, Aaron must live with the legacy of his deception. As Rabbi Tanchum bar Chanalai explains, Aaron "despises God" (Ps. 10:3), and we should be careful in venerating him because it provokes the Divine.[52] In other words, God remains angry about Aaron's act, so even if we agree that Aaron made the right call between the two terrible choices, we should refrain from proclaiming this fact.

It is a wonder that Aaron remains in his role for another generation. One could imagine he would face death after facilitating the building of an idol. At the very least, should he not have been speedily dismissed as High Priest? But he was not dismissed. It feels as if God understands Aaron's pragmatic calculation. Compromises may often be messy, but sometimes they stand as the best choice under the circumstances.

Not Leading Too Far Out in Front 3

Inasmuch as good leadership means pushing those we lead to be better, to grow, to act with integrity, it also means knowing when to stop pressing. A good leader must intuit people's breaking point and avoid crossing that line. If people are not ready for the message, however important it is, it is unlikely to penetrate. Instead, it is better to meet the people where they are and take them on their own journey.

As a congregational rabbi, I constantly confront the challenge of not leading too far out in front of my congregants. What can I expect of their religious practice? Can I push them to address certain social justice issues when they may feel less passionate about them? During the pandemic, too, I had to be sure I was not opening the synagogue so quickly that no one would come to an in-person service or that I was not instituting a mask-optional policy when my congregants were not ready to take off their masks and be in the presence of unmasked worshipers.

Today, surveys, polls, and focus groups are often mocked as pandering. Their critics believe that real leadership means taking a position and convincing a community to follow. If you have enough magnetism and charisma, they say, you can shape others in your image. But generally speaking, that is just not how leadership works. If you want to lead, you need a keen understanding of the people you are leading. You need to study them, understand them, know them. This way, you build trust, and you press them just enough to stretch themselves, but do not break their will in the process.

Sometimes being pragmatic means asking a little less of people in the hopes of getting more overall.

As we will see in this chapter, the Talmud is filled with examples of this delicate leadership. Generally speaking, the Rabbis had keen psychological minds. Acute observers of society, they understood what made people tick and behave in certain ways. Drawing upon their familiarity with the passions, motivations, and even hang-ups of their community, they could temper their own expectations of the people—and build sufficient flexibility into their legislation that would help people follow their edicts.

Setting Boundaries for Rebuke: Rabbis Zeira and Shimon

The Torah is clear that we must rebuke a wrongdoer. It states plainly: "You shall not hate your kinsfolk in your heart. Reprove your kinsman but incur no guilt on their account" (Lev. 19:17). Looking closely at these words, the Rabbis understand that if our neighbor is causing himself or others damage and we say nothing, our silence itself is a sin.[1] We are guarantors for those in our community.[2] Their moral failures become our burden. We build a better world when we stand up and proclaim what is right. As our Rabbis teach, "Rebuke leads to peace; a peace where there has been no rebuke is no peace."[3] In other words, our ability to be honest with others when they falter builds a more stable world. We might fear the sting that comes with candor, but only through truth-telling can we set others on a better course.

The same applies for society at large. If our ability to change hearts and minds reaches farther than persuading our neighbor, we have an obligation to stand firm in our principles and push for broader change. The Talmud teaches, "Anyone who had the capability to protest the members of his household and did not protest, he himself is apprehended for the members of his household. [If he is in a position to protest] the people of his town, he is apprehended for the people of his town. The whole world, he is apprehended for the whole world."[4] The Rabbis do not spell out what authority might catch and punish our silence. It might be God. It might be the Rabbis themselves. But here, they are clear: if we have power, we must use it. We cannot squander our chance to save the world.

Whether historically true or not, the Rabbis imagined themselves as possessing the power to shape those around them.[5] They believed it was imperative to correct the ills of their society. Even if they faced great resistance in doing so, keeping silent was not the answer.

For some, the ability to push, even against insurmountable odds, meant everything. In one talmudic passage, Rabbi Zeira speaks to Rabbi Shimon about how he should approach the Exilarch, the chief religious and political authority of the Jewish community in Babylonia, and reprimand him for his misdeeds. Hearing this, Rabbi Shimon is incredulous: "They will not accept reprimand from me." Yet Rabbi Zeira cannot be deterred: "Let my master reprimand them even if they do not accept it."[6] Rebuke may come with risks, Zeira seems to be saying, but doing the right thing matters more than the outcome.

However wonderful we might find this sentiment, as we will soon see, Rabbi Zeira's viewpoint is not mainstream. In fact, it is not clear that his counsel is even applied. The anecdote concludes abruptly, without mention of whether Rabbi Shimon does or does not speak to the Exilarch. The implication is that Shimon does nothing.

Rebuke is important, but it has its boundaries. And perhaps the most important limit the Rabbinic establishment places on it is that if rebuking another will not accomplish anything—or worse, if it might cause more trouble in the long run—it is better to remain silent. The Rabbis teach:

> Just as it is a mitzvah for a person to say that which will be heeded, so is it a mitzvah for a person not to say that which will not be heeded. Rabbi Abba says: It is obligatory [for him to refrain from speaking], as it is stated: "Do not reprove a

scorner lest he hate you; reprove a wise man and he will love you" (Proverbs 9:8).[7]

There are plenty of reasons one might choose to speak out. We want to preserve our integrity and not be the kind of person who remains silent in the face of injustice. We want it written in the annals of history that we were on the right side of a debate. At the same time, we need to consider why we might instead remain silent. We might prioritize maintaining peace in the home, workplace, or even society at large. We might privilege self-preservation if we dread a possible attack after we raise our voice.

Yet another strong reason to avoid a futile rebuke is to preserve our relationship with the person who needs correction. When we interact with others, we need capital. We need them to trust us, believe us. The more we rebuke someone or the louder our critique of society, the more we spend this capital. If we squander it, changing nothing in the process, the door closes on us. In the future, when we might be able to effect change, we no longer have the ear or the goodwill of others to be successful.

Rebuke is a delicate dance. The Rabbis understand that we need to choose which battles to fight. We have to be careful not to squander our opportunities to teach the most important lessons when these moments arise. Our task is to wait for the right time to make a point so it sticks.

Keeping Unknowing Sinners in the Dark:
The Nuanced Status of Meat, Wine, and Procreation

Our discussion of rebuke thus far has mainly considered situations in which a person knowingly sins. Yet many of our mistakes stem from ignorance. When these types of errors occur, is it a universal obligation to give others the opportunity to mend their ways? Or are there times it is best to hold our tongue even if we keep others in the dark? The Rabbis are unsurprisingly nuanced in their answer.

"DO NOT PUT A STUMBLING BLOCK BEFORE THE BLIND"

On the surface, Jewish law seems clear that we should always tell other people if they are erring. Keeping information from another if it might be useful in living an ethical life would itself be a moral failing. The Torah teaches, "You shall not . . . place a stumbling block before the blind" (Lev. 19:14). Although different authorities have read this prohibition in varying ways, including as a plain prohibition against tripping someone who is visually impaired, the Rabbinic understanding of the law goes to creative places.

Some see the prohibition as condemning anyone who gives false information to gain a profit.[8] An art forger or house flipper who has used shoddy materials would fall into this category. In this case, the individual misleads others and causes them to stumble over their mistaken impressions.

Others see the prohibition as warning against giving others an item they might abuse, perhaps because they lack control or do not understand their own limits. The Rabbis use the illustration of giving a Nazarite wine. Because a Nazarite is a pious individual who has vowed to avoid alcohol for religious reasons, giving him a drink or even taking him through a vineyard might lead him to break his vow.[9] This is somewhat akin to inviting a newly sober alcoholic to a bar. If we fail to safeguard such individuals against temptations beyond their control, we are responsible if they falter.

In both interpretations, "Do not put a stumbling block before the blind" exists to stop us from withholding from others crucial information that, if known, would protect them from harm. To illustrate the basic intent, the Talmud invokes this precept in reference to marking graves so that priests, who are prohibited from entering a cemetery, do not accidentally step on a burial plot and become impure. If their holy status is sullied, they cannot serve the Temple in purity.[10] Here, not sharing the location of a grave with priests who need to protect themselves would constitute a literal stumbling block.

In all of the above cases, knowledge is power. Shared with others, it gives them the tools to act ethically. Withheld, it provides avenues for sin.

LEAVE THE "STUMBLING BLOCK" IN PLACE

There are, however, times when following the right path means leaving the "stumbling block" in place. As with the recalcitrant sinner, we are ethically and legally bound to hold on to information we know will not be heard. Beyond this, a handful of times in the Talmud we are told that if society is inadvertently making a mistake, we can, and sometimes should, avoid alerting others to that fact.[11]

Perhaps the most famous example of this appears in a broader discussion of how we should behave in the wake of the Temple's destruction. Faced with the overwhelming loss of a ruined Jerusalem, the Rabbis advocate giving up certain joys as not befitting a society that ought to be in perpetual mourning. They try to prohibit many familiar Jewish practices that had brought their community an abundance of happiness.

At first some of the sages attempt to stop the public from eating meat and drinking wine.[12] Of all food and beverages, these are considered the most joyous.[13] Additionally, meat and wine are the most connected to the Temple service—priests sacrificing animals and pouring libation offers. Now without the Temple, it only makes sense to relinquish these two delicacies.

Yet in response to this decree, another countervailing voice of Rabbis responds that we "do not issue a decree upon the public unless a majority of the public is able to abide by it."[14] These Rabbis know that from the people's vantage point, giving up meat and wine will be too much to bear. If the people are made aware of the law, they will move from unknowing sinners to blatant ones. In the end, this latter voice prevails. Jewish law does not prohibit wine and meat, because it is better to keep the stumbling block hidden than remove it and allow society to fall anyway.

The Talmud, however, does not conclude the matter here. In the face of further Roman subjugation, the same sages who had called for abstinence from meat and wine attempt to take another, even more radical turn:

> And from the day that the wicked kingdom, [i.e., Rome] spread, who decree evil and harsh decrees upon us, and nullify Torah study and the performance of mitzvot for us, and do not allow us to enter the celebration of the first week of a son, [i.e., circumcision], and some say: To enter the celebration of the salvation of a firstborn son;[15] by right we should each decree upon ourselves not to marry a woman and not to produce offspring, and it will turn out that the descendants of Abraham our forefather will cease to exist on their own, rather than being forced into a situation where there are sons who are not circumcised.[16]

Here the abstinence-inclined camp of Rabbis is proposing outlawing procreation! If we are prohibited from performing the rituals associated with childbirth, they think, perhaps it is better not to bring those children into the world in the first place.

As it was with their suggested prohibition against eating meat and drinking wine, the countervailing voice of Rabbis quickly dismisses the radical prohibition against childbearing with this pragmatic retort: "Leave the Jews alone. It is better that they be unwitting sinners and not be intentional wrongdoers [who marry and procreate despite knowing that they should not]."[17]

Again this latter voice prevails. At no point later in the Talmud or in mainstream Jewish history do we hear about efforts to prohibit childbirth. In fact, one might say the opposite: Rabbinic Judaism becomes as dedicated as ever to producing babies.[18]

Notably, the most radical aspect of these two Rabbinic responses is that *neither rejects the substance of the prohibition; the Rabbis seem to agree with the proclamations in the first place.*[19] Their silence on the matter seems to condone prohibiting meat, wine, and childbear-

Too Far Out in Front   59

ing. Instead their objection comes down to one simple fact: if they stretch too far, if they ask too much, if they are too far out in front of the people, no one will heed them. The people will go right on eating forbidden food and having illicit offspring, and the Rabbis will have set society up to fail. So instead of telling the people how to behave, the Rabbis lie to them by omission.

Knowing that meat, wine, and procreation are technically forbidden but permitted for the general populace, why is it that the Rabbis seem not to follow their own advice? Why is the Talmud filled with numerous examples of later sages eating meat, drinking wine, and having kids? Is it ignorance? Hypocrisy? They might make concessions for others, but why do the Rabbis not hold themselves to their original, ideal standard? To answer this question, we need to return to the different theories of truth seen throughout the Talmud (see chapter 1).

If truth is simply what God ordains, as the correspondence theory of truth teaches, then even if the people are misled to keep rejoicing in the face of the Temple's destruction, their leaders should still practice abstinence. They might not publish it widely, but it is still "true" that meat and wine are off limits.

Yet here truth seems to function pragmatically—it is not what "is" but what "works." Because it would never work to ask people to give up so much in the aftermath of the Temple's ruin, it becomes de facto "true"—for Rabbis too—that one can eat meat, drink wine, and have children. Even if in an ideal world Jews ought to avoid these three things, the Rabbis do not legislate by conceiving the ideal but by grounding law in reality.

Not Fighting Folk Traditions: Acquiescing to Clapping and Stomping on Shabbat

As it happens, the sentiment that leaders need not tell the populace the full truth if the people cannot handle it appears a few other times in the Talmud. In one instance, a group of Rabbis is bemoaning that women in their town behave in clearly antithetical ways to the spirit of Shabbat and the holidays.[20] Some women engage in outward musical expressions, dancing, clapping, and slapping one's thigh as a sort of body percussion even though these actions are prohibited. These women do not realize that their acts might motivate people to play actual percussion instruments that might need repairing on Shabbat—actions that would then break the Rabbinic understanding of the biblical prohibition against working on the Sabbath.[21]

Likewise, these townswomen play loose with the laws of carrying on holidays and Shabbat. According to Jewish law, one can carry anything within one's own private domain, but one cannot transfer it into the public domain. For instance, I can carry a book from room to room on Shabbat, but I cannot bring that book over to my neighbor. As it happens, the same townspeople who inappropriately clap and dance on holidays also sit with their jugs right at doorsteps between public and private spaces, tempting fate that their jugs might roll away from them and as they snatch them up, they might end up carrying them in a place they should not.[22]

In both cases, despite their desire to stop their behavior, the Rabbis allow these women to keep behaving outside the law. The Rabbis respond as they did to the question of banning meat and wine after the Temple's destruction: "Leave the Jewish people alone, [and do not rebuke them.] It is better that they be unwitting [in their halakhic violations] and that they not be intentional sinners."[23] The Rabbis know their pleas will be ignored. This folk behavior is too ingrained into the townswomen's lives.

In later codes, some authorities would double down on the prohibition of clapping one's hands and stomping one's feet. In the sixteenth century, Sephardic Rabbi Joseph Caro writes in the Shulḥan Arukh, held by many to be the definitive statement of Jewish law:

> We do not clap nor do we slap our hand to our thighs nor do we dance. This is a rabbinic decree lest one come to fix a musical instrument. It is even forbidden to tap one's fingers on the ground or the board or to each other as singers do, or to shake

a nut for a child or to play with two nuts so that the child will be quiet.[24]

Yet the Rabbis' pragmatic thinking does open the door for other, equally important thinkers to encourage communal leaders to turn a blind eye to the behavior if the people cannot follow their dictates. The Shulḥan Arukh contains a gloss, right after Caro's statement, by Rabbi Moshe Isserless, the chief rabbinic authority in Eastern Europe in the sixteenth century, who channels his practical rabbinic predecessors by acknowledging he will only enforce what the people are ready to follow: "Today people clap and dance and we do not stop them because it is better that they sin unintentionally."[25]

Keeping a Leniency Secret: Not Telling the Whole Truth

A corollary of the above discussion appears in the Rabbinic adage *halakha v'ein morin ken*, meaning, "It may be the law, but we don't teach it."[26] In the previous situations, the Rabbis kept a *stringency* to themselves to prevent others from sinning. Here, halakha v'ein morin ken keeps a *leniency* secret to ensure that it does not result in an error.

NOT TEACHING ABOUT WEARING TEFILLIN AT NIGHT

To take one example, according to Jewish law, one is required to wear tefillin (leather-bound boxes containing the *Shema* and other scriptural readings) during prayer, binding them on one's forehead and bicep. During the Rabbinic era, however, tefillin were not just donned for prayer but worn as part of one's garb throughout the day. At night, though, many Rabbis hold that one should remove tefillin. Some say that God explicitly mentions the daytime when commanding the practice, saying, "You shall keep this institution at its set time from day to day" (Exod. 13.10).[27] Others reject this derivation but worry that if they fall asleep while wearing tefillin, they might inadvertently do something unbefitting of this holy item, like pass gas.[28]

As it happens, some Rabbis sanction the wearing of tefillin at night. However, they do not advertise this fact. Instead, they publish a middle-ground ruling to the masses. You should take off your phylacteries before sleeping, but if you are worried that damage might be done to the tefillin if you remove them,[29] or, if tefillin-snatching thieves are nearby, you can keep them on for safekeeping.[30] In ruling this way, the Rabbis safeguard against the worst-case scenarios on either end: that God's word will be abused either on or off the body.

The Rabbis introduce this claim through a story about two rabbis, Ravina and Rav Ashi. As the duo sits together, it begins to grow dark. Watching as Ashi dons tefillin, Ravina asks him explicitly, "Does the Master need to safeguard them?" Ashi answers affirmatively, but something does not sit right with Ravina. Ashi may be wearing his tefillin, but Ravina gets the sense from his body language and manner that his companion is not truly worried about them. If that is the case, why would he not take them off as required?

Probing deeper, Ravina realizes Ashi has lied to him. In fact, Ashi is one of the Rabbis who holds that the law permits him to wear tefillin to sleep, but he guards that opinion even from a contemporary out of concern that the masses who lack his control and wherewithal may fall asleep and abuse these ritual items. As Ashi sees it, preserving the sanctity of this holy ritual item requires him to keep his permissiveness to himself. "It may be the law," he says, "but we don't teach it."[31]

For the Rabbis, the democratization of information is not always inherently good. Yes it may lead to greater understanding and self-realization, but knowing the law without possessing the wisdom to use it properly will also lead to sin. The Rabbis have known this from the start. On this point, Hillel the Elder, one of the fathers of Rabbinic Judaism, envisions two scenarios: one in which spreading information is good and the other in which it should be hoarded.[32]

He explains that one should spread the Torah widely when the sages have power and influence. Because the masses need them as teachers, they will be open to following the sages' interpretations.

The general populous can engage with Jewish law because if they begin to err, the Rabbis will catch and fix their mistakes. In this scenario, avenues to knowledge are focused and streamlined. The sages can decide what gets taught, when it is taught, and how.

However, when knowledge is too diffuse, when it is impossible to correct the myriad of misunderstandings and misreadings that may arise when information is too available and the Rabbis' power is too weak, when people cannot tell the difference between fake and real teachings, the sages are obligated to step back and disengage from the conversation. Hillel conveys this with the cryptic phrase: "At the time of gathering, disseminate. At the time of dissemination, gather."[33] In other words, when you have control over the message, let others have it, but when it seems out of your grasp, keep it close.

NOT TEACHING TORAH KNOWLEDGE

This same spirit undergirds an additional teaching about the protection of knowledge:

> And if you see a generation for whom Torah is beloved, disseminate, as it is stated: "There is who scatters, and yet increases" (Proverbs 11:24). However, if you see a generation for whom the Torah is not beloved, gather; as it is stated: "It is time to work for God; they have made void Your Torah."[34]

As the Rabbis understand it, when we are told to disseminate Torah knowledge—to "impress them [i.e., God's teaching] upon your children" (Deut. 6:7)—the phrase should actually be interpreted more widely than its original context. Beyond parents teaching their children, all of us should be raising up disciples as we would our own offspring.[35] When we "scatter" Torah knowledge, our passion for it will "increase," and we will make the Torah beloved.

Yet even as the Rabbis uphold the mandate to spread the Torah's message, here they are also radically reminding us: *reconsider disseminating Torah if the conditions are unfavorable for its teaching*. The Rabbis attest to this by invoking the precept, "It is time to work for

God," which in later strata of Rabbinic thought indicates instances in which a person can set aside even the most important biblical laws for the needs of the moment. In our case, the crucial law is the dissemination of the Torah itself.[36] If you sense that Torah is liable to be misused in a given context, you have a right to withhold it, even if it means flouting God's command to teach the Torah widely.[37]

By summoning this precept, the Rabbis are making another important point about the power of Torah. Used wisely, it can shape society for the better. However, disseminating knowledge to those who are not ready for it or who might abuse it can be incredibly harmful. For instance, in the Rabbis' time, many people were influenced by Christianity, Zoroastrianism, and other religions. Ensuring that these people will not seek out evidence for these divergent practices in biblical writings might mean withholding the Torah's teachings. Another example: in the Middle Ages, some figures within the Catholic Church would inspect the Talmud in part to publicly dispute it and humiliate the Jewish community. Keeping Jewish wisdom close ensured less fodder for these disputations. For the Rabbis, one needs to know what to share, with whom, and when.

Avoiding Undue Burdens of Time and Money
Of all the undue burdens upon which the Rabbis seem to focus, two stand out as primary: burdens of time and burdens of money. In both, expecting too much may cause leaders to lose the confidence, trust, and patience of the people they serve.

PRESERVING THE PEOPLE'S MONEY
DURING TEMPLE SERVICE

In the Rabbinic imagination[38] and in the historical record as well, the Temple demanded a lot of its citizens. They had to pay tithes and taxes. They had to travel to Jerusalem for certain holidays on their own dime.

Yet even in the Rabbinic imagination, there were limits to what could be imposed upon the people. For example:

When casting lots for which animals would be sacrificed on Yom Kippur, the high priests were required to reach into a box. Though it was fitting that the box be made of gold and silver, because it was being used in service of God, the law stipulated that it should be made from plain wood so as to not burden the people with excess expenses.[39]

When priests would scoop out coal, they would use a cheaper silver pan rather than a more expensive gold one. Although a gold pan would more befit a holy act like a sacrifice, the heat of the coals would erode a gold pan considerably more than a silver one. Knowing gold pans would require replacement more often and not wishing to repeatedly ask the people to raise the funds for an expensive tray that would quickly degrade, the Rabbis ruled that a priest should scoop out the hottest coals with a silver pan, and once these cooled a bit, transfer them to a gold pan.[40]

While priests would blow rams' horns, or *shofarot*, on Rosh Hashanah and on all fast days, only on the New Year, a holiday to be met with majesty, could they blow shofarot with gold-plated mouthpieces. So as not to overburden the people with taxes, on regular fast days, priests had to use shofarot covered in silver.[41]

When priests brought "showbread"—twelve loaves of bread meant to be made from fine flour as a delicacy befitting the Temple—in keeping with the requirement that showbread be on display at the Temple at all times, the Rabbis, recognizing the prohibitive cost of purchasing fine flour and the tax burden that would have to be levied on the people to pay for it, asked the priests to buy worse quality flour and sift it to make it appear fine.[42]

Though there are other examples, these four cases suffice to show the Rabbis' concern that asking too much of a financial commitment of the people would sour their relationship even to the great

Temple in Jerusalem.[43] Tying the four examples together is a simple phrase capping each conversation: "The Torah spares the money of the Jewish people."[44]

To prove that "the Torah spares the money of the Jewish people," the Rabbis invoke the story of Moses's final days in the desert. The thirsty Israelites turn to Moses for aid. In turn, Moses seeks out God's guidance. The Eternal tells the aging leader to speak to a rock and it will pour forth water. However, God does not stop there. Not only should Moses slake the people's thirst, but also he should bring water "for their cattle" (Num. 20:8).

Because God did not need to offer up water for the people's animals, the Rabbis reason that God cares about their property as well as their person.[45] In those days, cows were of monetary value; therefore, preserving them must mean that God cares about preserving Israelite wealth. Drink, God seems to say, and allow yourself to keep your beasts alive in the process.[46] From this case, the Rabbis derive the mandate that leaders should emulate God in legislating against financial pain.

Later, the thirteenth-century French talmudist Menachem Me'iri puts a fine point on this:

> When a sage is required to make a halakhic decision, and it is possible for him to be permissive, it is not appropriate for him to be pious and to seek out excess restrictions—rather, he should take care for the money of Israel, for even the Torah takes care of the money of Israel.[47]

For anyone who has ever raised funds for an institution, there is no question about the validity of this statement. Woe be the leaders who waste money. Every person, every community has a breaking point, and when money is involved, the break is rarely clean. If you are going to ask for funds, it is best to do it thoughtfully. For the Rabbis it follows that we should spend when necessary, save when possible, and cut when practical.

RESTRICTING THE TIME BURDEN OF OVERLY PIOUS PRAYER

In crafting a prayer service, leaders walk a delicate line. On the one hand they want to preserve the integrity and historical legacy of the prayer book and to ensure that people fulfill their halakhic obligations—praying the right prayers, in the right way, at the right time. On the other hand, they want to create an atmosphere where people feel a connection to the ritual, enjoy the service, and feel spiritually elevated by the act of prayer. Often these two sets of goals work in concert with one another, such as when the feeling of having prayed correctly stirs people's personal connections to the liturgy and to God. Sometimes, however, the two objectives undermine one another, such as when leaders create a lengthy service in their quest to do everything by the book, but the unlearned feel alienated by it and may come to resent the very act of prayer. In the Talmud, the term for caring about the burden a religious decision might make on a community is known as *tirḥa d'tzibbura*. This principle even calls for breaking rules for the community's sake.

In one notable example, the Rabbis propose and then quickly reject the idea that the prayer service should include sections from Balaam's famous speech in praise of the Jewish people.[48] After a failed mission to curse the people, the foreign prophet makes a 360-degree turn, waxing extensively about the deep faith of the Israelites (Num. 22–24). Although it would feel fitting that these lines make their way into the *Shema*, the people's great proclamation of faith, the Rabbinic inclination, at least as understood by Rashi and other commentators, is to skip the section because it will add undue burden on worshipers. The service is long enough, and Balaam's speeches are unabating. However artful and thematically rich, reciting Balaam's words daily is too much to ask of a congregation that has myriad commitments outside of services.

In an equally telling example, the Rabbis mandate certain leniencies for prayer leaders to keep them on pace with their congregations. A long-held principle of classical Jewish law states that if a worshiper makes a mistake while praying, the person has to go back and redo that prayer. This is especially true when one is silently praying the Amidah, the central petitionary prayer in every worship service. However, this stipulation does *not* apply to prayer leaders reciting the Amidah. When they are praying silently, should they err, they are required to keep going. Because a congregation cannot continue the service until the leader is done, leaders must sacrifice the integrity of their own praying for the greater good. No one should have to wait because their leader falters.[49]

Finally, the Rabbis wrestle with this question: is it is fair to make a congregation wait while a Torah is rolled to a new section if the community only has one Torah scroll? Certain holidays and *Shabbatot* call for multiple readings in wildly different areas of the Torah. Ideally, the congregation waits while the leader rolls the scroll to the new section to be chanted, as the Torah is expected to be read, not memorized (in fact, in most cases, reading a Torah by heart invalidates the reading). However, if rolling the Torah might put an undue burden on the congregation by making everyone wait many minutes before the new section is found, the Rabbis rule that a community must either purchase a second scroll,[50] or, in certain select cases, the reader may recite the section by heart.[51]

These three examples demonstrate the serious weight the Rabbis give to communal psychology. They recognize the importance of intuiting a community's breaking point. They allow themselves to ask much of the people but also know where to draw the line, in keeping with human limitations.

This psychological sensitivity can perhaps best be seen in the way the Rabbis talk about the speed at which the High Priest must pray on Yom Kippur. In the ancient world, there was a belief that the priest faced mortal danger by entering the Holy of Holies to pray. God's presence there was too powerful; one false move might spell certain death. However, as much as a priest might wish to take his time to ensure his safety, his obligation was to move quickly through his prayers. If he extended his time in the inner chambers of the Temple, the people might grow anxious, assuming something horrible had happened to him.[52]

The Talmud tells the story of a group of Jews so scared by the High Priest's delay that it decides to go after him to save him. These people run into the priest just as he is exiting the Holy of Holies. He admonishes them for almost entering a holy section of the Temple they are not allowed to access, and they quickly scold him back for having taken his time, "Don't make a habit of doing this."[53] The Talmud ends with a postscript, "He would not extend his prayer, so as not to alarm the Jewish people." In finishing the story this way, the Talmud is agreeing with the people's critique. They may come off as impatient, rash, panicky, and reactive, but priests and other leaders who care about their flock need to take these attributes into account. Sometimes it is easier for leaders to bend to the people's needs than to expect the people to change for theirs.

Legislating for Perfection but Accepting Imperfect Reality: The *Leḥatchilah-Bedieved* Duality

In a similar vein, the Rabbis understand that law is not always a zero sum game. There is a middle ground between expecting others to reach for our goals and letting them fully off the hook. This means legislating for the ideal while accepting the imperfect when we humans fall short.

To illustrate this, the Rabbis conduct a thought experiment. Imagine you are walking down the street and spot a group of young chicks sitting behind a fence. Given the location and placement of these fledglings, you assess that though they may be wild and have wandered there, there is an equally good chance that someone left them behind the fence, planning to come back for them later. In that case, do you have license to take them?

According to Jewish law, you must leave them. Although they may be wild, the risk remains that you might be wrong and that they are someone's property. If they do indeed belong to someone else, you might be liable for stealing.[54]

With it firmly established that a person must leave the chicks, the Rabbis consider a second question: What happens if you take them either because you are ignorant of the law or you lack the cultural understanding about how people treat their livestock? If later you realize your mistake, is it your responsibility to return the fledglings? Here the law is equally clear: you may have erred, but what is done is done. You do not need to bring them back.[55]

This example illustrates two complementary principles in Jewish law. First, a law may exist *lehatchilah*, meaning as it is without any mitigating circumstances. It is normative law in the ideal—the answer authorities give when they are asked how people should behave in a vacuum. In the case of the chicks, we are told, lehatchilah, one may not take these fledglings.

Counter to lehatchilah is *bediaved*, a principle often translated as ex post facto, or after the fact. If you either tried to fulfill an ideal and fell short, or you did not know better and thought you were doing right, not only are you not punished for your error—your actions stand. In the case of the chicks, you do not need to give them back, something you would have to do if your actions are defined as stealing. Lehatchilah, you may not take the chicks, but bediaved, if you did, your acquisition was a valid one, and you can keep them.[56]

Note, however, that the Rabbis employ arguments like this sparingly, as giving license to behave out of ignorance can be a dangerous precedent. In such cases they weigh the burden of righting a small wrong (by giving those few chicks back) against a larger, impracticable burden (of hunting for an unknown owner who might have already moved on).

The lehatchilah-bediaved dichotomy appears in almost every corner of Jewish law. Ideally shofars must be curved, but if circumstances leave you no option but to use a straight one (or you use it by mistake), your blowing is valid and fulfills the mitzvah of sounding a shofar on Rosh Hashanah.[57] Likewise, Jewish law mandates scouring clay vessels with burning rocks and boiling water before Passover to ensure there will be no cross contamination with remnant ḥametz (residue from leavened products), possibly from wheat or barley previously stored in those vessels. However, if you fill your vessels with wine or honey (both kosher for Passover) right before the holiday but realize soon after that their containers were not properly scoured, provided they were cleaned well before these substances went in, you may eat their contents without worrying they are tainted.[58]

Although the Rabbis tend to employ leḥatchilah-bedieved in ritual matters, later authorities find ways to use it elsewhere in Jewish law. Joseph Caro rules that a woman who sees blood for two to three days is required to check herself for menstrual blood in the evening to distinguish spotting from a full-on period. But if she errs and only checks in the morning, finding nothing, she is considered pure because that checking counts, bedieved.[59] The twelfth-century scholar Maimonides applies similar thinking to the realm of medical law. Ideally, people performing medical care should not treat their fathers or mothers, because in the course of treating them, they may also hurt them and thereby violate the principle that one cannot cause harm to a parent.[60] However, Maimonides cautions, although this is the ideal, it need not be the practice:

> When a person lets blood for his father, or if he was a doctor and amputated flesh or a limb, he is not liable. Even though he is not liable, the initial and preferred option is for him not to perform the operation.... When does the above apply? When there is another person there who is capable of performing these actions. If, however, there is no one else there capable of doing this but him and they are suffering, he may let blood or amputate according to the license that they grant him.[61]

Here Maimonides makes two concessions. First, a child is allowed to do anything to aid a parent, provided that 1), only he is competent to perform the needed operation at the time and 2), he has the parent's permission to proceed. If both conditions are met, he may help his parent despite the pain he will inflict in the course of helping that parent. However, even in the case when another person is available to help and he is prima facia denied permission, should he choose to aid his parents, he is not held accountable for violating the law.

The dual concepts of leḥatchilah-bedieved provide an avenue of leniency and forgiveness to those who have erred. Leḥatchilah asks us to be our best. Bediewed gives us a cushion on which to fall short.

Bediewed does not mean that the ideal laws are irrelevant, that Jews can skip right to the accommodations bediewed offers. Jewish law does not encourage stolen fledglings, misshapen shofarot, or partially cleaned barrels. It does, however, acknowledge that there can still be holiness and even the fulfillment of mitzvot in our shortcomings. Bediewed is not permissiveness but compassionate resignation.

Although there is certainly a moral element to making room for our failures, there is also an important pragmatic consideration. Imagine trying to achieve something and failing over and over again. Some of us will persevere in that situation, but most of us will give up sooner or later, defeated by our own perceptions of inadequacy. Clawing our way back from failure requires way more resolve than many of us have. Our Rabbis understood this well. They allowed us to fall short while still saving face. In doing so, they kept countless of us committed and excited about engaging with Jewish law.

Building Compassion into the Rabbinic System of Law

Leaders today could learn something from the approach of the Rabbis. Be scholars in the psychology of your flock. Understand what those you lead are capable of and hold standards malleable enough to fit their needs. Expect that people are flawed: self-interested, stubborn, fickle, impatient, careless, selfish, quick to pronounce the truth of complex situations with only surface understandings. The Rabbis do not wholly reject these most human of traits (even if, to be fair, they, being human themselves, often bemoan that those they serve do not meet their standards). Instead, the Rabbis are inclined to legislate around humanness—to build compassion into their system of law.[62]

An oft-told story encapsulates this spirit of the Rabbinic mindset. A woman approaches a sage with a dead chicken in hand. Showing it to the rabbi, she asks if the way it was slaughtered makes it kosher or not. The rabbi looks closely at the chicken and then at the woman. He observes her clothing, her manner, her hygiene. The chicken was not slaughtered in the kosher way, but he will still tell her she can eat it. Better she eats, unknowingly erring, than goes without dinner that night. In this case, stringency would be an act of cruelty.

There is little as deeply and authentically Jewish as this Rabbi's lie. As Rav Abraham Isaac Kook, Israel's first Chief Rabbi, once wrote, "A leniency or [halakhic] adjustment which comes about as a result of extenuating financial circumstances or because of communal necessity is not a deviation from halakha, but is instead an integral part of the 'perfect/complete Torah.'"[63] Leaders need to learn to pause and study those around them before making proclamations. Only then will they be able to voice the values they seek to espouse in ways that others will hear and heed.

Abiding by the Wisdom of the Masses 4

A true account: modern scholars believe the Rabbis were a relatively small, largely powerless cohort that could not effect any significant change without the masses.[1] Often the general populace did not listen to them either. They constructed and used their own synagogues differently—some of their synagogues displayed human iconography and zodiac signs.[2] And the "folk" tended to have a more relaxed relationship with purity laws and different views on tithing.[3]

Imagine what this reality must have felt like for the Rabbis. The masses are always subverting their authority. People are flouting or ignoring their rules and regulations (including mandated regular Torah study) for holy living.[4] Sometimes the Rabbis get so infuriated that they disparage the people in the harshest of ways.[5] Even so, deep down the Rabbis understand just how much the people matter. As this chapter will show, the Rabbis proceed to honor—or, at the very least, accommodate—the communal will and vision.

However contradictory, this makes sense. Although Rabbinic history is not monolithic, with eras of more or less interaction between the Rabbis and the masses,[6] on balance the Talmud shows the Rabbis engaging consistently with the general populace around them. Sometimes this communication is an inevitable product of living in the same world. As Talmud scholar Jacob Neusner says, "The Rabbis came out of the bosom of the folk. They were brought up among the people and later lived among them."[7] Affected by the same vicissitudes of life, the Rabbis are shown in the Talmud to struggle with the same droughts,[8] fear the same foreign enemies,[9] and stand beside the *am haaretz* on the same lines in the markets.

At other times, their choice to maintain good relations with the masses is intentional. Local farmers might be uneducated, but the Rabbis need them to produce food. Communal tzedakah funds will remain paltry if only the Rabbis participate. And, as we will see throughout this chapter, the people are the keepers of collective wisdom and communal memory, which the Rabbis need as well if they are to legislate properly.

Ultimately, when the Talmud shows the Rabbis deciding to engage with the majority population around them, it shows deeply pragmatic engagement. The Rabbis' stance might be encapsulated in the oft-quoted phrase by contemporary business guru Ken Blanchard: "None of us is as smart as all of us."

Communal Prophecy:
Hillel's Solution for the Sons of B'terah

The Rabbis make this very point in a story about the Sons of B'terah. When the sons forget an important workaround surrounding sacrifice and approach Rabbi Hillel for the remedy, Hillel finds their solution not on his own, and not by consulting with his fellow rabbis, but by observing the actions of the people.

Some background: On Shabbat and holidays a Jew may use a knife to make a sacrifice, but one cannot transport that knife through the public domain, since it is forbidden to carry it outside one's home on a sacred day. Instead, Jewish law requires one to bring the knife to the Temple in advance and store it until needed on the holiday. If the knife is not already in place, one cannot deliver on an important obligation to offer animals to God in their proper time.

Although they are usually good about this, on one week, preceding the Sabbath, the sons of B'terah accidentally leave their knife at home. That Sabbath, stuck with the choice of either breaking Shabbat to transport the knife to the Temple or forgoing the sacrifice, they approach Hillel for help. They know a remedy exists, but they do not know what it is.

Hillel, who has just been promoted to head of the court, is stumped. He confesses: "I have heard this law but forgotten it." However, he quickly devises a plan to resolve the dilemma. He will watch for clues in the populace around him. Perhaps their behavior will point him in the right direction. "Leave it to the Jewish people" he says. "If they are not prophets . . . they are the sons of prophets."[10] In saying this, Hillel expresses a deep and oft forgotten truth: the people possess sagacity. They are "sons of prophets." Like their prophetic ancestors, God has endowed them with Divine wisdom, creativity, and imagination.

As the story continues, Hillel watches in wonder as the people face the same problem as Sons of B'terah but concoct their own creative workaround. When they forget their knives, they tie the blades onto the wool and horns of sheep and goats and then lead the animals up to the Temple mount for sacrifice. By not carrying the forbidden items themselves, the people preserve Shabbat, and by having their animals do the carrying, the knives make it to the Temple with the animals on time.

Seeing the people's ingenuity jogs Hillel's memory into recalling a teaching from his early years of study that affirms their actions. Recalling his teachers, he proclaims, "This is the tradition I received from the mouths of Shemaya and Avtalyon!"[11] The community had preserved a tradition that even the smartest thinker of their generation could not recall. Communal memory was a failsafe against rabbinic forgetfulness.

The Costs of Ignoring Communal Wisdom: Prelude to the Sons of B'terah and Story of Deborah

To reinforce their point that one must listen to those around them, the Rabbis follow up the Sons of B'terah story with a reflection on the costs of ignoring communal wisdom: "Anyone who acts haughtily, if he is a Torah scholar, his wisdom departs from him; and if he is a prophet, his prophecy departs from him."[12] Wisdom, according to this text, relies on humility. Arrogant individuals see themselves as the only source of knowledge. Yet we humans are leaky vessels; even the smartest of us forget salient information. If we rely only on ourselves, external sources of wisdom cannot replace what we ourselves lose. If, however, we open ourselves to the wisdom of those around us, our learning will endure—reinforced by the discourse and actions of those with whom we surround ourselves.

To prove this point, the Rabbis relate two anecdotes. The first is an imagined prelude to the above query from the Sons of B'terah. At the outset the group asks him a different set of questions about Passover, which he answers easily. Hearing about the exchange and amazed by his legal reasoning, the Rabbis seat him at the head of the academy and appoint him leader (*nasi*) of the community. But as soon as they do this, Hillel tears into his fellow leaders: *You are lazy in not learning the laws for yourselves. If you took your learning seriously, you would not need to rely on me for wisdom.* Upon hearing this rebuke, God proceeds to curse Hillel with forgetfulness. If he is too haughty to simply answer the straightforward legal questions that come his way, then he better learn humility, by needing to rely on the general populace to remember the most basic of laws.[13]

The second anecdote involves Deborah, a prophetess and war hero from the book of Judges. After a triumphant battle against the Canaanite general Sisera, Deborah famously sings a song of victory. Yet, rather than share the credit, she casts aspersions on previous generations:

In the days of Shamgar son of Anath,
In the days of Jael, caravans ceased,
And wayfarers went,
By roundabout paths.

Deliverance ceased,
Ceased in Israel,
Till you arose, O Deborah. (Judges 5:6–7)

Speaking about herself in the third person, Deborah contrasts her success with the failures of other leaders. The Israelites face enemy ire, closed roads, disappearing wayfarers, even God's own withdrawal from the battlefield. Nonetheless, when she enters the fray, the Israelites are victorious.

The Rabbis imagine that God punishes Deborah for taking undue credit. As soon as she disparages other Israelites and claims victory fully on her own merits, God causes Deborah to lose her train of thought. She no longer has words to continue her famous song. Rather, she calls out to herself, "Awake, awake, O Deborah! Awake, awake, strike up the chant!" (Judg. 5:12)—a pep talk of sorts aiming to bring back the Divine inspiration God took away from her. Indeed, as the Talmud teaches above, haughtiness causes one's prophecy to depart. Like with Hillel, God has wiped clean the mind that puts itself above others.

These two anecdotes undergird the point that real leaders cannot and do not do everything on their own. All of us are products of the trailblazers who come before us and the society that more or less sustains them. Even if Israelite society struggled under previous leaders, they laid a foundation that allowed Deborah to enter into leadership and thrive. Different leaders, a different people, different circumstances might have meant Deborah never would have found her voice.[14]

The Rabbis' Need to Listen to Rumors

The Rabbis hold fast to the biblical prohibition, "Do not go about as a talebearer among your people" (Lev. 19:16).[15] In Hebrew, the word "talebearer" (*rakhil*) can also be translated as "peddler," a reason this text has become the central Torah command prohibiting gossip.[16] No one should peddle information as ware; no one should make others' business into a means for furthering one's social standing. In fact, gossip is so harmful, the Rabbis liken it to murder:

> The person who listens to gossip is even worse than the person who tells it, because no harm could be done by gossip if no one listened to it. It has been said that lashon ha-ra [disparaging speech] kills three: the person who speaks it, the person who hears it, and the person about whom it is told.[17]

And yet, the Rabbis realize, sometimes there is truthful and highly important information in the people's chatter. However harmful, gossip should not always be ignored. At this point the Rabbis wrestle with whether one can act, and even legislate, on the basis of rumors.

CRITERIA FOR HEEDING RUMORS

Sometimes the answer is no. The reasons vary. If gossip is unjust, a legal decision should not be rendered on its basis. Similarly, since certain rumors are tantamount to "stolen information," they are thus impermissible. A rumor's veracity may be too difficult to authenticate. Even a fairly reliable rumor may not contain all the kernels of truth needed to make a sound legal decision. And the rumor may be old news. In the time it took to hear of the problem, the parties involved might have reached a solution.

The stakes may also be too high to gamble on a mistaken assumption. In capital cases, when a person's life is at stake, a judge must implore a witness, "Perhaps what you say in your testimony is based on conjecture, or perhaps it is based on a rumor, perhaps it is testimony based on hearsay."[18] Unless the evidence is incontrovertible and the person saw the defendant commit the crime firsthand, the legal system must ignore witness testimony.

The Rabbis know all too well the costs of specious rumors. When King Yannai (103–76 BCE) learns the sages of Israel have been spreading the unsubstantiated rumor that his mother was taken captive before he was born and raped, he executes the sages.[19] The Talmud instructs that it took generations to retrieve the wisdom lost on that fateful day. The sages' failure to guard their tongues led to immeasurable tragedy.

Still, even with all this in mind, the Rabbis remain open to making use of rumors under select circumstances. They develop criteria to help them decide which rumors to follow. First, they explore the longevity of a given report: are the tales "rumors that stop" or "rumors that do not stop"?[20] In their eyes, the former category, short-lived rumors, are the kind of falsehoods that, as the adage goes, can "travel halfway around the world before the truth can get its boots on."[21] These usually last a day or two, and move so quickly that they rapidly burn out. By contrast, the Rabbis maintain, "rumors that do not stop" have staying power, in part because they are based in fact. If, after a month, people are still talking about some event, it likely happened, even if the details might morph in society's game of telephone.

To cite perhaps the most famous example of this distinction, the Rabbis discuss a case of a suspected adulterous wife. Can her husband divorce her on the basis of his strong suspicion that she is unfaithful? If, for example, he sees a man leaving their home and then walks in to find her wearing disheveled clothing or he finds another man's shoes under his bed, should he be allowed to dissolve the marriage?[22]

Surely something untoward seems to be happening under the husband's nose. One might argue that he should be able to act on his suspicions in order to avoid being cuckolded. Jewish law, however, prohibits this knee-jerk response. Hearsay in law can be a slippery slope, and the burden of proof falls on the husband so he does not rashly overreact. According to *halakhah*, one needs witnesses to prove a claim as serious as infidelity.

That is, unless a rumor is strong enough. According to the Rabbis, if there is a short-lived rumor of infidelity, a court needs an extra burden of proof to authenticate the husband's hunch. He must go the extra mile and aid the court in finding witnesses, as Jewish law dictates he would need to with his suspicion alone. However,

Wisdom of the Masses   81

if the rumor persists for longer than a day and a half, it means his worst fears are likely realized.[23] The court may grant him a divorce on the strength of the rumor, provided there is no evidence the rumor was circulated in bad faith.[24]

Like a rumor's strength, the Rabbis viewed its simplicity as an equally telling sign of its veracity. The more straightforward the rumor, they decided, the more likely it is true. To explain this, the Rabbis imagine a man hearing two simple rumors: first, that a woman claiming to be unmarried is actually betrothed; and second, that a woman who he thought was married is in fact divorced. In both cases the man can act on this information, not courting the betrothed woman or beginning to court the divorced one.[25] To the Rabbis, the simplicity of the rumors lends a degree of truthfulness to them even without corroborative evidence.

However, as the rumor gets more complicated, one ought to begin to doubt its validity. If, the Rabbis say, the rumor is that the divorce was conditioned on something that may or may not have happened, such as the divorce document (*get*) possibly not having been delivered in the correct manner, a man should ignore the rumor and not proceed to court the woman.[26] There are two many "ifs." It is enough to take the leap on the rumor itself. One should not also have to assume other variables fell into place for the rumor to be true.

ACCEPTABLE ACTIONS IN RESPONSE TO RUMORS

The Talmud speaks of severe actions taken in light of rumors, all of which seem to be fine in the mind of the Talmud's editors, among them flogging someone who is the subject of a bad report[27] and banishing someone from the study hall due to a communal suspicion that he revealed a long-held secret.[28] One Mishnah requires someone to take an oath—a big deal at the time[29]—that he did not steal an item in question if there is a rumor that he did.[30]

Other times the Rabbis do a delicate dance to honor rumors while preserving their own integrity. In one instance, a group of citizens from the Galilee approach Rabbi Tarfon.[31] Gossip is spreading that they have killed someone and they are worried for their lives. It is not known whether Tarfon already knew about their plight or heard it from them. Regardless, their request leaves Tarfon at a loss. He suspects they are innocent and wants to help them. If he does nothing, their pursuers will kill them in retaliation, but if he does hide them, he will be guilty of listening to "malicious speech." One has to be very careful before acting on rumors, even if doing so will save lives.[32]

To make his decision, Tarfon considers how others treat rumors. He concludes: "Even though one should not accept it [i.e., a rumor], one is required to be concerned [about the harm that might result from ignoring it]." He therefore implores the Galilee Jews to hide themselves. The Talmud does not say whether he aids them in this effort, which implies that he does not.

Even if Tarfon wants to avoid involvement in the intrigue around him, he has to take some action. The rumor may not be true, but it is working. Yet, Tarfon knows not to jump headfirst into action either. He tries to remain neutral, perhaps even to find a pragmatic middle ground: giving the group encouragement (and maybe even advice?) to hide, but not doing the work himself.

The People Help to Decipher Lost Meanings: Tales of Rabbi Judah the Prince's Maidservant

It is a truism that the meanings of words are often lost to history. For instance, open to almost any section of the JPS Tanakh, the standard Bible translation in many academic circles, and you will quickly find the phrase "meaning of word uncertain" in the footnotes. Even the most heralded Bible scholars need to rely on educated guesswork from time to time.

Likewise, in the oral culture the Rabbis inhabit, certain words passed down through the ages have opaque meanings as well. How do the Rabbis handle these confounding terms? Some guess. Some knowingly misread words to make them say what they want. But others listen closely to the speech of common folk to point them in the right direction. The most famous case of this appears in a number of anecdotes about Rabbi Judah the Prince's maidservant. One telling story surrounds the confusing word *seirugin*.

Some background: because the Rabbis' laws were first composed orally, well before redaction in the Mishnah in 200 CE, occasional terms, like seirugin, have been preserved without their definitions. Thus in one instance, the Mishnah says, "If one reads the Megillah *seirugin* they have fulfilled their obligation," without elucidating what seirugin means.[33]

As additional background, various laws govern reading the Megillah (the scroll traditionally read on Purim).[34] Reading the Megillah out of order negates the reading; reading it by heart, though not ideal, is accepted. Reading a scroll written on certain kinds of leather requires a redo; reading it in one's native language does not. What, then, is the text saying by adding, "If one reads the Megillah *seirugin* they have fulfilled their obligation?" At first, the Rabbis of the generation directly after the Mishnah are content to leave it a mystery. But then a random event lets them in on the meaning of the word.

One day, as the Rabbis are entering into Rabbi Judah's house in small groups rather than walking in together, a violation of the decorum of the time, Rabbi Judah's maidservant scolds them, "How long are you going to enter *seirugin seirugin*?"[35] Suddenly, they realize what the term means. In the context of their entering, *seirugin* must mean trickles or breaks. Then that must be what the Mishnah is saying: one is not supposed to read the Megillah in drips and drabs, pausing often and then resuming. However, if one does so, he has nevertheless fulfilled his obligation. The less than ideal reading still counts.

Other stories like this follow. The Rabbi discover that the unknown word *ḥalogelogot*, which appears in several places in the Talmud, must mean purslane, a small, fleshy-leaved plant that grew in ancient Israel, after they hear Judah's maidservant utter ḥalogelogot while scolding a man who has been scattering the leafy-green vegetable haphazardly.[36] In another tale, the sages learn what the book of Proverbs means when it implores the reader to "*salseleha*" wisdom (Prov. 4:8) as a result of overhearing the same maidservant say to a certain man, "How long will you go on twirling [*mesalsel*] your hair?"[37] Clearly, the text must be saying that each of us must turn and twirl wisdom, to wring it of all its majesty. Only then will the Torah yield its fullness to us.

These stories are not anomalous. In a different part of the Talmud, Rava Bar Bar Hana tells of stumbling upon Arab merchants who reveal to him deep-held secrets, like the place where earth and heaven touch.[38] In certain episodes he learns the meaning of obscure biblical terms.[39] At another time, a bedouin reveals to him the precise location in the desert where the generation of Jews who died while wandering for forty years after the Exodus are lying peacefully for all eternity.[40] Later, the bedouin shows him the exact place where the earth swallowed Korach's children after Korach rebelled against Moses during their wanderings.[41]

Undoubtedly, there is a fantastical quality to these stories that makes even the most ardent believer skeptical. Yet in my view, these tales exist in part to show that esoteric wisdom lives with the surrounding cast the Rabbis interact with daily. In doing so, the stories open the possibility that the everyday people the Rabbis interact with will also add something important to the Jewish conversation. The message then extends to us. People we might not expect to guide us may well help us find that which is most hidden and precious.

Furthering the Rabbinic idea that encounters of all kinds can be platforms for wisdom, Rabban Yochanan Ben Zakkai is famously lauded for searching for knowledge anywhere he can find it. In addition to studying the Torah, Yochanan seeks out "the conversation of ministering angels; the conversation of demons, and the conversation of palm trees; parables of launderers [possibly folk tales that explain the Torah or the musings of people doing housework], parables of foxes; [and more generally], a great matter and a small matter."[42] Yochanan finds meaning in the banter of laborers around him as well as the minutiae of Scripture and the esoterica of the heavens. In a way, all of this wisdom is Torah.

The Rabbis Repeat the People's Folk Sayings

The Talmud is filled with folk sayings. Maxims appear hundreds of times in the Talmud alone, and in almost equal amounts in midrashic literature.[43] In many respects, the presence of these adages constitute some of the greatest evidence of the Rabbis' reliance and even respect for the communal wisdom of the masses around them.

Here are a few examples:

> "Either friendship or death."[44] This is used to explain why, in one of the most tragic episodes in Rabbinic literature, Honi the Circle Drawer chooses to end his own life when he awakens after 70 years of sleep to a world that fails to recognize or acknowledge him. With his whole community dead and no one believing that he is who he says he is, he prays for death to cease a lonely life not worth living. God grants his request and Honi is allowed to die.
>
> "One who steals from a thief has a taste of theft."[45] This proverb appears in the Rabbis' rebuke against Rav Huna, who decides to get even with the sharecropper who is stealing from him by withholding the stolen amount from the sharecropper's wages.[46] Although Rav Huna is technically within his right to do this, the Rabbis reprimand him that responding to his worker in such an underhanded way perpetuates a culture of stealing. Eventually, and perhaps due in part to the force of the folk-saying's rebuke, Rav Huna realizes the error of his ways and vows never to withhold money from his sharecroppers again.
>
> "The ewe follows the ewe."[47] After a long passage telling the story of how Rachel allows her husband Rabbi Akiva to leave home for years on end to pursue his rabbinical studies at major

financial and emotional expense to her and her family, the Talmud adds a postscript about how their unnamed daughter does the same for a rabbi named Ben Azzai: she betroths Ben Azzai and then sends him to find himself by studying abroad with the best Sages of their generation. In other words, a child tends to follow in the footsteps of one's parents.

"One spicy pepper is better than a basketful of squash."[48] In the Rabbinic world, if you make a hasty vow or oath, you can appear before an authority and get it nullified. This idea is very important to the Rabbis—a whole talmudic tractate is dedicated to it—and yet the Torah says very little about how nullification works. Hence the Talmud tells a story that gets to the heart of how one can rescind one's vows. An oath-taker asks the Rabbis to nullify his former vow which he now regrets. Various Rabbis offer shaky proofs for the nullification until one rabbi, Shmuel, finally proposes what all consider to be good, strong proof. Then the question arises: should the Rabbis rely solely on Shmuel's solid proof, or should they piece together all of the weaker proofs which provide more cumulative support? They bring in the folk saying to prove that Shmuel is enough. One "spicy pepper" to support an idea is better than multiple uninspired sources.

It is hard to pinpoint why the Rabbis emphasize these folk statements. Perhaps in the absence of a biblical verse to prove a point, adages bestow authenticity. Maybe the proverbs are pedagogical tools; in an oral culture, they are easy to remember. They also pack a punch, delivering a desired message even better than the Rabbis could articulate. I would add a fourth pragmatic reason. If part of the Rabbinic project is to change the hearts and minds of the populace, then speaking in the familiar folk language of the masses seems like an optimal strategy. When the masses hear these proverbs, they are likely to feel like the Rabbinic teachings behind them are theirs too.

Praising the Masses: Rabbi Simon ben Lakish's Analogy

One particularly moving Talmud passage acknowledges just how interconnected the Rabbis feel with the multitudes. Rabbi Shimon ben Lakish likens the Jewish people to a vine:

> The branches of [the vine support the clusters of grapes, the leaves, and the tendrils]; these are represented among the Jewish people by the homeowners, [who provide financial support for the entire nation]. The clusters of grapes on the vine, these are the Torah scholars. The leaves on the vine, [which protect the grapes], these are the ignoramuses, [who protect the Torah scholars]. The tendrils of the vine, [which do not directly serve the grapes themselves], these are the empty ones of the Jewish people.[49]

Even as the Rabbis imagine themselves to be the grape clusters, the juiciest segment of the plant, they also praise the other parts. The branches which support the vines are the homeowners who keep the economy going. The leaves are the *amei haaretz*, the people unlearned in Torah. Just as the leaves protect the clusters from the harsh rays of the sun, the amei haaretz do the normal labor of society like farming, trading, and building, which ensures that the Rabbis do not have to worry about daily subsistence and can concentrate on their studies. Even the tendrils, which symbolize the people who seem to serve little to no real purpose, those whom the Rabbis call "empty ones," also matter. They add stability to the vine and extra surface area for capturing the sunlight, a process later generations will call photosynthesis.[50] These people are still part of the mosaic of culture surrounding the Rabbis: carrying communal wisdom, telling folk tales, teaching their children too.

Rabbi Shimon ends his metaphor of the plant with a moving testament to the people: "Let the clusters of grapes pray for the leaves, as were it not for the leaves, the clusters of grapes would not survive."[51] Although the Talmud does not explain why or how this is so, the whole of this chapter is devoted to demonstrating the wisdom of this teaching. The clusters of grapes (the Rabbis) need the leaves (the people). The people do the jobs the Rabbis cannot or will not do. All the more, the people are carriers of wisdom in an oral culture. The more voices that speak, the more likely it is that someone we might never expect will say the very thing that will help us solve a pressing concern.

Even if we, like the Rabbis, spend most of our time in conversation with likeminded human beings, it behooves us to follow their lead and peek out of our enclaves once in a while. There is no telling what we might learn.

Keeping the Peace with Neighbors   5

For as long as Jews have existed, somewhere in the world, Jews have been strangers among a non-Jewish populace. To maintain good relationships within the broader society, they have needed to walk a fine line between changing to fit their surroundings and preserving their independent identities. Although diverse factors may have animated the Rabbis' relationships with their neighbors in their day, this chapter explores how the Rabbis navigate the challenge of coexistence with a pragmatism that makes keeping the peace a priority.

Drinking Non-Kosher Wine: The Tale of the King's Cupbearer

The Rabbis uphold as an example of this delicate dance a throwaway line in the book of Nehemiah. In telling his story, Nehemiah explains:

> I was the king's cupbearer at the time. In the month of Nisan, in the twentieth year of King Artaxerxes, wine was set before him; I took the wine and gave it to the king. (Neh. 1:11–2:1)

At issue for the Rabbis is the fact that Nehemiah, a Jew, has a professional obligation to drink what would be tantamount to today's non-kosher wine. In their imagination, a cupbearer, one who serves wine to royalty, is also the first line of defense against poison. Consequently, daily, Nehemiah took sips of a forbidden beverage.[1]

In examining the story, the Rabbis make a pun out of Nehemiah's official title, *tirshatha*, meaning an official governor of Judaea.[2]

Noticing that the word sounds similar to the Hebrew word *hitir*, to permit, they imagine Nehemiah was called tirshatha because he was permitted to break certain laws in service of the crown.

Jews and Gentile Governments:
The "Drawing Near to the Kingdom" Principle

Over the course of time, this permissibility coalesced into an important legal principle known as *kerovin l'malkhut*.[3] Literally meaning "drawing near to the kingdom," kerovin l'malkhut allows the Rabbis to make certain legal exceptions if these help the Jews forge or maintain close ties with the gentile governments around them. When the Jewish community rises and falls at the behest of the foreign regimes in their midst, such exceptions become necessary.

For Nehemiah, it means drinking non-kosher wine. For others, it may mean dabbling in Greek philosophy to better speak the cultural language around them, something at least some Rabbis believe should prima facie be forbidden.[4] Perhaps most famously, it allows Rabbis to cut their hair and dress like the general population, to blend in and lend themselves a level of credibility.[5]

So, too, it means carefully navigating social dynamics to remain in a ruler's good graces. For instance, Rabbi Judah the Prince, who had cultivated an incredibly close relationship with Emperor Antoninus,[6] is nonetheless vigilant about how he approaches the ruler:

> Our teachers instructed Rabbi Afes, "Write a single letter in my name to our lord the Emperor Antoninus." Thereupon he rose and wrote, "From Rabbi Judah the Prince to the Emperor Antoninus [greetings]," [Rabbi Judah] took it, and read it, and tore it up. He said to him [R. Afes], "This is what you should write: 'From your servant Judah to our lord the Emperor Antoninus.'" He protested to him, "My master, why do you abuse your honor?" [Rabbi Judah] replied, "Am I better than my ancestor? Didn't Jacob say in this manner, 'Thus says your servant Jacob' (Gen. 32:5)."[7]

The biblical scene Rabbi Judah is quoting takes place after the brothers Jacob and Esau have been apart for twenty years and are about to be reunited. Earlier in the narrative Jacob had stolen Esau's birthright and blessing. Now Jacob sends a request to his brother asking for safe passage through his territory in which he humbles himself, calling himself a "servant" and raising Esau up to the status of a master. (He receives a reply that Esau will be coming to greet him personally.) Rabbi Judah seems to be saying that Esau may not have deserved his brother's respect, yet Jacob still had to be careful and build him up to preserve their relationship. Jacob also did not know the kind of army at his brother's disposal and whether Esau was still angry with him. It is better to feign reverence than risk offending someone who might do you harm.

According to tradition, Esau is the forebearer of Rome and, by extension, many non-Jewish ruling powers. By invoking his story, the Rabbis remind the Jewish community, Jacob's progeny, to follow in his footsteps, engaging politely with Esau's children. Knowing this, Rabbi Judah compels Rabbi Afes to act humbly toward Antoninus. The Jews are under the thumb of Rome. Good relations mean more freedom and safety. Offense means fear and violence.

Rabbi Judah is considered a master at preserving the peace. He is said to be constantly in contact with Rome, always in the hope of keeping up good relations.[8] In this instance, perhaps all Antoninus needs is a simple greeting. But if the emperor takes offense, even at the way he is addressed, the letter will no longer be effective. Pragmatically, the safest course is to flatter.

One sage goes so far as to not observe Jewish practices to avoid provoking a fickle, impulsive, violent monarch. The Rabbis relate an apocryphal[9] story of King Shapur, who, furious over the simple sound of Jews playing a harp in the city of Laodicea, decides to attack it.[10] His troops massacre twelve thousand people.[11] After hearing about the slaughter, a sage named Shmuel does not mourn for these fallen Jews. Although the Talmud jumps through hurdles to explain his reluctance to tear his garment in mourning,[12] one likely explanation is that he does not want to further enrage the king. A king who destroys a city of Jewish civilians over the sounds of a musical instrument would think nothing of murdering an individual who upsets him.

A generation after Shmuel, the sage Rava sends bribes to the king proactively to keep the peace. These payments are secret. Not even his fellow sages know; they mistakenly think the king leaves him alone because somehow he is a favored subject. But Rava's clandestine gifts work for only so long. Eventually, the king sends for Rava and imprisons him, hoping to force him to increase the level of payments. As the story ends, Rava is in prison waiting for someone to deliver him the additional funds. Thankfully he does not die there, suggesting that he either finds someone to help him pay the king or the king changes his mind. The reader leaves the story with the strong sense that even the craftiest of the sages cannot plan around a capricious ruler.[13]

Thus it is imperative to do everything to avoid such outcomes, even if it means changing Jewish law to fit a king's need. Sometimes these changes are small. In designing roads, for example, Jewish law requires builders to conform to local norms, which generally means keeping roads relatively narrow and hence minimizing costs of labor and supplies. However, the Rabbis permit a king to demand whatever width he wants from the public thoroughfare because his travel takes precedence over every other concern.[14]

Rabbinic accommodations toward kings can be even more extreme. Jewish law holds that Jews must not only seek to destroy idolatry but also the pedestals that idols sit upon, as these retain the stain of idolatry. In planning for a future time when Jews will have autonomy and sovereignty, Jewish leaders need to root out any such existing symbols now. However, the Rabbis rule that any pillars belonging to a foreign king—even those that once staged idols—should remain along the side of the road. The Jewish community should not petition the king to take them down or to remove them when the king is not there. Kings want to erect their idols on pedestals when they visit, and it is in the Jewish community's interests to facilitate this regardless of the Jewish mandate to destroy idolatry.[15]

Gaining Aid from One's Neighbors: The Case of the Roman Matron

In one talmudic episode, the Rabbis seek out a Roman matron after the Roman government signs a decree prohibiting Torah study and circumcisions.[16] It is telling that they choose this matron, whom the Talmud describes as keeping "the company of all the prominent people of Rome."[17] This not only shows her influence but also the Rabbis' savvy in knowing the Roman power players.

She tells them, "Arise and cry out at night."[18] With only this counsel, the Rabbis head into the public square, crying, "O Heaven! Are we not brothers? Are we not children of one father? Are we not the children of one mother? How are we different from any other nation and tongue that you single us out and issue against us evil decrees?"[19] Moved by their plea, the Romans annul the decree.

It is not clear from the story whom the Rabbis beseech with their words. If they are speaking to God who hears their cries and moves the hearts of the Romans, then this story is radical in that the Rabbis can imagine a Roman matron somehow understanding the workings of heaven better even than they do. More likely, their protest is aimed at the Romans, but the Rabbis address their plea to God to make it feel less threatening. Because demonstrating against an oppressive force is risky due to the threat of retaliation, they have to be careful to choose the right message and deliver it in just the right way so that, if it fails, it will not endanger them all the more. Being able to consult with a Roman matron who knows what actions will be effective proves invaluable. Knowing she believes they will not face violence for speaking out gives them the confidence to advocate for what they need.

It is impossible to know why the Roman matron helps these Rabbis. The Talmud does not spell out the precise nature of their relationship; one only knows from context that the Rabbis have garnered enough goodwill from her to know that she is open to helping them in their time of need. Yet one can surmise a variety of factors that might have led to their success in enlisting her aid. Below are two characteristics of Rabbinic life that might lead them to be in a position to gain her kindness and those of other Romans when needed.

ENGAGING CONSTANTLY IN DIALOGUE

The Talmud is full of Rabbinic dialogues with Romans about any number of issues.[20] Together the Rabbis and the Romans explore such diverse issues as why God chooses to reward good and punish evil,[21] why God chooses to make Eve out of Adam's rib,[22] and the importance of keeping kosher.[23] Although these debates provide a framework for the Rabbis to explore important ideas, their form suggests a deeper lesson about the Rabbinic worldview. The Rabbis keep in close contact with their non-Jewish neighbors, especially with Roman matrons who are often the focus of these dialogues.

One of the most famous of these involves a conversation between Rabbi Yosi and a Roman matron about how God spends time now that God has finished creating the world. Rather than sit back and relax, Rabbi Yosi explains, God devotes the rest of eternity to making romantic matches.[24] At first the matron belittles this Divine feat—but when she tries it herself, pairing up her male and female slaves, all her matches end in disasters. Amazed, she compliments God, "There is no God like your God; your Torah is true, pleasing, and praiseworthy. You spoke wisely."[25] Rabbinic dialogues with neighbors can open minds and hearts.

EMBRACING MARKERS OF ROMAN CULTURE

Despite their sometimes fraught views toward non-Jewish pathways to knowledge,[26] and in particular their fear that foreign wisdom may lead the populace astray, the Rabbis speak Greek, know Greek lore, and are conversant in Western philosophy.[27]

One famous example of this involves the use of the "fox parable" as theorized by Burton Visotzky of the Jewish Theological Seminary in his study of Hellenism's influence on Rabbinic culture.[28] In his view, the Rabbis interact so much with the non-Jewish world that they internalize Aesop's methodology of using animal stories to frame moral lessons. In Greek lore, the most famous of these stories concerns a fox walking by a river with a fish in his mouth. Mistaking his own reflection in the water for another fox holding a similar fish, he lunges toward the image, but when he opens his maw to bite his imaginary nemesis, he drops the fish, and it swims away. This story is so emblematic of the Greek way of telling these animal tales that the practice as a whole becomes known as "parables of foxes."

That gives us new insight into why, when Rabban Yochanan ben Zakkai searches for knowledge, he marries traditional Torah study with "the conversation of ministering angels; the conversation of demons, and the conversation of palm trees; parables of launderers, *parables of foxes*; [and more generally], a great matter and a small matter."[29]

The Rabbis understand the power of using Roman motifs and metaphors when interacting with their neighbors. In fact, through a fox story of their own, they teach one another about the importance of speaking the Romans' "language." Multiple factors may account for why the Rabbis draw on non-Jewish teachings.[30] In the parable that follows there is Rabbinic recognition of the utility of doing so:

> Once the lion was angry with all the animals. They asked one another, "Who will go and reconcile with him?" The fox said, "I will lead the way, for I know three hundred fox fables which can assuage him." All the animals said, "Let's go!" They walked a bit and he stopped. The animals asked the fox, "Why have you halted?" He confessed, "I have forgotten a hundred fables." They said, "No matter, two hundred fables are a blessing." They walked a bit and the fox stopped again. The animals asked the

Keeping Peace   97

fox, "Why have you halted?" He confessed, "I have forgotten another hundred fables." They said, "No matter, even one hundred fables are a blessing." When they arrived at the lion's lair, the fox cried, "I've forgotten them all! Every man for himself!"[31]

Here the lion is meant to symbolize Rome and the fox, the Jews.[32] The moral of the tale is that to assuage Rome, the Jews need to be armed with the very rhetoric that will speak to their oppressors. As long as they can adopt aspects of Roman culture, symbolized by the motif of telling their stories, they will be fine. But without it, pandemonium will ensue—all Jews will be left to fend for themselves.

Subterfuge for Peace: Reuven ben Isterobeli

Knowing they need to tread lightly when stating an important case to a foreign regime, the Rabbis sometimes turn to subterfuge. When Rome issues a decree that the Jewish people "may not observe Shabbat, may not circumcise their sons, and must engage in intercourse when wives are menstruating"[33]—all three decrees being violations of deeply held Jewish religious precepts—Rabbi Reuven ben Isterobeli, who is living in Rome, proceeds to cut his hair in a *komei*, the hairstyle in vogue with the non-Jewish population at the time. Hoping that appearing like a Roman will convey the false impression that he is one, he proceeds to infiltrate conversations with Roman leaders to convince them not to legislate in a way that oppresses the Jews.[34]

Sitting with Roman leaders, he first attacks the Romans' hatred of Shabbat. But rather than make a case for religious freedom or the sanctity of the day, he instead explains how letting the Jews observe the Sabbath will benefit the regime:

> He said to them: One who has an enemy, [does he want his enemy] to become poor or to become rich? They said to him: He wants his enemy to become poor. Rabbi Reuven ben Isterobeli said to them: If so, with regard to the Jewish people as

well, isn't it better that they will not perform labor on Shabbat in order that they will become poor? The gentiles said: That is a good claim that he said; let us nullify our decree. And they indeed nullified it.[35]

Reuven ben Isterobeli reminds the Romans that in their desire to hurt the Jewish people, sometimes letting them keep their traditions may be just as harmful as outlawing them. Here, their forgoing a day of work means they lose a day of pay. Ben Isterobeli then employs the same approach to preserve circumcision. The ritual, he claims, only makes the Jews weaker. This resonates, too. The seat of a man's virility is understood to be in his genitals, and an enervated Jewish population is in the Romans' best interests.

He finally tackles family purity. When Jewish women are menstruating, he says, their husbands abstain from sexual relations with them in order not to violate the laws of purity. Fewer sexual encounters means fewer opportunities to conceive children and fewer Jews to contend with in the long run.[36] This, too, is of benefit to Rome.

Moved by all of his arguments, the Roman leadership retracts the full decree. Soon, however, the Romans learn that despite the haircut, Reuven ben Isterobeli is Jewish. They quickly reinstate all the previous rulings. Because one of their own has been discovered trying to dupe the powers that be, and the Romans will not easily trust them again, the Rabbis are left with little recourse. A delegation of two Rabbis, Shimon Bar Yochai and Elazar bar Rabbi Yosei, heads to Rome to take the Rabbis' plea directly to Caesar.

From here the story gets strange. A demon named Ben Temalyon offers to help make the Rabbis' case for them. He will possess the emperor's daughter. With the emperor unable to cast out the demon, Rabbis Shimon Bar Yochai and Elazar bar Rabbi Yosei will play the heroes. They will command Ben Temalyon to leave the emperor's daughter, he will depart, and in gratitude, the monarch will grant them their wish.

The plan goes off without a hitch. The extraordinarily thankful emperor offers the duo anything it wants. The two ask him to tear up the decree that outlaws Shabbat, circumcision, and menstrual purity, and he does. This is a huge accomplishment. Although Reuven ben Isterobeli's initial act of trickery only exacerbates the Jews' plight, the two Rabbis' subterfuge saves the day. Without bloodshed, the Jews have gotten their way.

This story teaches the important lesson that sometimes it is necessary to do the wrong thing (i.e., lie to and fool another) to keep the peace. Imagine what might have happened had the Rabbis done nothing. Each decree would foment resentment—and possibly incite rebellion. Jewish history has well taught us that the Jewish community tends to lose when that happens.

That said, the story does conclude on an ominous note. The Talmud describes Rabbis Shimon and Elazar standing in the emperor's treasury, looking mournfully at the spoils Rome took from Jerusalem less than a century earlier during the Second Temple's destruction. The Rabbis' hearts break on seeing the sanctuary curtain stained with the blood of sacrifices, tattered, and cast aside.[37] No dialogue is recorded; evidently the two Rabbis say nothing.

How can this be? Taking in the ravaged remnants of their most sacred artifacts, would they not be compelled to scream or weep or run from the treasury? Compelled, yes—but they do nothing of the sort. It is too dangerous. All that ultimately matters is being allowed to live as Jews for another day. This final image reminds the reader that though Rabbis Shimon and Elazar got lucky in their mission, not every interaction with Rome will end well. Reflecting on the story as a whole, the reader is left with the sense that in the face of oppression one should do whatever one can to overcome it—to lie, cheat, or scheme one's way past the powers that be and, to preserve peace, learn to hold one's tongue.

Entering "Idolatrous Spaces": Permitting Visits to Bathhouses and Gladiatorial Events

Keeping peace also enters into the Rabbinic picture when the Rabbis discuss what to do about Jews entering public spaces when doing so would seem to contravene Jewish law.

ENTERING ROMAN BATHHOUSES

Walk around during the early days of the Rabbis and you will find idols everywhere, from the roads (per noted earlier) to the markets to the bathhouses, which the Rabbis frequent because these are not only places of sanitation but also meeting quarters where business and politics are discussed. In a perfect world, the Rabbis would ask their followers to stay far away from sites like bathhouses where statues are on display. If they or their students visit these bathhouses it would send the wrong message of tolerance for something they view as intolerable. However, the Rabbis live in anything but a perfect world.

Knowing they have no choice but to learn to coexist with the idols, the Rabbis employ feats of logic to prove that although the Bible prohibits idolatry and even commands us to smash idols,[38] we might need to learn to tolerate them. Halakhah prohibits gaining even a cursory benefit from idolatry, like walking into a store and smelling the pleasing scent of incense someone is offering to a foreign God.[39] Even visiting a place where people are known to make idolatrous offerings is prohibited, as this may set a person up to be suspected of idolatry.[40] On the other hand, if Jews take these laws to their logical conclusion, it might lead them to boycott Roman businesses and distance themselves from Romans, two outcomes antithetical to the project of peaceful coexistence.

The most famous discussion of the issue of public idolatry appears in a second-century conversation between Rabban Gamliel and Proclus ben Plospus, a Roman, about the presence of an Aphrodite statue at the bathhouse the two men are enjoying in Akko.[41]

As they bathe, Proclus asks Gamliel: how can you, a rabbi, enter a building adorned with the Greek goddess, since the Torah is so explicit about avoiding even the hint of idolatry?[42]

Gamliel answers him shrewdly, making three arguments for why he may enter:

1. The bathhouse existed well before the statue was erected, and he has been going there long before anything was suspect in the building. Thus, he should be grandfathered in and his visits permitted.
2. The main activity of the bathhouse is bathing, not idol worship. While he would be at fault for spending time in a Roman temple, a bathhouse is different insofar as his intention is not to pray but to bathe. His motives are pure. To him, who does not accept her divinity, Aphrodite is just decoration, a simple adornment he passes by on the way to attend to his hygiene.
3. By going into the bathhouse he is actually disgracing Aphrodite, since he joins others in urinating and defecating, all the while naked, right next to her image. True idols are imbued with meaning by people's behavior toward them. Aphrodite may have the shape of an idol, but until someone treats her like one, she is just a simple statue.

Eventually the later strata of the Talmud do qualify Gamliel's permissiveness, allowing him to enter the bathhouse but prohibiting payment for its use if that payment will help idol worshippers purchase additional idols or if the funds will eventually pay the wages of idolatrous priests.[43] Yet even with later generations complicating Gamliel's simple sanction of the Aphrodite statue, the fact that no one fully walks the law back is astounding. Not only are we not told to deface the idol, as our biblical ancestors would ask of us, but also we are allowed small cursory benefits from it, since Aphrodite's presence invites in Romans with whom the Jewish community can interact and find safety and security in our strengthened bonds. It certainly flies in the face of the above concern with optics (at the very least), as one Jew walking into the bathhouse might ignore the statue while a second secretly venerates it.

Gamliel is being pragmatic here. Jews have to maintain good relations with their gentile neighbors. It is a reality of life that business is done and relationships are forged in Roman bathhouses. If Jews are not allowed to enter bathhouses, they will be deprived of important avenues of communal and business connections. Because of this, moreover, even if he prohibits Jews from going to bathhouses, many Jews are liable to rebuff him and go anyway. The Rabbis are careful not to legislate more than the people can handle (see chapter 3). Thus, knowing he has little choice but to issue a permissive ruling, he explains away Aphrodite's statue and gives the Jews of his time license to remain engaged with the outside world.

TOLERATING ATTENDANCE AT GLADIATORIAL EVENTS

According to Rabbinic law, one is not allowed to attend gladiatorial matches or army entertainment shows.[44] The Rabbis give multiple reasons for this:

(1) There are diviners who cast spells there;
(2) One who watches these matches participates in a system that sheds innocent blood;[45]
(3) Going to the games is time wasted that could be used for Torah study.

Each of these three reasons was likely sufficient to prohibit Jews from attending these games. Taken in the aggregate, they provide a strong rationale for why no rabbi should ever step foot in a Roman stadium. Yet despite this, the Talmud tells us of a subset of Rabbis that permits its brethren to attend the spectacle:

> Rabbi Natan permits [attending stadiums] due to two reasons; one is because he can scream and save [the life of someone who would otherwise be killed], and the other one is because [even

if he cannot save the man's life], he can provide testimony that a woman's [husband died], which will enable her to marry again.[46]

To understand Natan's reasoning, a little background is needed. At a certain point in the games, an emperor might ask the audience to weigh in on whether a gladiator who lost but has not yet died should be put to death. Both sides would shout, and the king would listen to whichever was louder and more passionate. Because a single stadium-goer may be the crucial voice who pushes the "no" position over the top, Rabbi Natan believes he may attend. He himself may save a gladiator's life.

As for Natan's second rationale that even if one is not successful and the person is killed, the court may still need your testimony to prove that the husband died. Here Natan is pointing out that not every gladiator who dies will be returned to his kin. When there is no physical proof of a death, witnesses are needed to prove that the death actually occurred. This proof will allow the gladiator's wife to remarry. Without such proof, she would still be technically "married" to a missing husband, and any future union would be considered adultery. In this instance, Rabbi Natan himself may save the life of a gladiator's wife. Potentially saving their neighbors' lives: could there be better examples of how Jews might keep the peace with neighbors?

Ultimately the Talmud does not affirm Natan's permissive view, upholding instead the majority Rabbinic opinion prohibiting stadium attendance. Nonetheless, by including his reasoning, the Talmud is acknowledging the lengths many in the Rabbinic world will go to ensure they and their students can remain engaged with the Roman world.

Stretching the Law: Accommodations to Foster Peace and Avoid Animosity

The Rabbis stretch the law in yet other ways to ensure good and peaceful relations with their neighbors. To help them decide when to bend halakhah to social pressures, they anchor these extensions/exceptions in a number of legal frameworks.

PIKU'AḤ NEFESH: THE NEED TO SAVE LIVES

One such principle is *piku'ah nefesh* (saving a life), which allows Jews to break any law in the Torah for reasons of survival, provided one does not murder, worship idols, or commit any of the sexual sins outlined in the book of Leviticus in the process.[47] Although some later rabbinic authorities limit the law's scope, claiming it only applies during times of religious persecution or for sins perpetrated in private, other Rabbinic decision-makers throughout time have called on the precept in broader circumstances, such as when non-Jewish persecution has forced Jews to violate deeply held religious principles. In one particularly moving example, the Jews of Bergen-Belsen invoked the principle in a radical prayer over the eating of bread on Passover.[48] Although consuming *chametz* (leavened food) is traditionally forbidden on Pesach, they knew that without the bread the Nazis had dispensed, they would likely starve and therefore choose to sanctify the act.

DINA D'MALKHUTA DINA: THE NEED TO ACCOMMODATE FOREIGN RULES

Another important principle, *dina d'malkhuta dina* (the law of the land is the law), stretches Jewish law to accommodate the realities of Jews residing under foreign rule. Appearing four times in the Talmud, this precept requires Jewish communities to behave in ways that Jewish law might not permit or mandate but are demanded by the kingdoms in which Jews live.[49]

For example, although Jews are only obligated to provide monetary support to their own communities, dina d'malkhuta dina requires Jews to make an honest accounting of taxes owed to foreign tax collectors when they approach the Jewish community for its periodic contribution to the king, provided the collectors show they are his legitimate representatives.[50] In another instance, the precept requires abiding by the Persian laws of property transfer, even if in certain cases these do not comport with Jewish law. Because, technically, only documents overseen by Jewish courts and with Jews as signatories effect transfer, dina d'malkhuta dina requires Jews to accept all documents that are approved by the kingdoms in power, no matter who oversees or signs them.[51] Additionally, the precept corrects a technicality in Jewish law that prohibits a person from benefiting from anything a king takes in eminent domain, as according to halakhah, anything a king takes by force is technically stolen property. However, because kings will often cut down trees to make important societal goods, like bridges, Jews are allowed to benefit from such acquisitions without fearing they are party to a sin.[52] Here, dina d'malkhuta dina stands to keep people from holding so fast to Jewish law that they ignore the social costs of exempting themselves from the law held by the rest of society.

MIPNEI DARKHEI SHALOM: THE NEED TO FOSTER PEACE

Generally speaking, when making legal decisions, Jews are permitted to privilege their own people. For instance, Jewish law prohibits charging a fellow Jew interest when lending money but permits it in the case of a non-Jew.[53] Jews are also allowed to consider a person's background when disbursing charity, giving first to fellow Jews in need.[54] Likewise, there are opinions that if you find the lost item of a non-Jew, you should return it, but you need not expend the great effort required by Jewish law to track down the owner as you should if you are confident the owner is Jewish.[55] Provided that one meets one's basic moral obligations to all humans, halakhah demands a higher standard of care for members of one's own people.

At times, however, Jews are asked to ignore the ideological technicalities of law and act as if they are obligated in caring equally and fully for the non-Jew. Most of the time these cases involve some kind of relationship that will be preserved or strengthened by going above and beyond. When laws are stretched to further include non-Jews in the fold, the Rabbis explain that they are acting "for the sake of peace" (*mipnei darkhei shalom*). Although this term is often employed in other scenarios (see chapter 6), the legal precept packs the largest punch when discussing how Jews should treat their non-Jewish neighbors:

> A city which includes both Jews and Idolaters,[56] the leaders should collect money from both Jews and Idolaters for the sake of peace, and they should support the poor of both Idolaters and Jews for the sake of peace. And they should eulogize and bury the dead of Idolaters for the sake of peace. They should comfort the mourners from among the Idolaters for the sake of peace.[57]

Technically, Jewish law does not obligate a Jew to collect and distribute charity, attend to the dead, or comfort the mourners of non-Jews. All these are religious obligations existing squarely within the Jewish community. Nonetheless, as the text explains, Jews should still take care of their neighbors in these ways "for the sake of peace," to preserve their relationship with the gentile world. Peace, as a value, is enough to reorient a Jew's obligation toward the other.

Over time, the Rabbis add other behaviors to the mix. We should visit non-Jews who are sick for the sake of peace.[58] We should visit Jewish and non-Jewish mourners and comfort both equally.[59] We should let both Jews and non-Jew make decisions about the communal charity fund.[60] Jewish farmers should allow people of any religion onto their land (hence admitting strangers onto their property) to pick from the corners of their field and gather up sheaves accidentally left behind during harvest, an act biblically required for one's Jewish neighbors but expanded by the Rabbis to include non-Jews.[61] Despite the resources and time, we should even launder both Jewish and non-Jewish clothing for the sake of peace.[62]

That said, scholars are torn about whether mipnei darkhei shalom, acting for the sake of peace, is entirely pragmatic.[63] Some see it as an "intrinsic moral value."[64] Because this talmudic teaching is derived from a line in Proverbs, "[The Torah's] ways are ways of pleasantness, and all its paths are peace" (Prov. 3:17), they believe the Rabbis are upholding peace as its own virtue and saying that all aspects of Jewish law should get us closer to peace. Regardless, one cannot help but marvel at the pragmatic effect of the maxim. It works. Done well, it preserves the fragile coexistence of Jews and non-Jews in the ancient world.

MISHUM EIVAH: THE NEED TO AVOID ANIMOSITY

Whereas the Rabbis' intent in mipnei darkhei shalom ("preserve peace") may be open for debate, there is no disputation concerning the Rabbis' motives behind its inverse principle, a Rabbinic maxim that also appears throughout the Talmud: *mishum eivah*, "avoid enmity" between Jew and non-Jew. Mishum eivah is entirely pragmatic: it exists to keep Jews safe. In precarious times, ones where wrong moves might spell communal punishment and persecution of the Jews, the Rabbis recognize that sometimes one has to break laws to survive. Stretching a precept now may ensure future opportunities to keep it.

Sometimes the outcome of this law looks similar to mipnei darkhei shalom. For example, Jews are commanded to take care of a non-Jew's animal as they would their own "because of fear of animosity."[65] More often, however, the Rabbis use it as rationale for more radical changes.

According to the earliest strata of Rabbis, a Jewish woman cannot serve as a midwife to non-Jewish women, "because she [the midwife] is birthing a child for paganism."[66] However, later talmudic authorities reverse this. They know that refusing to help an ailing pagan neighbor during a difficult birth will make the Jewish people appear cold, distant, uncaring. To combat the inevitable enmity that will arise from denying non-Jews needed aid, they permit Jews to help, even if doing so will add more idolaters to the world. Their only qualification: the Jewish midwives must ask for pay.[67]

In their discussion of childbirth, the Rabbis permit an even greater transgression for the sake of preserving relations. Jewish law permits a Jew to violate Shabbat to save the life of a Jewish woman and her baby during a difficult childbirth. However, this law does not extend to non-Jewish women. Realizing the harm this double standard would cause, talmudic authorities began permitting Jews to desecrate Shabbat to assist a non-Jewish woman in labor.[68] Because few commandments are as precious to Jewish law as preserving Shabbat,[69] the fact that the Rabbis allow one to violate it to avoid hostilities means that the latter is of more paramount value.

Perhaps the greatest test of mishum eivah's strength comes in how it permits one, in certain cases, to aid non-Jews in idolatry. During the early eras of Rabbinic history, Jews were proscribed from doing business with non-Jews right around their holidays. The Rabbis feared that after a successful business deal, non-Jews would make sacrifices to idols at their Temple, thanking their gods for the Jews' business. Because their Jewish business partners' funds and goodwill facilitated the sacrifice, Jews would now be unwitting parties to idol worship.

Later, however, the Rabbis and medieval commentators weaken this prohibition, allowing business and gift giving, mishum eivah, because of the animosity aroused if Jews were to fail to do business with their neighbors.[70] The Rabbis even allow Jews to attend non-Jewish weddings despite the potential presence of idolatry, ubiquitous at pagan weddings, provided that Jews abstain from eating and drinking, acts then directly associated with pagan practice.[71]

An instructive episode takes place between the two time periods. Before later authorities relax the prohibition against doing business with non-Jews prior to their festivals, Rabbi Yehudah is seemingly left with an impossible choice: accept a dinar (local currency) from a pagan before a festival and thereby facilitate idol worship (the pleased gift-giver will surely go on to thank his foreign Gods for the opportunity) or return the coin and risk fostering animosity:

> A certain heretic sent a Caesarean dinar to Rabbi Yehuda Nesia on the day of their festival. Rabbi Yehudah Nesia said to Reish

Lakish, who was sitting before him: What shall I do? If I take the dinar, he will go and thank [his idol for the success of his endeavor], but if I do not take the dinar, he will harbor enmity toward me. Reish Lakish said to him: Take it and throw it into a pit in the presence of [the heretic]. Rabbi Yehuda Nesia said: All the more so, this will cause him to harbor enmity toward me. Reish Lakish explained: I said, [i.e., I meant], that [you should throw it] in an unusual manner, [so that it looks as though the dinar inadvertently fell from your hand into the pit].[72]

Here the Rabbis attempt to uphold two seeming contradictions: their original precept not to engage with non-Jews before holidays *and* good relations with those very neighbors. They counsel artifice and subterfuge as much as they protest against facilitating idol worship. Further, their advice—take it (the money) and fake it (accidentally lose it)—violates numerous other Rabbinic precepts. The first, of course, is lying, which is generally frowned upon in the Talmud. Second is a violation of an idea known as *ma'arit ayin* (appearance of the eye): if onlookers might confuse your action as permitted, you cannot engage in it for fear that it might mislead them. In this case, others might see you accept money without knowing that you planned to purposely lose it and make assumptions that they could do the same.

Though these precepts matter, good relationships with non-Jews matter more. The Rabbis walk a tightrope of coexistence and with few exceptions, almost always greet the challenge with considerable pragmatism.[73] They show surprising flexibility and openness when the hour calls for it. They accept the need to compromise some of their values in order to live another day to uphold the rest of them. And in doing so, they provide a model for us on how to negotiate our own tensions in this day and age.

Avoiding Infighting 6

The Rabbis know the true cost of communal discord. In the first century of the Common Era, preceding the Second Temple's destruction, Jewish sects like the Sadducees and Pharisees dispute theological matters (such as whether predestination exists or if we will one day arise from the dead[1]) so intensely that according to one Rabbinic telling, the two groups invalidate one another's purity and divorce practices.[2] Even the Pharisees themselves accuse one another of only following the law for financial gain or marriage opportunities.[3] Zealots murder other Jews in the streets: one subgroup, the Sicarri, wields hooked knives at public gatherings to covertly assassinate those they consider Roman sympathizers.[4] Shammai's students attack and kill many of Hillel's students over the particularities of Jewish law (see chapter 1). One Rabbinic opinion holds that the people are responsible for the Temple's destruction because they openly mock the Torah scholars of their generation.[5]

The Rabbis recognize that few ideals are ever worth these high costs. This chapter looks at specific tools they use to pursue peace and minimize intrareligious conflict. Taking a pragmatist stance, they temper their own followers' absolutist impulses and even retract their own sincerely held legal principles if it means averting communal disunion.

Stressing Jewish Unity and Cohesion

In one particularly famous adage, the Rabbis teach, "All Jews are responsible for one another."[6] Notably, the Hebrew word for "responsibility," *arevut*, shares the same three-letter root with two seemingly unrelated terms, the verb "to mix" (*l'arvev*) and the noun "guarantor" (*arev*). By choosing this root to spell out communal responsibility, the Rabbis are implying that the fates of each Jew are "mixed up" with one another. We are interconnected. If one of us sins, it becomes everyone's problem.

There is more. We need each other to solve these problems. When my neighbor is struggling, it is my duty to help her, as it is her duty to help me when I am in my time of need. What will it take for all of us to hold ourselves sufficiently accountable to act on each other's behalf? The Rabbis hammer home their answer: Jewish cohesion.

GOD'S PRESENCE REQUIRES COHESION

The Rabbis teach that a divided Jewish people cannot survive. They imagine a unified Jewish community as two boats tied together that God builds the Divine palace atop:

> Rabbi Shimon bar Yochai says: This is likened to one that brings two boats together and ties them with anchors and iron and stands them up in the heart of the sea. Then [God] builds upon them a palace. As long as the boats are tied together the palace stands, but if they are separated the palace cannot stand.[7]

As the metaphor explains, when the Jewish people are acting together as one, God can dwell in their midst. Their bond provides a platform on which the Divine can rest. However, as we lose touch with and drift apart from one another, our tradition floats away, and God's palace comes tumbling into the sea. The Rabbis are telling us straightaway: Judaism cannot survive if its people are at one another's throats. Infighting makes it impossible for God's presence to remain among us.

INFIGHTING IS A STAMPEDE ON THE JEWS

The Rabbis also make their case by pointing to a particularly horrifying episode in the Torah. The end of the book of Leviticus contains a series of curses that will befall the Jewish people if they do not listen to God. Alongside the calamites of hunger, disease, and violence is the horrifying image of a frightened stampede:

> As for those of you who survive, I will cast a faintness into their hearts in the land of their enemies. The sound of a driven leaf shall put them to flight. Fleeing as though from the sword, they shall fall though none pursues. *With no one pursuing, they shall stumble over one another* as before the sword. You shall not be able to stand your ground before your enemies, but shall perish among the nations; and the land of your enemies shall consume you. (Lev. 26:36–38)

For the Rabbis, the worst image in this protracted scene is that of Jews stumbling over one another, legs tangled in a chaotic mess of limbs.[8] When Jews are pushed and turn against one another, they cannot stand their ground. They will perish among the nations. Unity, on the other hand, will be our salvation.

Mipnei Darkhei Shalom for Intra-Jewish Harmony

Although its most famous iteration appears in discussions of how and when to accommodate their non-Jewish neighbors (see chapter 5), the Rabbis also use the justification of *mipnei darkhei shalom*, acting for the sake of peace, in their efforts to promote intra-Jewish harmony.

RECALIBRATING THE LAWS OF ACQUISITION

Consider this particularly famous example of inadvertent olive snatching:

> If a poor person gleans olives at the top of an olive tree and olives fall to the ground under the tree, then taking those olives that are beneath it is considered robbery on account of the ways of peace.[9]

According to halakhah, to acquire ownership of an object, you have to do something that asserts control over it, like picking it up or dragging it.[10] Simply spotting it first does not mean you own it. Thus, if you are knocking olives off a tree by shaking its branches but do not touch the olives themselves, technically speaking, they are not yours, no matter how hard you are working to glean them. Legally, whoever can get to them first will assume ownership. If another Jew who happens to pass by gathers the olives while you are hanging by a limb, that passerby is the beneficiary. But even if you know the laws of acquisition, you are probably going to be angry at the passerby who has prospered from your hard work.

Here is where the Rabbis invoke mipnei darkhei shalom. To stave off discord, the Rabbis introduce a new law making it illegal to pick up produce one might find on the ground if it is clear someone else has done the work to place it there. Taking it would be akin to "robbery."[11] For the sake of peace, the Rabbis stretch the laws of acquisition. In this select case, one can add, "doing the work to get the fruit down from the tree" to the other legally admissible ways a person may acquire an item.

What makes mipnei darkhei shalom revolutionary is that it redefines the criteria for what makes a law good. The Rabbis understand that strict legal formalism—the idea that laws should not be changed for social or political reasons—can be dangerous. Instead, their outlook is more akin to legal realism, which acknowledges that outside forces and motivations inevitably play a role in lawmaking. Therefore, one should not pretend that law is neutral but rather lean into those outside forces, making law fluid and employing it to respond to real-world needs.

Mipnei darkhei shalom does just this. Rather than throw up their hands when they realize a person has exploited a loophole in the laws of acquisition, the Sages bend halakhah to accommodate communal cohesion.

Likewise, the Rabbis modify the law of animal ownership for "the sake of peace." They prohibit a person who comes upon an animal caught in a trap from keeping it, even though, as in the example above, most likely the trap's owner has not taken an action that officially counts in acquiring that animal as his own.[12]

PROTECTING THE PROPERTY OF PEOPLE WITH DISABILITIES

One of the harder aspects of Rabbinic law for us moderns to stomach is the way in which the Rabbis view people with disabilities. According to halakhah, people who are deaf and mute (*ḥeresh*) and those with intellectual deficiencies (*shoteh*) are treated like minors (*katan*) in a host of ways. They are not allowed to participate fully in Jewish life because they are not deemed "mentally competent."[13]

This discrimination was supposed to carry over to their ability to acquire lost property. In Jewish law, someone who finds an item must do everything possible to return it to the owner, but if finding the owner is impossible because the object is too generic or without distinguishing marks (think a Yankees hat on a New York City sidewalk), the finder may keep the item. Yet in principle this should not hold true for *ḥeresh*, *shoteh*, and *katan*. As we saw above, an item is only acquired through an act of acquisition like dragging or lifting—and, the Rabbis would add, someone mentally competent enough to pursue the act of acquisition. Since in the Rabbis' eyes these three categories of people lack this competence, each would have no agency to acquire an item, known in the Hebrew as a "yad" (an acquisitional hand). Thus, if one were to learn that such an individual found an object, one could technically walk up to the person and take it. Ostensibly the object would currently be as "ownerless" as if it had been left on the street.

Knowing the animosity these callous acts might cause, the Rabbis make it illegal to take objects from people identified as *ḥeresh*, *shoteh*, and *katan*, also "for the ways of peace."[14]

Mipnei Tikkun Ha-Olam—Healing in the World

Changing halakhah for the sake of *tikkun ha-olam* is yet another important tool in the Rabbis' arsenal. Note that the Rabbis understood the phrase tikkun ha-olam (literally, "healing the world") very differently from how many of us view it today.[15] Rabbi Jill Jacobs explains their thinking:

> This phrase is invoked in response to a situation in which a particular legal detail threatens to cause the breakdown of an entire system. . . . By invoking the concept of tikkun ha'olam, the Rabbis repair the flaw that endangers the stability of the system as a whole, and in doing so, they improve the system.[16]

To the Rabbis, no single law is more important than the system as a whole. If a specific legality, enforced at the wrong time, might endanger the entire enterprise, the pragmatic solution is to make an exception to ensure that society continues to function.

PROTECTING A DOCTOR WHO ACCIDENTLY ERRS

In one telling example, the Rabbis rule that a doctor who accidently errs and injures someone while intending to help that person cannot be punished, provided the physician is properly credentialed. Although technically the patient has the right to sue, the doctor is protected "due to *tikkun ha-olam*."[17]

This approach is a change to prevailing law. In mainstream halakhah, a person is liable for harm done to another. If you injure someone, you must pay five categories of damages ranging from the victim's loss of income from the injury to medical costs incurred to the victim's monetary assessment of what payment they might be willing to accept to experience the same level of pain from the injury again. All of these and more are added together, and you as the liable party must pay the damages in full.[18] However, a well-credentialed doctor is exempt from any of these charges. Here the rationale is twofold. First, the change exists to encourage doctors to take risks. If doctors are too conservative in their approach to medicine, people who might be healed may be undertreated. Second, it promotes tranquility. Avoiding litigious lawsuits and keeping well-meaning doctors out of the courtroom make for a more amicable society.

PROTECTING THE FINDER OF A LOST OBJECT

In a similar vein, the Rabbis legislate that if people find a lost object, like a coin purse, and return it, they are not obligated to prove, through taking an oath or any other means, that they did not steal from it, even if it is missing funds.[19] As with the previous example, this leniency fixes a flaw in the system. According to Jewish law, there are numerous times when an individual or a court can compel another person to take an oath. For example, a worker can be compelled to take an oath if their wages are in dispute[20]; likewise, a landlord who suspects a tenant stole from them may take an oath that their property was in their house up to the time of their arrival and get it back.[21] Since the thrust of the law is to require oaths whenever there is a question about foul play, it would be natural to require one in the case of returning lost property. The Rabbis, however, exempt it in the case of finding a lost object "due to *tikkun ha-olam*." In doing so they ensure that society does not abandon the biblical mandate to reunite owners with their misplaced property.[22] Knowing they will not be accused of theft will make finders more apt to do the right thing—and provides the secondary benefit of preserving the peace, say, if the coin purse the finder returns to the owner is missing some of its original, precious contents.

PREVENTING A WIFE FROM INADVERTENTLY COMMITTING ADULTERY

In a more technical example, the Rabbis work hard to fix a major issue that could cause problems in the divorce process. At the time, if a husband wished to get divorced, his wife lived elsewhere, and he did not want to travel to her, he could appoint an agent to travel in his place, act as a stand-in for him, and deliver the divorce document (*get*) on his behalf. If, though, the husband changed his mind after he had sent the stand-in, he could go to the court to get the divorce annulled. So long as he could get the court to agree on the annulment before the get was delivered, in principle he could turn that get into a meaningless piece of paper and keep his marriage intact.

Still, the Rabbis register concern. What if word does not get to the agent that the husband annulled the get? Not knowing the get is invalid, his wife would assume the divorce has gone through. She might remarry, causing her to accidentally commit adultery, as Jewish law prohibits a woman from being married to two men. Not only is this a sin in its own right, but any child produced would be considered a *mamzer*, a tainted designation that keeps the child from marrying all but the most outcast in society.[23] Not only would mistakes like this make every divorcee who attained a get through an agent suspect, corrupting the trust in the system, but it would also sow discord. Imagine the wife's anger when she learns that her husband put her in such a precarious position. Imagine her new husband's fury when he learns he has been an unwitting party to adultery. Future children might blame their parents for not adequately investigating the validity of the divorce. The future couple's respective families might hold a grudge against the "ex-husband" for changing his mind at the last minute.

To forestall such disastrous consequences, Rabban Gamliel outlawed the practice of allowing a husband to call upon a court to annul a divorce when his agent was enroute to deliver a *get* and used tikkun ha-olam as his justification.[24] As with other instances of tikkun ha-olam in Rabbinic literature, he repaired a flaw in the system that might cause unneeded suffering and discord. Although technically a husband should be able to annul an undelivered document at any time, he is denied that right for the good of the wider legal system. Instead, the husband would have to chase down the agent himself or accept the divorce he initiated, however rashly, in the first place.[25]

Lo Titgodedu—Avoiding Factions

Yet another legal tool that attempts to avoid internal Jewish disputes takes its name directly from the fear of factionalism. Some background, or foreground, is needed. Imagine you are living in Switzerland in the late 1940s, in the shadow of the Holocaust. The Nazis have been defeated, but turmoil in the Jewish community is ongoing. Many Jews are displaced. Poland and Germany are no longer viable places to live. The majority of survivors have immigrated to America, Israel, or Canada. Others have settled within Europe, and some have migrated to your community in Zurich. They have brought with them their own practices, rites, and rituals, some of which directly contradict your own.

This was the problem faced by Rabbi Mordechai Yaakov Breisch, head of the rabbinical council Agudas Achim in Zurich. Sometime after the end of World War II,[26] he wrote an urgent letter to the chief Swiss legal authority at the time,[27] Yechiel Yaakov Weinberg, also known as the *S'ridei Eish*. The issue: these strangers had different kashrut practices. His community was more lenient in how they checked animals for the types of defects that make them unkosher, whereas this new community was stringent.[28] Rabbi Breisch rightfully feared that such a discrepancy in practice might foment mistrust and infighting between the two communities. At the very least, it would set up rival butchers and complicate the practice of communal eating.

The question Breisch put forth to Weinberg was whether he should invoke an ancient Rabbinic precept known as *lo titgodedu* (do not make factions) to demand that one of the two communities, preferably the newcomers, conform to the other's practice, adopting the other's legal positions to create unity and harmony in the city.[29]

Breisch's query was not new. Throughout Jewish history, persecutions, blight, expulsions, and economic opportunities had compelled Jews to relocate, and sometimes they encountered distinctly different Jewish cultures where they settled. Diverse communities had divergent customs. Certain groups observed holidays for seven days, whereas others celebrated them for eight. Some refrained from marrying at select times of the year, whereas others encouraged wedding in those same months. Some Jewish communities permitted polygamy; others condemned it.

For the most part, as long as Jewish communities remained far away from one another, these variations were met with tolerance. However, when migrations forced these differences to coexist in one locale, Jewish authorities had to decide whether to allow or prohibit them.

Often the existing residents used the legal precept lo titgodedu, literally "do not make factions," as a tool to compel conformity. They would command newcomers with different practices to abandon their communal norms and embrace the longstanding community's approach to the Jewish religion.

Early on in the Rabbinic era, the discussion of lo titgodedu became a testing ground for a number of issues related to religious pluralism. Is it a problem for a town to contain two courts, each ruling differently?[30] (Answer: It is up for debate.[31]) Can two people, living in the same locale, celebrate the holiday of Purim on different days if one came from a place where it is traditionally observed earlier or later? (Answer: No, one must abide by the custom of the place one is traveling to.[32]) Can one authority permit a marriage that another considers incest? (Answer: Yes. [33]) If one travels to a city on a business trip that has a different religious norm around work in the hours leading up to Passover, should one retain one's own practice or adopt the practice of one's new home? (Answer: One does whichever is stricter.[34])

As you can see, sometimes the Rabbis leaned toward conformity, whereas other times they promoted diversity. It is not clear why. Although our tradition preserves these case-by-case rulings, there is no talmudic discussion unpacking the scope, rationale, and boundaries of lo titgodedu. A given practice was either deemed an accepted variation or a faction—with the latter lo titgodedu ("do not make factions") was usually employed to compel conformity to entrenched practices.

It would take a few hundred years after the Rabbis stopped offering their wisdom for authorities in the Middle Ages to produce two competing rationales as to why lo titgodedu belongs in the Jewish cannon of law. Knowing the purpose of the precept would then give future authorities guidance as they navigated novel problems of legal variation and potential factions.

Some saw lo titgodedu as entirely pragmatic. Too much diversity within a community can kindle conflict. Disagreements on the right way to pray in which one faction is not forced to cede to the other may foment disputes, failed friendships, and in extreme cases even violence. If the goal of religious practice is to unify rather than divide, then any allowance that might deepen rifts needs addressing.

The major voice on this side of the debate was Maimonides, who wrote in the twelfth century in his legal opus *Mishneh Torah*:

> There should not be two rabbinic courts in one city, one behaving according to one custom (minhag) and one according to another custom, for this thing causes great disputes as it is said, *lo titgodedu*, do not make factions.[35]

For Maimonides, peace is the lens through which such a disagreement must be mediated. Because differences in custom can foment great disputes, only one rabbinic court should prevail in a given place.

Yet another camp advocated a different reason for the law: universality. Asher ben Yechiel, the thirteenth-century Spanish scholar known as the Rosh, explains: "If a resident of a community travels to another community he must behave like them, so that it not appear as if there are two Torahs."[36]

However variable Jewish laws and practices might be, the Rosh thought it was our obligation to make them appear immutable. Two groups, each behaving contrary to the other, would subvert the nature and appearance of Truth. If God gave one Torah to Moses, would not disparate practices and religious variations make it appear as if multiple revelations took place atop Sinai? To the uninitiated eye, it might seem that God allows haphazard variation. God's revelation must appear whole.

This reading of lo titgodedu is also indicative of Judaism's pragmatic spirit. Notice that the Rosh does not say there can be no pluralism in Jewish practice. Instead he is concerned with perception, "so that it not *appear* as if there are two Torahs."[37]

These dual pragmatic rationales, avoiding both conflict and the appearance of a muddled revelation, would become salient factors in modern halakhic decision-making.

In the end, Rabbi Yechiel Yaakov Weinberg permitted the variation of practice in his Swiss community. He intentionally read the scope of lo titgodedu narrowly. For him, the postwar period necessitated a tolerance of pluralism. One can surmise that with European Jewry destroyed and many people left with nothing but their religious practices, letting them keep those practices was an act of kindness. They needed something foundational in their lives. They could behave as their ancestors had, taking a small piece of their shattered home with them to a strange land.

Weinberg was sensitive to social factors as he pursued a path of peace. Here, too, law had to yield to the needs of the people who performed it.[38]

Takkanat Ha-shavim: Embracing Imperfection for Peace

The Rabbis also worked to address another cause of infighting: wrongdoers who did not make amends for their misdeeds. When we wrong another, Jewish law expects us to engage in *teshuvah*, the process of self-reflection and repentance that culminates in tangible acts (apologies, monetary payments, the return of stolen items, etc.) to make things right.

Yet, the Rabbis saw, sometimes personal roadblocks got in the way of doing real teshuvah. Sometime, even when people wanted to make things right, doing so involved a lift they could not muster, such as giving back money they did not have.

The Rabbis considered whether to lower the bar to repentance. If making things right were a little easier, would more people do it? Might that bring people closer and heal the rifts the misdeeds caused in the first place?

Taking a gamble, they developed an idea known as *takkanat hashavim*, literally "the proclamation of the penitent." To explain this concept, they brought forward a famous thought experiment. They invited us to imagine that a person steals a strong wooden beam and builds it into his house. Later, whether on his own volition or because he is caught, the thief seeks to make things right. According to classical Jewish law, the pathway to teshuvah is straightforward; if you steal something, you must give it back.[39] But in this case, if the thief were to give back the exact beam he took, it would require dismantling his house to get at it. Should the Rabbis expect a person to go to those ends to do teshuvah?

As one might expect, the Rabbis develop a leniency for cases like this. They allow the thief to return the "value" of the beam rather than the wood itself.[40] This ensures that thieves can do teshuvah without completely upending their lives and destroying their pocketbooks.[41]

This pragmatic decision prioritizes the less perfect outcome to get at the spirit of repentance. If part of teshuvah is to help reconciliation, then making it easier on sinners to find their way back into their victims' good graces means more people are likely to engage in the process. If expecting too much of a person might lead Jewish law to fail in this endeavor, perhaps it should be softened to allow it to work better.

Radical as takkanat hashavim may be, the Rabbis even go one step farther. They actively dissuade a person from collecting money from a thief if he comes to them with an item or money to return. They teach:

Avoiding Infighting   123

With regard to robbers or usurers that returned [either the stolen item or the interest to the one from whom they took it], one should not accept it from them. And with regard to one who does accept it from them, the Sages are displeased with him.[42]

The reason for this worldview is found in a story that follows directly after this proclamation in the Talmud. A thief approaches his wife, looking to make amends for his past misdeeds. Knowing that much of what he owns he amassed through thievery, she admonishes him, "Empty one, if you repent [you will have to return all the stolen items to their rightful owners], and even the belt that you are wearing is not yours."[43] Hearing that doing the right thing will make him destitute, he gives up his quest for repentance. From that day forward, the Talmud reports, people were asked not to accept money or items from thieves who offered to return them.

The Rabbis held that having to apologize and vow not to continue stealing was hard enough for thieves. Already, ethical living would be a new enterprise for them. Repayment on top of that would make for too high a hurdle, impeding them from repenting and apologizing to their victims. The Rabbis knew they had to open the door wide for reconciliation and the prevention of further sins.

Takkanat Ha-Shuk—Ensuring Trust in the Marketplace

A companion principle to *takkanat ha-shavim* is known as *takkanat ha-shuk*. It too seeks to effect reconciliation by removing barriers when a person seeks to right a wrong. In this case, however, the wrong done is an accident.

Imagine that a thief steals an item from a person and it ends up in the hands of a third party, either by selling it directly or selling it to a second party, who resells it to a third party. In time, the new owner (third party) learns that the goods are tainted. Once this comes to light, the new owner must return the object to its original owner.[44] However, and herein lies the innovation: when the final purchaser returns the item, the original owner must reimburse that purchaser in full for the expense incurred when buying it. With things made right with the purchaser, the original owner can then go after the thief for repayment.

The reasoning behind this Rabbinic innovation is twofold. On a personal level, asking a person who unknowingly buys stolen goods to return them and then pursue the thief to be reimbursed is too onerous. Knowing how difficult it would be to make things right, the purchaser might keep the stolen merchandise, the victim of the original theft would never get the goods back, justice would remain undone, and no party would take the opportunity to do *teshuvah*. Without people choosing to right wrongs, interpersonal cohesion unravels.

On a communal level, takkanat ha-shuk also aims at preserving society's trust in the markets. Trust is the bedrock on which economies are built. If one has the double headache of returning stolen goods and finding the thief who stole them, one might avoid the market altogether.

Takkanat ha-shuk is an imperfect solution and a good illustration of the messiness of legislating for competing values. On the one hand, it seems to punish the original owner of the goods. He is the victim of theft, and yet he is forced to repay the final purchaser of the stolen goods *and* redress his grievances directly to the thief. However, the Rabbis judge, the dual goals of creating pathways for reconciliation (for communal harmony) and protecting people's trust in the markets (for economic stability) supersede the fairness of the law to all parties involved.

God's Prayer for Unity

We have now seen the lengths our tradition will go to promote cohesiveness. It will add laws, stretch laws, and even ignore laws to keep the community together. Over time, theology learned to follow sociology. When the Rabbis' great fear was factionalism, they imagined a God who views factionalism with great concern. They imagined God praying alongside us. Every time we don tefillin (small boxes containing the Shema) and recite the Shema, "Listen Israel, Adonai is our God, Adonai is One" (Deut. 6:4),[45] God puts on a Divine pair of phylacteries containing a different verse with a parallel sentiment, "And who is like your people Israel, *a nation one in the earth*" (2 Sam. 7:23).[46] There is an artistry to this Rabbinic imagining. The Shema contains the Jewish aspiration that in a world that believes in many gods, our God is one. God's tefillin throws that aspiration back at us. Every time we make peace, every time we avoid dispute, we live out God's chief wish for the Jewish people: to be united, to be one. All the while, God's prayer for our tranquility adds authenticity and holiness to our quest. Might this be the Rabbis' topmost tool: imagining that their wish for Jewish unity is written into the cosmos?

Employing Tools to Transform Law　　7

To date we have examined the "whys" and "whats" of the Rabbis: why they feel it is necessary to make revisions to existing laws and customs and what modifications they make. We have yet to look closely at the "how," namely the tools the Sages employ to make these changes.

Although at times the Rabbis are able to radically transform law, they are careful not to make their changes appear haphazard. Because they believe the Torah is God's divine word, they couch their changes carefully. They know they have flexibility to transform law, but at the same time they cannot touch the language of the Torah.

This chapter will explore the methods the Rabbis utilize to make revisions. Their Rabbinic toolbox ranges from Rabbinic decrees (*takkanot*) to searching for loopholes to reading the Torah's words out of context. They are careful to employ the right legal method, as the way they derive laws will determine whether others sanction their innovations as authentic and authoritative. In taking such care to prove their points, the Rabbis create a new and revolutionary way to read Torah, and they do so in a deeply pragmatic fashion—one designed to have a substantive influence on Jewish life.

Using Proof Texts to Make Legal Change

To the Rabbis, the Bible's text is meant to address their pressing needs of the day. They read its words with a set of assumptions summarized in four key points by Bible scholar James Kugel:

1. The Bible is fundamentally cryptic, meaning that there are hidden messages within the words. Just because the Bible says something doesn't mean it can't be read in an opposite way.
2. The Bible is meant to speak to us in our day, about our concerns. It's not fundamentally history and miraculously can speak with authority about events that occur centuries or millennia after its production.
3. There are no mistakes in the Bible. If it seems so, it invites the reader to create interpretations that smooth out these mistakes. The Bible also cannot contradict the reader's religious norms and creeds. Thus if it says something about God or Jewish practice that no one believes today, the reader is invited to explain away these errors.
4. The Bible is God's word, whether directly or through inspiration.[1]

Taken together, these assumptions explain why the Rabbis are able to be widely creative while simultaneously careful to point back to the Bible during those times of creativity. If the Bible is from God, the Rabbis can't just change its text willy-nilly. Its words are eternal.

However, counter to its actual text, the Bible's message may change. Because God is God, God's Divine text can prefigure the Romans, a civilization not yet born at the time of Sinai. The Torah can guide us on how to shake a lulav, even though there is no evidence that Sukkot was celebrated with the waving of four species in biblical times.[2] It can teach us the laws of marriage from certain verses even though those verses focus exclusively on divorce.[3]

To prove that their most radical readings are still authentic, the Rabbis rewrite history, claiming that God actually gives two Torahs on top of Sinai. The first is the written one, contained in the biblical text itself. The second is an oral Torah, passed down through the ages, which eventually manifests as the Rabbis' own insights.[4] The Rabbis point at the Torah itself for proof of this dual revelation.

Looking closely at the wording of a biblical line which pluralizes the word Torah (*torot*), they derive that God gave two related revelations at Sinai:

> "These are the laws, rules, and instructions (*torot*) that Adonai established, through Moses on Mount Sinai, with the Israelite people" (Lev 26:46).... This teaches us that two [sets of] instructions (*torot*) were given to Israel, one written, and one, oral.[5]

Rooting Rabbinic innovation in the moment of revelation means that God ordained even the Rabbis' most radical turns. Because they have God's stamp of approval, their changes are as authentic as anything written in the Torah. In fact, if their words seem to contradict the plain meaning of the written text, they may still be correct because the oral Torah can dictate how one interprets the written Torah.

Yet the Rabbis are not happy with simply claiming authority on their own. They want the written and oral Torahs to speak in harmony, ensuring the appearance of one seamless revelation. To do this, they consistently go back to the Bible and quote verses to support the very innovations that might undercut the Bible's original meaning. Scholars call these "proof texts." Often introduced with statements like "as it is said" or questions like "from where do we know," proof texts lend authenticity to the Rabbis' words and root their changes in God's Divine revelation.

To understand how proof texts work, let's closely examine the above midrash and how the Rabbis quote the Torah to make their point. In the Bible, the word *torah* often plainly means "instruction" or "teaching."[6] Over time, it came to take on two additional meanings: (1) a physical scroll that contains God's law that we are instructed to read each Shabbat and (2) the collective knowledge contained in the scroll.

If *torah* is read as the generic term for instruction, it makes sense that it would be understood as plural, as God gives many instructions atop Sinai. However, rather than read it in its original context, the

Tools to Transform Law 129

Rabbis provide what may be called a hyperliteral reading—ignoring the metaphors and context and instead applying a more common meaning to words. They therefore drop the plain meaning of the verse and read the word *torah* as the collected teaching and laws of the Jewish people. Because there is only one collected teaching, pluralizing *torah* would be odd, since it would have to connote at least two bodies of knowledge. Left with this textual wrinkle, the Rabbis make the logical leap that Leviticus 26:46 points to the existence of both written and oral law because it's the only adequate way to explain more than one *torah* without venturing into heretical territory.

Although sometimes proof texts are straightforward readings of the plain meaning (*peshat*) of a text, many times in the Torah, as with our above example, proof texts diverge wildly from the original biblical context. When that happens, the Rabbis choose to use them to bolster radical Rabbinic innovations—entirely different ideas from the apparent original biblical intent. Beyond the hyperliteral reading example above, two other famous approaches are creative misreadings and narrow readings.

CREATIVE MISREADINGS

One of the earliest examples of creative misreadings appears in a conversation between Yochanan ben Zakkai and his study partner Rabbi Joshua ben Hananiah after the Temple's destruction:

> It once happened that Rabban Yochanan ben Zakkai was leaving Jerusalem with Rabbi Joshua, and they witnessed the destruction of the Temple. Rabbi Joshua said, "Woe to us, for the place where the sins of Israel were atoned for has been destroyed." Rabban Yochanan ben Zakkai said, "Do not be bitter, my son, for we have another form of atonement which is as great, and this is acts of love and kindness" (*gemilut ḥasadim*); as the verse states, "for it is kindness I desire and not burnt offerings" (Hos. 6:6).[7]

Walking together and viewing the ruins of Jerusalem, Rabbi Joshua cannot help but break down. Without the Temple, he asks, how can the Jewish people find expiation from their sins? Sacrifice is the only way people know how to communicate with God. Without a central place to perform sacrifice, the people are bereft of their chief tool to engage with the Divine.

Yochanan answers him with a novel idea. Rather than sacrifice, God will accept our acts of love and kindness. If we do good in the world, these actions will lead us to God's forgiveness.[8] To prove this, Yochanan offers a "creative misreading": quoting a proof text from the book of Hosea that proves his point but diverges wildly from its original context.

As background, the quote comes as the prophet Hosea is rebuking the people. Seeing that the people are acting immorally and that their "goodness is like morning clouds / Like dew so early gone" (Hos 6:4), Hosea warns them that God will not accept their sacrifices unless their offerings are matched by ethical living. This familiar refrain appears throughout the Bible.[9] Rituals like sacrifices and fasting matter to God but only by people who are walking the good path. For Hosea it is hypocrisy to seek Divine connection when you sow division within your society.

Yochanan, however, creatively misreads Hosea. When God says, "It is kindness I desire and not burnt offerings," Yochanan knows that Hosea is still affirming sacrifice. Hosea is solely telling the people: "God just wants the context of your sacrifice to change; you should rise to act morally before you approach the Divine altar." However, Yochanan rereads Hosea's speech as a message of comfort in the post-Temple era: there is no Divine rebuke, sacrifice is not needed, and it can be replaced with acts of love toward others. By creatively misreading Hosea's words, Yochanan is able to honor his textual heritage while making the Bible speak to a post-Temple world. In doing so, he contributes to the Rabbinic revolution of giving Divine sanction to the Rabbis' creative reinvention of Judaism.

NARROW READINGS

Another important way the Rabbis are able to change the plain meaning of a biblical text is by defining its terms so narrowly that the words lose much of their power. Perhaps the most notable example of this appears in the Rabbinic discussion of a *ben sorrer u'moreh*, an insolent and rebellious son. In its original context, in Deuteronomy, any son who is disrespectful to his parents can be brought to the village gates and killed:

> If a man has a wayward and defiant son, who does not heed his father or mother and does not obey them even after they discipline him, his father and mother shall take hold of him and bring him out to the elders of his town at the public place of his community. They shall say to the elders of his town, "This son of ours is disloyal and defiant; he does not heed us. He is a glutton and a drunkard." Thereupon the people of his town shall stone him to death. Thus you will sweep out evil from your midst: all Israel will hear and be afraid. (Deut. 21:18–21)

For the Rabbis, this text is deeply disturbing. How can a just society kill a child for acting out? Don't most sons go through stages of defiance and disloyalty? Don't most teens act like gluttons (and even drunkards) at least once in their lives?

The Rabbis decide to attack the text, first by narrowing the time window for a child to become a ben sorrer u'moreh. Because the Torah does not specify the age of this son, the Rabbis restrict the age by invoking a paradox: a young person is not really called to task for his moral decisions until he is thirteen,[10] yet once he becomes a "man," the Bible wouldn't call him a "son," as that connotes a juvenile. Thus they conceive a compromise position: a ben sorrer u'moreh must be between twelve-and-a-half and thirteen with at least two pubic hairs.[11] During this six-month period, the young person has reached a physical age of maturity and hence should be held to adult standards, but chronologically he remains a child who is still beholden to parental authority.

In a similar way, the Rabbis narrow the scope of the son's gluttony. He is a glutton only if he consumes kosher meat in large quantities.[12] The Rabbis quote the number at "a *tarteimar* of meat,"[13] which in today's language might be well over four and a half pounds.[14] The meat can only be purchased with money stolen from his parents, and it must be eaten somewhere other than his home.[15]

The Rabbis then put one final death knell in the law. When the parents bring their son to the town square, they must speak as one, saying, "He does not heed us" (Deut. 21:20).[16] The Rabbis read the word "us" (*b'koleinu*) literally as "our voice." The fact that the parents speak in one voice indicates that their voices must sound precisely the same. "If his mother was not identical to his father in voice, appearance, and height, he does not become a stubborn and rebellious son."[17]

To summarize, the Rabbis' creative rendering of this story requires the ben sorrer u'moreh to be just short of thirteen but undergoing puberty, to eat outside the house excessively large quantities of stolen kosher meat, and to have virtual vocal clones as parents. From this vantage point,[18] it's no surprise that the Rabbis conclude, "There has never been a stubborn and rebellious son, and there will never be one in the future."[19]

The Rabbis' penchant for conveniently narrow readings likewise enables them to do away with other harsh biblical injunctions. Deuteronomy 13:13–19 calls for utterly destroying an Israelite city that turns to idolatrous worship (*ir ha-nidaḥat*). The Rabbis say that only a court of seventy-one judges can declare the city worthy of destruction, that it cannot be a frontier city, that it cannot be next to other similarly idolatrous cities, and that religious items like Torahs, mezuzot, and prayer books cannot be present in the city.[20]

We find a similar Rabbinic methodology in response to the death penalty for certain capital crimes explicated in the Torah.[21] Although the Rabbinic world is sometimes mixed about the morality of the death penalty, the thrust of halakhah seems to point to the Rabbis' deep discomfort with its use.[22] The Rabbis construct a myriad of barriers to prevent a person from being sentenced to death. Two witnesses not only need to see the perpetrators perform the very acts that would be liable for the death penalty—the witnesses *need to warn the potential perpetrators in advance* about the exact kind of punishment the potential sinners will face (for example, stoning vs. burning) if they take these actions,[23] and *the sinners themselves need to publicly acknowledge the risks and continue immediately with the actions nonetheless*.[24] The Rabbis even build barriers around the sentencing process—if a panel of twenty-three judges rules unanimously to convict a defendant, the defendant is instead freed because in the Rabbis' minds, the defendant was not given talented enough counsel to have planted the seed of doubt into at least one of the twenty-three judges.[25] All of this compounds to make it nearly impossible (with few exceptions; see chapter 8) to carry out capital punishment.

For ben sorrer u'moreh, *ir ha-niḏaḥat*, and the death penalty, the Rabbis are able to undo the prescriptions of the Torah text without changing the Bible's wording. They take advantage of the Torah's terseness and ambiguity to read meanings into the words that conform to their understanding of the law's spirit.

Rabbinic *Takkanot*

Whereas most Rabbinic innovations point back to proof texts, the Rabbis occasionally make their changes without looking to biblical precedent. Often these changes are so radical that citing the Torah as validation would seem disingenuous. When this happens, the Rabbis employ different tools[26]—the most famous one known as a *takkanah*, a proclamation without biblical justification that modifies an existing legal norm.[27]

Sharing the same root with the word *tikkun*, which means to fix, a takkanah is a Rabbinic decree meant to repair a law that no longer works. Unlike changes rooted in proof texts, a takkanah's authority lies outside of the Bible, in the authority of the person making the changes and in the needs of the hour.

Takkanot were present from the first moments of Rabbinic innovation. Yochanan Ben Zakkai uses them to rethink post-Temple religious practice from the earliest moments of Yavneh (see Prologue). In one instance, Yochanan changes an important rule about blowing the shofar on Shabbat. Before the Temple's destruction, if Rosh Hashanah fell on Shabbat, one was allowed to sound the shofar solely in the Temple complex—the site of the Sanhedrin (primary Rabbinic court) responsible for deciding when a new month would begin—but not outside.[28] Most likely this law had been instituted to make sure far-flung communities did not accidently blow the shofar on the wrong day if Rosh Hashanah fell on Shabbat. If word of the New Year did not reach those in the outskirts in a timely manner, Jews might accidentally blow the shofar on a Sabbath day that the Sanhedrin had not declared to be Rosh Hashanah—a violation of Jewish law.[29]

This approach works until the Temple is destroyed. Without the Sanhedrin's presence and with Jerusalem no longer the focus of ancient Jewish ritual, Yochanan is forced to innovate: "After the Temple was destroyed, Rabban Yochanan ben Zakkai instituted (*hitkin*) that the people should sound the shofar on Shabbat in every place where there is a court of twenty-three judges."[30]

Yochanan knows the people need the power and authority that the Temple and its institutions once afforded. Rather than take that authority solely for himself, he decentralizes it. Every neighborhood court will attain the lost authority of Jerusalem. Without a centralized cult, judicial power will become regional and diffuse. Any learned set of judges can make the decision whether or not to sound the shofar on Shabbat.

In this instance, Yochanan has to resort to a takkanah, because his ruling is unprecedented. Takkanot, in the words of Yale professor Christine Hayes, are tools to "respond to an unmet need poorly served by the present state of the law."[31] Yochanan's need to figure out how to vest authority when no clear group is in control is unique to Jewish history. Ever since the shofar had first sounded on Rosh

Hashanah, there was always a central power to look toward that could designate the new month.[32] Simply finding a proof text and claiming his ruling as an authentic expression of Torah law will fail in light of the differences between the communal circumstances envisioned by the Torah and the historical context that Yochanan was attempting to address.[33]

Later authorities, well past Yochanan's death, would find a set of proof texts for him.[34] However, these two proofs would not be about the authenticity of blowing the shofar on Shabbat but about the Sages' authority to make takkanot in the first place. The first text reads: "You shall act in accordance with the instructions given you and the ruling handed down to you; you must not deviate from the verdict that they announce to you either to the right or to the left" (Deut. 17:11). The original context of this statement is the biblical requirement to heed the court's judgments, but the Rabbis read the text out of context as a reference to their own authority. Thus, when they hand down a ruling, one must listen closely to the verdict and not deviate from it.

Their second proof text is also from Deuteronomy: "Ask your parent, who will inform you, Your elders, who will tell you" (Deut 32:7). In the biblical context, this text is part of Moses' last speech to the people before they enter the Promised Land. He is reminding the people to learn and remember their history. In the Rabbis' creative rereading of the text, the Rabbis themselves are the "parents" and "elders" who will inform the people of the right path, and the people must follow their edicts.

Returning to Yochanan's shofar ruling, in the future it will become a religious imperative to follow the Sages' takkanot. For now, Yochanan knows that simply asking the people to change their ways will not be easy. Jerusalem still occupies a coveted place in the people's consciousness; they are still grieving their ruined Holy Place. If he replaces Jerusalem entirely with local courts, the people might not accept the change.

Thus, the story continues with an emendation to his ruling. Although the shofar must be blown in the presence of the court at places like Yavneh, Yochanan allows a leniency for anyone living in Jerusalem. If a Jerusalem court declares a new moon, the shofar can be blown anywhere within earshot of the city, even if miles away from the court, thus giving a nod to the sanctity of Jerusalem lost in the siege:[35]

> And Jerusalem [in earlier times] had this additional superiority over Yavne [after Rabban Yochanan ben Zakkai instituted this practice], for in any city whose residents could see [Jerusalem] and hear [the sounding of the *shofar* from there], and which was near [to Jerusalem] and people could come [to Jerusalem from there], they would sound [the *shofar* there as well, as it was considered part of Jerusalem]. But in Yavne they would sound the *shofar* only in the court [itself, not in the surrounding cities].[36]

This ruling mimics the Temple practice of sounding the horn near the authority that allowed it. It also makes a distinction between Jerusalem, which is holy enough to warrant blowing anywhere within its walls, and a place like Yavneh, where Jews are now living, where courts are now functioning, and which might otherwise not be seen as holy enough to allow for sounding the shofar.

Ultimately, to persuade people to listen to him, Yochanan speaks to their sense of loss. He puts constraints on his revolutionary legislation, limiting where the shofar can be sounded, to honor the legacy of the Temple cult, now in ruins.

Moving forward, and again using takkanot, Yochanan will go on to reimagine many of the most sacred practices in the Jewish tradition: when the lulav can be shaken on Sukkot,[37] how to judge the new moon,[38] and how converts enter into the Jewish fold.[39] Where some leaders might be crippled by the desire to return to a world newly snatched away, Yochanan makes the painful decision to change the law to match the new reality. In doing so, he not only

Tools to Transform Law   137

saves an endangered faith but also sets the example for countless other takkanot from his disciples.

Responding to the Hour of Need: Invoking *Sha'at Ha-deḥak* or *Sha'at Ha-sakanah*

One of the reasons Rabbis like Yochanan ben Zakkai are able to institute such radical changes is because they are living in extraordinary times, described by the Rabbis as a *sha'at ha-deḥak* (lit. a pressing hour) or *sha'at ha-sakanah* (hour of danger). These phrases appear in Rabbinic literature a few dozen times, each time describing a dire situation that forces the Rabbis to innovate.

In one classic example, the Rabbis forgo the requirement to place a Hanukkah menorah (*hanukkiah*) in a window if displaying it is dangerous:

> It is a mitzva to place the Hanukkah lamp at the entrance to one's house on the outside, [so that all can see it]. If he lived upstairs, he places it at the window adjacent to the public domain. And in a time of danger, [when the gentiles issued decrees to prohibit kindling lights], he places it on the table and that is sufficient to fulfill his obligation.[40]

For the Rabbis, one of the key reasons one lights a hanukkiah is to teach the world about the miracle of Hanukkah: namely that after the Hasmoneans reconsecrated their Temple, their one-day supply of oil lasted for eight days. Jews are required to publicly mark this holiday observance. However, if remembering this episode through the public display of lights is dangerous—say, if governmental authorities have outlawed core Jewish practices, or if antisemitism is rampant and broadcasting one's Jewishness to the world might threaten one's well-being—the law allows Jews to forgo this practice.

Although physical threats are common reasons for legal innovations, the Rabbis also invoke the sha'at ha-deḥak rationale in times of scarcity or economic hardship:

There was an incident involving city dwellers [who lived in an area distant from the region where the four species grow], who would bequeath their *lulavim* to their grandchildren, [even though they were completely dry]. The Sages said to him: Is there proof from there [that species that are dry remain fit for use]? Actions taken in exigent circumstances are not proof. [In typical circumstances, it would be prohibited to use those species].[41]

According to Jewish law, under normal circumstances, one may not shake a lulav[42] that has become too dry, because it is unbefitting of Sukkot holiday observance.[43] Nonetheless, the Rabbis understand that sometimes using a desiccated lulav may be the only option. Perhaps you are enduring a drought, living too far away from nature, or danger keeps you from traveling to buy one or more of the species from your supplier.[44] In such cases, if you cannot find the four species that compose the lulav, the Rabbis proclaim it is better for one to perform the mitzvah incorrectly than to forgo it altogether. You may use last year's lulav or pass down an old, dry lulav so your descendants do not lose touch with the practice.

Sometimes the Rabbis did hold the line against using the "pressing need" rationale, but on the whole they were quite willing to call a moment a sha'at ha-dehak and to permit legal flexibility.[45] As they did, they kept in mind that their changes were time limited. When the exigencies of the moment disappeared, so too would their leniencies.[46]

Loopholes

Jewish law is full of legal fictions and loopholes the Rabbis sometimes exploit to make legal changes. Some loopholes are so commonplace in traditional Jewish practice today that Jews forget how radical they were in the first place. One can carry keys and push strollers through certain public streets on Shabbat despite the fact that Jewish law prohibits carrying items more than four cubits (about 6 feet) in public on the Sabbath because in those locales Jews have set an *eruv* (a zone often delineated today by fishing wire and telephone lines that designates a larger geographic area as being part of one private residence). One can take a "Shabbat elevator" that stops on every floor of a hotel despite Jewish law prohibiting operating electrical devices (by one common understanding, akin to the biblical prohibition against lighting a fire).[47] One can "sell" *hametz* (leavened products) to non-Jews right before Passover so as not to be "in possession" of hametz on the holiday, on the understanding that the non-Jewish "buyers" sell back the leavened goods right after Pesach.[48]

Often, when the Rabbis resort to loopholes, it is because of some pragmatic concern they are addressing. A few examples:[49]

> Jewish law does not permit a person to run back into a burning building to rescue personal effects on Shabbat, since it violates the rules against carrying items in public on the Sabbath.[50] However, this prohibition does not extend to clothing one is wearing. Knowing this, the Rabbis allow a person to wear as many layers of clothing as one can fit on one's body in order to save them from the fire. In fact, they even allow a person to leave the house, strip, and run into the burning house for more items to wear.[51]
>
> Anyone who belonged to the ancient caste of *kohanim* (priests) was allowed to eat *terumah*, gifts of produce given to the Temple by ordinary Israelites to sustain the priests in the Temple since they themselves could not own land. Once, during a famine, Rabbi Tarfon, who was a *kohen*, betrothed 300 women. Since any woman betrothed to a kohen could eat terumah and there was no limit then to the number of women who could be betrothed to a single man, Tarfon was able to utilize public stores of food that these women would not otherwise have access to in order to sustain them during the time of scarcity.[52]

In ancient times, people were required to periodically[53] bring to the Temple a certain tithe known as *ma'aser sheni* which consisted of grain, wine, and olive oil.[54] Because carrying the heavy ma'aser sheni was challenging, people were allowed to change it out for money where they lived and then use those coins to purchase an offering when they arrived in Jerusalem. In exchange for this convenience, Jewish law imposes a penalty of a fifth of the value of one's ma'aser sheni.[55] Worrying that this penalty would dissuade people of limited means from coming to Jerusalem at all, the Rabbis create a loophole. Reading the Torah closely, they note that the penalty only applies if you bring your own funds to Jerusalem.[56] If you give your funds to another, that person is not subject to the added fifth.[57] Hence, that other person can buy ma'aser sheni for you in Jerusalem, and you can do the same for that person, without either of you being subject to the penalty.

Although the Rabbis are not universally in favor of these types of loopholes, they tend to welcome them if the loophole will help the community as a whole.[58] These three examples preserve the essence of each of their laws while ensuring that people will be able to protect their property in a crisis, find food in a famine, and not grow distant from the Temple cult.

THE *PROZBUL*

Another loophole helps support the needs of both lenders and debtors in society. According to biblical law, one is required to forgive debts every seven years (Deut. 15:1–2). The apparent rationale was to ensure that no person would remain economically bound to another forever; rather, every seven years, all debtors would get a fresh start and a chance to begin amassing wealth anew. In time, however, the Rabbis came to realize that this seemingly good social policy was having a negative economic effect. Free-flowing capital is necessary for a society's economic well-being: it allows people to buy property, invest in new economic enterprises, regroup after a setback, and more. Yet as the date of debt forgiveness neared, lenders would grow wary of lending money, lest the balance on their loan be erased before being paid back, hampering a lender's willingness to loan money.[59] This would have widespread ramifications on the society at large.

Hillel thus realizes that the biblical law has run its course. So he exploits a loophole found in the biblical law.[60] He observes that the Torah says, "You must remit whatever is due you from your kindred" (Deut 15:3). Concentrating on the fact that you, the lender, have to forgive debts that are "due you," he devises a plan known as the *Prozbul* (a Greek word likely meaning "before the assembly of the councilors") whereby the lender will transfer the debt owed to the Jerusalem court. Because a court is not a person and hence is not the "you" that the Torah is addressing, it is outside the law and not subject to the laws of debt forgiveness.

Hillel is careful to legislate the appropriate formula and ritual for this title transfer:

> I transfer to you, so-and-so the judges, who are in such and such a place, so that I will collect any debt that I am owed by so-and-so whenever I wish. And the judges or the witnesses sign below.[61]

By reciting this formula and signing the requisite paperwork, a creditor could return to the court following the year of forgiveness and take the debt back. Thus, instead of having to forgo the debt, the lender would extend the grace time for repaying it by an extra seven years.

The *Prozbul* encourages lenders to more graciously open their hands. Although the Torah tells lenders explicitly that they should not refrain from lending as the seventh year draws near,[62] the Rabbis understand that even a command from God cannot compel human beings to risk their economic future.

OTZAR BEIT DIN

Much like the Prozbul, the Rabbis develop the concept of the *otzar beit din* (literally a "court-owned storehouse"), which likewise protects a person's hard-earned assets from being taken away by transferring them to the court. As background, Jewish law requires field owners farming on their lands to let their lands lie fallow every seven years, in what is known as a *shemitah* (lit. release) year. At that time, anyone could come onto a person's property to pick what grew naturally on the trees and vines. Owners no longer owned their own produce. They had the same foraging rights as everyone else. But because people were treading on other people's property, they were not careful to safeguard it, to the consternation of the field owners, who were powerless to stop them.

In response, the Rabbis create the concept of otzar bein din, whereby the courts assume ownership of the fields and, not being beholden to the same laws as individual field owners, arrange for guards to monitor the premises.[63] The courts also hire workers to till and harvest the fields. Because the workers they hire are often the owners of the fields, the courts are able to pay them for the produce by disguising the payments as labor costs. Provided they don't "pay" for the produce itself, as that produce belongs to everyone during a *shemitah* year, otzar bein din allows field owners to survive economically and to protect their crops for the following year, at which time the courts transfer the land ownership back to them.

Both the Prosbul and otzar bein din are revolutionary in that the courts themselves are participating in the legal ruses. One could imagine the Talmud quietly countenancing loopholes for individual cases while holding firm to societal norms. Yet the fact that the Rabbis specifically call for the judiciary—the institution tasked with the upkeep of social justice—to facilitate these workarounds demonstrates the Rabbinic commitment to weaving halakhic flexibility and creativity into all of society.

Subterfuges

A close cousin of the Rabbinic loophole is the subterfuge. Though this is a little harder to find, the Rabbis will often use similar logic and craftiness to mislead others if doing so preserves themselves and their people.[64]

In one talmudic episode, Rabbi Yochanan learns a secret medical remedy from a Roman matron who makes him swear he will not reveal it to anyone. His promise seems clear. He tells her, "To the God of the Jews, I will not reveal it." The next day, he goes against her wishes and teaches the remedy in a public lecture. Although we don't hear the matron's reaction, the anonymous editor of the Talmud interrupts the story to ask in wonder why Yochanan was allowed to go against her wishes after he gave his solemn promise not to reveal the cure.

Answering its own question, the Talmud notes that Yochanan words his promise in a crafty way; he promises he will not reveal the secret "to the God of the Jews," but he doesn't say he will not tell the Jews, themselves.[65] As with the loopholes above, this lie ensures that Yochanan's society will have access to the best medical remedies.

In another example, the Rabbis permit the courts to intimidate and confuse witnesses who claim to have seen the new moon so that they will renege on their testimony and the court can shift the start of a new month by a day.[66] The reason given for this trickery surrounds the unfortunate possibility of Shabbat falling directly before a holiday like Yom Kippur. Because both days require rest and certain actions, like burying the dead or harvesting vegetables, are not permitted on them, it is helpful to have a weekday to recover after Shabbat ends and the holiday begins.[67] In fact, some opinions even permit this intimidation when others can authenticate the witnesses' original testimony. Here the need not to let a body rot or a good crop wither takes precedence over the "truth" of celestial time. These subterfuges too were the subject of much talmudic debate, but when employed well, they helped the Rabbis stretch the law to improve society.[68]

Playing with Intent

One of the reasons otzar bein din works is that it creates a loophole using intention. The courts give money to the field owner pretending it is only for the labor and not for the goods produced. Although one could say there isn't a difference between paying one hundred dollars for labor or one hundred dollars for produce, the different rationales make one act permitted and the other forbidden.

This willingness to parse a person's intent is another key tool the Rabbis employ to stretch the law's bounds. For our Sages, sometimes the intention behind a given act can change its implications. For example, if two people eat the same forbidden food, one intentionally and the other accidentally, thinking it is permitted, each receives different punishments.[69] Even one's motivations when intentionally sinning matters. Some Rabbinic opinions hold that a person who eats a cheeseburger because of a craving for it is less accountable than a person who eats it to flout Jewish law and scorn God.[70]

Sometimes the Rabbis even find ways to permit a sinner's act if they believe the intent is noble. In one place, they allow a person to do some light hoeing around a tree during a festival, something usually considered "work" and thus prohibited, if the intent is to preserve—rather than strengthen—the tree.[71] Elsewhere the Rabbis allow a person to pick vegetables during the intermediate days of holidays[72]—something usually considered prohibited because it violates the command to refrain from "reaping" on Shabbat and holidays[73]—provided the intent is to eat the produce and not thin out the garden to help it grow. And despite this prohibition, people who want a cleaner and more manicured garden can pick more produce than they can eat, so long as they begin with the intent to eat what they reap.[74]

Both of these workarounds allow a person to preserve property. In a similar vein, the Rabbis radically rule that based on one's intentions, one can save an animal as well. Specifically, if an animal falls into a pit on a festival day, one is allowed to save it, even though by law animals are not to be handled on festival days unless the handler intends to use them for food:

> An animal and its offspring which fell into a pit, Rabbi Eliezer says, "One raises up the first on condition to slaughter it but does not slaughter it, and for the second, one provides food while it is in its present location, so that it does not die." Rabbi Joshua says, "One raises up the first on condition to slaughter it but does not slaughter it, and, practicing cunning, one then raises up the second. [If] he wanted to slaughter neither one of them, he has the right [to refrain]."[75]

Imagine you see the animals fall into the pit and want to rescue them right away, not when the festival ends. You don't need the animals for food. According to Rabbi Eliezer, if you tell yourself you intend to slaughter one of the animals, you may raise it up and then conveniently change your mind.[76] Rabbi Joshua takes an even more unconventional position. He allows you to play this mental trick for both animals.

There are, of course, limits to how far one can stretch intentions. At times the Rabbis categorize intention games that go too far as *pesik reisha*. Meaning "cutting off the head," this idea prohibits doing a permitted action if the unintended side effect is against Jewish law. Pesik reisha comes from a Rabbinic quip that one cannot intend to cut off a chicken's head without it inevitably dying.[77] A classical example prohibits keeping a Shabbat candle near an open door or window.[78] You may not mean for the flame to be extinguished—perhaps your intent is to beautify the room or show others you are religiously observant—but if you position the lit candle in a precarious place where a passing breeze will quench it, Jewish law treats your act as if you intentionally extinguished the flame.

Though pesik reisha is an important counter to loopholes of intent, the concept is not applied universally. When needed, the Rabbis still have the freedom to creatively innovate based on a person's internal monologue and motivations. Because people act for a myriad of reasons, this gives the Rabbis tremendous flexibility.

Legislating around a Fluke

As keen observers of everyday traditions, the Rabbis often craft the law around what the people are already doing or might be able to do in the future. The challenge with legislating broadly on communal norms, however, is that most of their observations are ballpark estimates. They do not send out surveys. When they state that a majority of people think or act in a certain way, they are either following their guts or thinking wishfully, neither of which stands up to scientific scrutiny. Nonetheless, the Rabbis are able to take their unfounded observations about the practices and traditions around them and exercise them into law. They are able to claim that something that might be a fluke is actually common and thus legislate with that in mind.

As we will see, their use of unfounded observations often involves cases centering on women's experiences—instances in which the Rabbis' firsthand knowledge would have been complicated at best. Regardless of how we might view these issues today, it is striking how the Rabbis attempt to attend to what they see as the dynamics of everyday life.

MENSTRUATION AND SEXUAL INTIMACY

In one example, the Rabbis know that most of the time, when a woman discovers menstrual blood, it is because she is either menstruating or spotting. Because the law states that a woman who is menstruating is impure and thus not available for sex with her husband, and because the Rabbis value sexual intimacy both for the sake of procreation and sometimes as a mitzvah in its own right,[79] the Rabbis tried to find alternative explanations for occasional blood stains that would ensure husband and wife could remain physically intimate together:

> And [a woman who discovers a blood stain on her body or her garment] may attribute its existence to any matter to which she can attribute it: If she slaughtered a domesticated animal, an undomesticated animal, or a bird; or if she was occupied with [the removal of blood] stains [from the garments of other women or from her own garment, from any source, such as blood that originated from a wound elsewhere on her body or even her own menstrual blood from a prior menstrual cycle]; or if she sat alongside others who were occupied with [removing blood stains]; or if she killed a louse; in all of these cases, that woman may attribute the blood stain to it.[80]

There is an adage in medicine that "when you hear hooves, think horses, not zebras," meaning that most often a symptom is caused by the most prevalent ailment. In this case, menstrual-looking blood is almost always caused by menstruation. However, the Rabbis give permission for any number of zebras, including the leftover blood of lice, if it can create a narrative that will bring husband and wife together.[81]

A WIFE'S TESTIMONY ON HER HUSBAND'S DEATH

Legislating around an anomalous case also appears in Rabbinic discussion surrounding a wife's testimony on her husband's death. As background, most testimony requires two witnesses, neither of whom can be related to the person about whom they are testifying.[82] What, then, should be done about a wife who is the sole witness to a husband's death and whose body cannot be recovered (say, because he died during their trip abroad)? Can she be believed? Or is she doomed to wait for who knows how long until two other unrelated people can prove her husband passed away before she is permitted to remarry?[83]

Early in the Rabbinic era, this question was up for debate:

> With regard to a woman who went, she and her husband, overseas[84] . . . and the woman came back by herself and said: My husband died, she may marry on the basis of her own testimony. . . . Rabbi Yehuda says: She is never deemed credible when she testifies that her husband died, unless she came crying and her clothing was torn, [in which case it is apparent that she is speaking the truth]. They said to him: [This is an incorrect distinction]. Rather, both this woman who cries and this woman who does not cry may marry on the basis of their own testimony.[85]

To counter Rabbi Yehudah's assertion that a woman has to look like she's been through an ordeal to be believed, the Sages create an implausible scenario:

> The Rabbis said to Rabbi Yehudah: According to your statement, a crafty woman [who knows how to deceive will come with torn clothes crying], and it will be permitted for her to marry. However, a foolish woman [who does not know how to deceive] will not be permitted to marry. [Is this a fair outcome?] Rather, both this woman and that woman may marry.[86]

Here the Rabbis choose an uncommon argument to defeat Rabbi Yehudah. Rather than say the obvious—most wives do not invent the deaths of their husbands, and if widows don't appear to be mourning, it might be because they are in shock or simply stoic—the Rabbis prove their case with an ostensibly much less common scenario. They raise the prospect of a wife who pretends to mourn her husband to trick the court into sanctioning a subsequent marriage. This more unusual scenario undercuts Rabbi Yehudah's argument because it makes all testimony suspect. Because there is no way to know for sure whether a given woman's testimony is true or false, the court no longer has to consider whether it is being tricked. The

Rabbis discount the concern and simply err on the side of compassion, allowing the wife to remarry.

As with most of the workarounds in this chapter, the Rabbis' propensity toward exploiting flukes to legislate is not without controversy in the Talmud.[87] However, while up for debate, the tactic proves useful. There will always be outlier scenarios. Rarities open the doors for the Rabbis to imagine alternative paths to necessary rulings.

All Creativity Is Essential

The Rabbis draw a distinction between three types of laws:

1. Rabbinic rulings that have no basis in the Torah itself: These laws are complete Rabbinic innovations. One cannot find them anywhere in scripture. They "fly in the air and have nothing to support them."
2. Rabbinic rulings that have only scant support in the Torah: These laws, which include the laws of Shabbat and certain festival practices, are only mentioned a handful of times in the Torah, even though huge tractates are written about them. They are likened to "mountains suspended by a hair."
3. Rabbinic rulings that have a firm basis in Torah: These laws, which include the laws of purity and of ritual sacrifice, receive extensive coverage in the Torah and warrant equally significant treatment in the Rabbinic corpus.[88]

One might think that the third of these categories is the most important: those laws that God states explicitly must matter more. However, the Rabbis go out of their way to acknowledge that all three categories matter. All form "the essential parts of the Torah."[89]

In speaking this way, the Rabbis are making a bold claim about their own authority. Their project is essential. They have a right to innovate, to reimagine, even to "misread" when their understanding of what is right for their society clashes with a plain reading of Torah. All the more, as our next chapter will show, the Rabbinic toolbox can allow the Rabbis to advocate for the gravest of sins, provided they do so with the care and logic they bring to all innovation.

Sinning for the Greater Good   8

Moral living is sometimes a balancing act between two competing values. And often there is no ideal choice. Truth will often compete with kindness. Principle will clash with compromise. Loyalty will butt up against independence and self-determination. Transparency will contend with privacy.

To understand how it is that moral dilemmas convey contesting values, it's helpful to look at one of the most famous examples in history, one that many philosophy students encounter early in the course of their studies. Jean-Paul Sartre famously wrote about a student of his who lost his brother during World War Two.[1] Angry at the Nazis, the student sought to enlist and fight against the regime. However, this young man was also tending to his grieving mother, and he knew that if he went to fight, with the many risks involved, it would break her. Should he fight for his country and avenge his brother or stay home and care for his bereft parent? He approached Sartre, hoping the philosopher would help.

Yet Sartre would not help him choose one path over another. Ultimately, Sartre reports, his student metaphorically threw up his hands and said, "All things considered it is feelings that matter; I should choose what truly compels me to follow a certain path."[2]

Reflecting on the student's answer, Sartre explains that moral dilemmas are too situationally dependent to rely on grand ethical theories. When values are in tension, one cannot turn toward a moral system for guidance, hoping some algorithm will spit out the right answer. Though many philosophers have tried to create these systems of moral thought, Sartre held that the world is too complicated, and moral systems too abstract or otherwise flawed, to rely on predictable patterns and solutions. Even seemingly straightforward sources of guidance, like the Christian idea that we should "be charitable, love our neighbor, sacrifice ourselves for others, choose the narrow way," fall flat for Sartre, since for the student it is up for debate which is the "narrow way" and who is more of a "neighbor," his mother or his countrymen.[3]

Rather than view this as a bad thing, Sartre sees the fact that moral conundrums are circumstantially dependent as actually freeing. It means we humans often get to make our own moral choices. We get to read the facts of a situation and chart a course we decide is right. As he writes, "No general code of ethics can tell you what you ought to do."[4]

Somewhat like Sartre, the Talmud tends to shy away from systematically legislating morality in complex cases.[5] When values are in tension, the Rabbis often vacillate between poles. When negotiating social pressures, they commonly choose messier paths and privilege pragmatism alongside moral law. As this chapter will demonstrate, sometimes the Rabbis even go so far as to countenance immorality and sin for the sake of some other moral good. In their world, acting rightly can sometimes mean doing wrong.

Intent and Transgressions for the Sake of God: Lot's Daughters, Tamar, and Yael

Adamant that one's intentions matter (see chapter 7), not only in ritual realms (where such discussions of intent appear most often) but also when deciding the integrity of ethical actions,[6] the Rabbis engage in spirited debate on "which matters more, intention or action?" If two Jews eat the Paschal offering on Passover for different reasons—one to fulfill the commandment to "offer the Passover sacrifice at its set time" (Num. 9:2) and another to fulfill his craving for meat by "excessive eating," is the craver equally righteous?

Rabbi Yochanan condemns the craver, comparing him to a "transgressor" who "stumbles" over the commandments,[7] but Resh Lakish accepts him, saying, "Even though he had not performed the mitzvah in the optimal manner, he has at least performed the mitzvah of the Paschal offering."[8] To Resh Lakish, a consequentialist voice in Rabbinic literature, one should be judged by the effects of one's actions. Both offering a sacrifice for God and bringing an animal to the Temple to partake of its meat result in a completed Temple rite. God is honored by the scent of burning meat either way.

However compelling Resh Lakish's argument may be, his view will not win the day. To the majority of Rabbis, intention matters, as much as—if not more so than—its effects. Only a half-page later, the Talmud's discussion climaxes with the provocative statement by Rabbi Nachman Bar Yitzhak: "Greater is a transgression committed for its own sake, [i.e., for the sake of Heaven], than a mitzvah performed not for its own sake."[9] In one statement, the Talmud explodes the notion that actions speak for themselves. Intent counts for so much that having the right mindset when sinning can turn a transgression into a righteous act.

The Talmud bolsters this claim subtly. Rather than bring direct proof, it surrounds Nachman's statement with a series of case studies of biblical characters: all women who sin in deed but are held in high regard for it. In every case, as we will see, the women transgress, ignore, and even rebuff traditional Jewish moral and legal norms because they believe failing to act will result in dire consequences for themselves, their families, and the future of the Jewish people. Seeing their careful and sometimes painful calculations, the Rabbis generally consider their sins meritorious.

LOT'S DAUGHTERS

The first case study arises in the aftermath of the razing of Sodom and Gomorrah. God condemns the two cities to destruction after observing their moral corruption and depravity but in an act of mercy, God sends an angel to the home of Abraham's nephew Lot to warn him of the impending conflagration and compel him to escape. Eventually, Lot, along with his two daughters, find their way out of the city and settle in the hill country, camping out in a cave. There the story takes a morally problematic turn.

Assuming they are the last people on earth, Lot's two daughters get him drunk and sleep with him. Their explicit goal is clear: they want to repopulate the world. "Let us lie with him," they say, "that we may maintain life through our father" (Gen. 19:32). Their intent is actualized. One daughter gives birth to the forefather of the Moabites and the other to the forebearer of the Ammonites.

The Rabbis criticize Lot for allowing himself to be duped by his daughters. They especially take him to task because he is violated a second time after a second night of drinking; he should have learned his limits after his first mistake, and abstained.[10] They speak somewhat disparagingly of the daughters as well, but they are careful not to wholly condemn the women.[11] Despite their clear discomfort with this rape and accompanying incest, they focus on Lot's daughters' intent.[12] Because they witnessed the destruction of their town and assumed the same had happened across the world, the two daughters believed sleeping with their father was the only way to save humanity. And this—their intent to preserve the species—makes their sin virtuous. The Rabbis apply to the two a verse from the prophets: "For the paths of God are smooth, and the righteous [i.e., Lot's daughters] can walk on them" (Hos. 14.10). According to the Rabbis, then, the daughters' incestuous rape can be seen as God's path because it was carried out for the right reasons.

TAMAR

The second case involves Tamar's seduction of her father-in-law, Judah. After losing her first husband, Er (for reasons the Bible does not explain), Tamar marries Er's brother Onan in accordance with the requirement that if a man dies childless, his brother should marry his widow, both to take care of her and to continue the line in his name. Soon, though, Onen also dies (as punishment for spilling his seed rather than impregnating her). Now Tamar is promised to the third and youngest brother, Shelah. She waits and waits for her chance to marry Shelah, but a date for the wedding is never set. Eventually Tamar realizes her father-in-law, Judah, is the impediment. Judah blames Tamar for his two older sons' deaths. Despite his promise to one day give her Shelah in marriage, he will never follow through. He isn't willing to risk his one remaining son's life by allowing him to marry her.

Now Tamar takes it upon herself to trick Judah into sleeping with her to have a child she will never have with Shelah. Dressing up as a harlot, she seduces her father-in-law. In the process she keeps proof of her liaison with him, including his staff. She becomes pregnant, and an incensed Judah, not realizing he himself is the father, grows furious at her for "cheating" on his son. "Bring her out," he says. "She should be burned" (Gen. 38:25). In response, Tamar quietly hands Judah's staff back to him, proving that the child soon to be born is his. This assuages Judah's anger. Realizing she intended to perpetuate his family seed, he acknowledges, "She is more in the right than I, inasmuch as I did not give her to my son Shelah" (Gen 28:26). She eventually gives birth to twins.

Like Lot's daughters, Tamar commits incest. She also lies and flouts the laws of the day by cheating on Shelah to whom she is promised.[13] Yet, the Rabbis teach, because Tamar commits to the command to be "fruitful and multiply" (Gen 1:28) and honors her dead husbands by continuing their line, she merits that kings and prophets descend from her. And that's what happens. Tamar's children become the ancestors of King David and great seers like Isaiah. Moreover, we are told, even the Messiah will descend from her.[14]

The Talmud also contrasts Tamar's licentiousness for the sake of good with a male character's fornication with a Midianite woman for the release of his carnal appetite in, of all places, the Tent of Meeting, God's holy dwelling place on Earth.[15] Tamar's children become the ancestors of King David; Zimri is killed for his depravity.

Sinning for the Greater Good   157

YAEL

The third scenario centers on Yael, a Kenite woman whose husband has ties to Sisera, general of the Canaanites.[16] When the Israelites' battle against the Canaanites turns to their advantage, Sisera flees the front to take refuge in Yael's husband's tent. Yael invites him in, gives him milk, woos him to sleep—and then drives a tent peg through his skull. When Yael brings the leader's limp body to the Israelite command, it cements their victory (Judg. 4:17–22).

Yet the Rabbis are baffled by Yael's ability to lull Sisera asleep simply with warm milk and a kind countenance. They surmise that Yael must have figured out another, more crafty way to exhaust the general. She could have only accomplished this though sex. Through a careful misreading of the verbs used in Sisera's death scene, where he "lay at her feet" and "sank" and was utterly "destroyed,"[17] they postulate that Yael, in great vigor, slept with him no fewer than seven times.[18]

This liaison is adulterous and hence an overt sin. All the more, Yael sleeps with a foreign general! But to the Rabbis, the fact that she transgresses to aid the Israelite army makes her blameless. (That she also murders Sisera is not at all problematic; the Rabbis view spilled blood as a byproduct of war.) In fact, the Rabbis elevate Yael above the matriarchs, Sarah, Rebecca, Rachel, and Leah. These four women enjoyed sexual relations with their husbands, they say, but Yael did not savor her liaison.[19] Her acts solely benefitted the Israelite campaign.[20]

Yael also transgresses in flouting the ancient norms of hospitality. For Jews, as with other nomadic peoples, the simple gesture of inviting someone into one's tent was a holy act. The Talmud is filled with folk wisdom on how to treat guests,[21] to the point that one could argue that ignoring the mandate of hospitality is grievous enough to warrant punishment in nearly every case. But this is not so for Yael, whom the Rabbis praise as committing a transgression in the name of heaven.[22]

In this regard the famous Talmudist Ephraim Urbach called the Rabbinic mindset a "revolution in intention."[23] Lot's daughters, Tamar and Yael, all take morally problematic actions, but on the whole the Rabbis esteem them because their intent-filled acts lead to good.

Killing Informants to Preserve More Lives: Weighing Bar Kamtza, Rabbi Kahana's Act of Strangulation

Sometimes the Rabbis assent to taking reprehensible actions to stave off great suffering or achieve other paramount goods.[24] As we will see in the cases that follow, at times the Sages go so far as to call for killing *moserim*, Jewish informants who pass on harmful information to non-Jewish authorities. Mindful of the ever-present possibility of extreme violence against Jews, the Rabbis periodically calculate that preserving the life of informants—who are said to descend "to Gehenna [hell] and are judged there for generations and generations"—is liable to ultimately cost many more Jewish lives.

WEIGHING BAR KAMTZA

Perhaps the most famous example of this calculation appears in the Rabbinic telling of the lead-up to the Second Temple's destruction.[25] As the story goes, when a Jew sends out invitations to his upcoming feast, an invite intended for his friend Kamtza mistakenly ends up in the hands of his enemy, bar Kamtza. Surprised but touched, bar Kamtza goes to the party, unaware he is not the intended recipient. When the host sees his nemesis sitting and eating, he demands that he leave. Bar Kamsa pleads with him to let him stay, but to no avail. He is forced out.

Irate, bar Kamtza blames everyone for his humiliation, including the Rabbis at the party who did nothing. He becomes a *moser*. To exact revenge, he tells the Roman rulers an insidious lie: the Jews are preparing for rebellion. And, bar Kamtza adds, he knows just how to prove this. He counsels the Romans to give the Jews a test. They are to send the Jews a gift of an animal the Jews are to sacrifice as an offering in the name of the Roman government. If the Jews do not receive this act of friendship with gratitude and proceed to sacrifice the animal, it will confirm that the Jews hold Rome in contempt.

The Romans agree, not realizing that bar Kamtza plans to exploit a priestly rule that prohibits Jews from offering an animal with a defect on the altar of God:

> While [bar Kamtza] was coming, he made a blemish on [the calf's] upper lip. And some say it was on its eyelids, a place where according to us, it is a blemish, but according to them [gentile rules for their offerings], it is not a blemish. The Sages thought to sacrifice the animal as an offering due to the imperative to maintain peace with the government. Rabbi Zekharya ben Avkolas said to them: If the priests do that, people will say that blemished animals may be sacrificed as offerings on the altar.[26]

Once the Rabbis acknowledge Rabbi Zekharya's point, they face a dilemma. Not accepting the sacrificial calf is liable to unleash Roman anger. What should they do?

Knowing that bar Kamtza himself added the blemish, thereby putting them in this impossible situation, the Sages explore a considerably more extreme measure, saying:

> If we do not sacrifice [the calf], then we must prevent bar Kamtza from reporting this to the emperor. The Sages thought to kill him so that he would not go and speak against them. Rabbi Zekharya said to them: If you kill him, people will say that one who makes a blemish on sacrificial animals is to be killed.[27]

In the end, Rabbi Zekharya prevails on both accounts: the Sages let both the calf and bar Kamtza live. Bar Kamtza reports to Rome that the Jews have failed the test, and Rome attacks Jerusalem.

This episode takes place before the true birth of Rabbinic Judaism (see Prologue), when the Rabbis have not yet learned that maintaining peace with the government is a paramount value (see chapter 5). Here they privilege the integrity of the altar, to disastrous results. Even so, the Rabbis do not come across as moral absolutists. To keep bar Kamtza from informing on them, they not only consider making a blemished sacrifice but also entertain murder.

CONDEMNING RABBI ZEKHARYA

In the third century, the Rabbis condemn Rabbi Zekharya for his fundamentalist commitment to religious and ethical purity. Rabbi Yochanan writes: "The excessive humility of Rabbi Zekharya ben Avkolas destroyed our Temple, burned our Sanctuary, and exiled us from our land."[28]

Note that the Rabbis choose to attack Rabbi Zekharya's humility. In essence they malign him for shirking hard decisions (i.e., the murder of one informant) when bad and worse options are the only possibilities. Because he retreats from formidable action in the face of anticipated calamity, the Jews pay the ultimate price of losing their Temple and their sacred land.

RAV KAHANA'S ACT OF STRANGULATION

Elsewhere in the Talmud, Rabbi Kahana does what Rabbi Zekharya would not permit: he commits murder to protect the Jews from gentile authorities:

> There was a certain man who desired to show another individual's straw [to the gentile authorities, who would seize it]. He came before Rav, who said to him: Do not show it and do not show it, [i.e., you are absolutely prohibited from showing it]. The man said to him: I will show it and I will show it, [i.e., I will certainly show it]. Rav Kahana was sitting before Rav [and, hearing the man's disrespectful response], he dislodged the man's neck from him, [i.e., he broke his neck and killed him].[29]

Sinning for the Greater Good

From this one incident, Rav Kahana's response appears overly callous. He seems too quick to take this man's life. Yet this story follows a series of cases in which gentile authorities force Jews to inform on fellow Jews and then seize these Jews' property.[30] By contrast, this informer *has* a choice: he turns over the straw of his own free will. Furthermore, to the Rabbis, one of the great risks of *messirah* (informing) of any kind is that it would accustom gentile authorities to take further advantage of the Jewish community; non-valuable possessions like straw might induce them to seek out other, more valuable property.

Likening themselves to prey, the Rabbis write, "Just as with regard to this antelope, once it falls into the net, [the hunter] does not have mercy upon it, so too with regard to the money of a Jew, once it falls into the hand of gentiles, they do not have mercy upon him."[31] Here the Rabbis are claiming that their enemies will tread carefully, ostensibly cooperatively but essentially craftily, until the Jews are in their grasp. Then they will do whatever they want to the Jews' possessions and to their bodies. The Rabbis appear to sanction Rav Kahana's perpetration of murder to ensure the Romans do not grow accustomed to taking Jewish property. As this part of the story concludes, Rav Kahana flees his home in Babylonia for Israel, knowing that if he remains in Babylonia, the gentile authorities will press charges against him for killing the informant. In Israel, however, Rav Kahana becomes one of the great sages of his generation. He is not at all tainted by his act of violence, further evidence that he acted correctly.

OTHER PUNISHMENTS FOR INFORMERS

Elsewhere the Talmud discusses penalties for informers. If moserim fall into a pit, are we obliged to save their lives? The Rabbis are clear: Not only are we not obligated to "raise them up," but also if we assess they are dangerous, we are allowed to proactively lower them into the pit.[32]

Destroying a moser's possessions is also on the docket. One camp holds that confiscating or wrecking an informer's property is acceptable. The other camp disagrees—not out of concern for the moser, but rather for his descendants, as "perhaps he will have good children."[33] Notably, neither side seems to have an issue with physically harming the informant.

Permitting the Killing of Thieves

Relatedly, the Rabbis also allow us to kill first before being killed. The Torah instructs (without explanation): If you find a thief in your home, as long as "the sun has[n't] already risen," you may kill the intruder:

> If the thief is seized while tunneling and beaten to death, there is no bloodguilt in that case. If the sun had already risen, there is bloodguilt in that case. (Exod. 22:1–2)

To modern scholars, the Bible is distinguishing between daytime and nighttime break-ins,[34] but the Rabbis read "the sun has risen" differently: as a metaphorical statement about certitude. If you know for certain that the thief intends violence, you can kill him.

The Rabbis cite two texts that say this but disagree about what to do if you don't know the thief's intentions. The first reads:

> If the matter is as clear to you as the sun that the burglar is not coming to you in peace, [but rather his intention is to kill you, arise and] kill him first. But if you are not [sure about his intentions], do not kill him.[35]

Here the Rabbis allow you to kill a burglar at any time, if and only if you are certain he intends to hurt you.

The second text says: "If the matter is as clear to you as the sun that [the burglar] is coming to you in peace, do not kill him. But if you are not sure about his intentions, arise and kill him."[36] Here you must spare a thief's life, if and only if you are sure he means

Sinning for the Greater Good 163

you no harm. Whereas in the first text, uncertainty requires letting a thief go, in the second text, uncertainty allows you to take his life.

Needing to harmonize these texts, both authoritative in the Rabbis' eyes, the Rabbis imagine scenarios for when each might be true. In the first case, the Rabbis envision the thief is someone you know, like a parent or teacher. To break into your home, this person must really need the money but would not be prepared to harm you to get it.[37] In the second, the thief is a stranger to you and might naturally turn to violence when confronted:

> Rava says: What is the reason for this *halakha* concerning a burglar [who breaks into a house?] He explains: There is a presumption that a person does not restrain himself when faced with losing his money, and therefore this burglar must have said to himself: If I go in [and the owner sees me], he will rise against me and not allow me [to steal from him], and if he rises against me, I will kill him. And the Torah stated a principle: If someone comes to kill you, rise and kill him first.[38]

In that moment of panic and fear when a burglar who'd falsely presumed he wouldn't be caught finds himself challenged, he is likely to resort to violence, so for self-protection, the Rabbis permit you to kill him first.

This permissiveness is further underscored by a comment earlier in the discussion that a thief can be "sentenced on account of his ultimate end."[39] Hence you may take a thief's life for the *future* sin of killing you—one that you fully believe would otherwise be subsequently, inevitably, committed. Moreover, the Rabbis assert, this act of killing even benefits the perpetrator: "The death of the wicked is beneficial to them, [because they can no longer sin], and it is also beneficial to the world [which is now rid of those who do it harm]."[40] Ultimately the Rabbis allow us to kill thieves in self-defense—but, wary of the human tendency to act rashly, do caution us to do our best to determine the true nature of the threat before striking.

Taking the Life of a *Rodef*

Jewish law allows for still other instances during which you may kill a person in the midst of a crime. A bystander may kill someone who is attacking another if that bystander thinks the attacker will kill or rape them. Known as the law of the *rodef*, which means pursuer in Hebrew, this law gives license to good Samaritans to take extreme measures:

> And these are the ones who are saved [from transgressing even] at the cost of their lives; that is to say, [these people may be killed so that they do not perform a transgression]: One who pursues another to kill him, or pursues a male [to sodomize him], or pursues a betrothed young woman [to rape her]. But with regard to one who pursues an animal [to sodomize it], or one who seeks to desecrate Shabbat, or one who is going to engage in idol worship, they are not saved at the cost of their lives.[41]

The likely thinking behind these sets of laws (which in their framing toward women, many of us would consider inadequate today) is that murder and rape are irreversible. Unlike other grievous sins like profaning the Sabbath or bowing down to idols, where one can make amends, in these cases *teshuvah* is almost impossible. No amount of repenting on Yom Kippur can erase the lasting scars. For this reason, everyone benefits—even the pursuer—when a bystander steps in to impede the transgression.

Some of the earliest discussions of the rodef seem intentionally vague in their phrasing. The early midrashic collection known as the Sifra reads: "[If you see] a man pursuing another . . . you must rescue him at the cost of his life."[42] One could read this statement in two ways: (1) You must save the victim at the cost of the pursuer's life, or (2) you must save the rodef himself, precluding him from turning into a murderer or rapist. Because both interpretations are true, the Rabbis do not clarify and let both stand.

Later on, however, Maimonides tempers these more open-ended Rabbinic statements granting bystanders license to kill. Rather than fighting a rodef immediately, Maimonides rules, Jewish law requires a bystander to approach a pursuer with words of rebuke. If that doesn't work, one should pursue other physical means of stopping the pursuer before resorting to taking the pursuer's life:

> If the rodef was warned and continues to pursue his intended victim, even though he did not acknowledge the warning, since he continues his pursuit he should be killed. If it is possible to save the pursued by damaging one of the limbs of the rodef, one should. Thus, if one can strike him with an arrow, a stone or a sword, and cut off his hand, break his leg, blind him or in another way prevent him from achieving his objective, one should do so. If there is no way to be precise in one's aim and save the person being pursued without killing the rodef, one should kill him, even though he has not yet killed his victim.[43]

Sanctioning Torture

Strong physical or mental coercion designed to achieve a "positive outcome"—what many of us today might call "torture"—appears throughout Rabbinic literature, sometimes without critique.[44] The Rabbis are *not* saying we can inflict physical injury upon others without cause. Generally speaking, our Sages hold that one is solely allowed to hurt another if the second person has been proven guilty. Jewish law only permits a court to extend physical suffering on a person, usually through lashes, if that person is found guilty in due process—and even then, the law limits a person's punishment to exactly the prescribed number of lashes. The agent of the court can be held liable for exceeding that number.[45] So, too, one is not allowed even to raise one's hand and threaten a person who has not been proven guilty. The Talmud teaches, "[One who raises his hand to strike another] is called a sinner." [46] On the whole, the Rabbis also come out strongly against shaming others.[47] Rav Naḥman bar Yitzḥak states, "Anyone who humiliates another in public, it is as though he were spilling blood."[48] Elsewhere the Talmud teaches, "It is preferable, [from an ethical perspective], for one to throw himself into a fiery furnace rather than humiliate another in public."[49]

At the same time, as we will see in the cases that follow, the Rabbis do appear to endorse physical and psychological coercion or torture in cases in which they believe it is possible to achieve what they consider to be a greater good. Most of these cases fall into two camps: (1) The perpetrator has not technically sinned but by violating a norm is causing undue suffering; one tortures in the hope of getting the individual to cease causing pain (see divorce example below); and (2) the perpetrator is tortured in order to elicit a needed confession, and thereby reveals the truth, allowing justice to follow. Thus when the Rabbis make the decision to permit such coercion, one has to imagine that they do it with at least some degree of ambivalence. They may sanction the act but with the understanding that it is by no means ethically pure.

TORTURE TO ACCEDE TO DIVORCE

The Rabbis countenance torture in cases in which a recalcitrant husband refuses to divorce his wife, as by not granting her a divorce, he traps her in her marriage and forces her to either remain alone or commit adultery (see chapter 6). In one such instance, the instrument of torture is left to the court, which "coerces him until he says: I want to do so."[50]

However, the Rabbis do not stop there. Knowing that the torture might invalidate a divorce because a husband must grant it of free will, they image a case whereby a husband admits before giving a *get* that he is only granting it due to coercion. To get him to retract that statement, the Rabbis allow a court to torture him a second time, until he lies and admits to giving it willingly.[51]

In one final example, the Rabbis imagine a case whereby a woman makes a vow that would make it impossible for her to marry her brother-in-law[52] if her husband dies before they have children, an act required by biblical law known as *yibbum* (levirate marriage).[53] If her husband does die, her vow holds, and she is entitled to marry whom she pleases. But first, to fully free her from the obligation to marry her brother-in-law, he must undergo a humiliating quasi-divorce ritual known as *ḥalitzah* (extract) whereby she removes his shoe and spits in his face. Whether to punish her for not wanting to marry him or because he doesn't want to undergo ḥalitzah, the Rabbis imagine that the brother-in-law may refuse to free his sister-in-law from the marriage and might trap her in it. To get him to agree to ḥalitzah, one can "coerce him until he performs ḥalitzah with her."[54]

BINDING TORTURE TO ELICIT CONFESSIONS

The Rabbis relate many accounts involving the torture of "binding" to elicit needed confessions. In one such case, Mar Zutra Ḥasida, a highly respected figure whose name (*hasida*) connotes piety,[55] utilizes binding to yield a confession from a thief:

> A silver goblet was stolen from the host of Mar Zutra Ḥasida. Mar Zutra saw a certain student of Torah who washed his hands and dried them on the cloak of another. Mar Zutra said: This is the one who does not care about the property of another. He bound that student [to a post], and the student then confessed that he stole the goblet.[56]

The Talmud is silent on the extent of suffering provoked by this "binding." Some later commentators assume the binding includes lashes—that Mar Zutra beats the student until he confesses.[57] Others declare that the Rabbis who "bind" threaten the student with impending lashes to elicit a confession, a sort of psychological torture.[58] In another tethering episode, after a Babylonian rabbi with the simple name Abaye discovers that a groom has erased and altered sections of a *ketubah* (marriage contact) to his own advantage, Abaye binds the groom until he confesses.[59]

A third binding ensues after two Rabbis, Rava and Rav Aha bar Adda, learn their names have been forged (on an unnamed document). Aware that such a forgery threatens their reputations—

making them appear in favor of things they might otherwise not be—and concerned that the forger might do this to others, they find—and bind—the suspect. He not only admits to the forgery but also reveals part of his tradecraft. To mimic the signature of Rav Aha bar Adda, an elder rabbi known to have shaky hands, he would sign the document while standing on a rickety footbridge.[60] Knowing how he did this allows his interlocutors to look out for future copycats.

In a fourth instance, a woman miscarries, and the fetus is brought to Mar Shmuel, who is responsible for dating the fetal remains.[61] He determines the fetus died at forty-one days—and, doing the math, that the husband violated Jewish law by having sex with his wife while she was menstruating. The husband denies this claim, not wanting to admit to the sin, putting Mar Shmuel on the hot seat. Unless he proves he is correct, people may lose faith in his expertise around pregnancy loss and not seek out his authority when it happens. Mar Shmuel brings the husband to the local court, which "bound [the husband] and he confessed."[62]

LAWS OF THE *RODEF* AND *MOSER*

The laws of the rodef and moser also seem to bolster the permissibility of torture. As some modern commentators have argued, if Rabbinic law permits taking a life for some greater good, then it must also allow the "lesser" punishment of torture if it can bring similar benefits.[63] All this is certainly not to say that Rabbinic precedent should be used carte blanche for permitting torture today.[64] Yet a fundamental issue behind the Rabbinic sanction of torture is still salient. For the Rabbis, even seemingly sinful behavior has the potential to be for good.

A Hedge against Thinking like the Rabbis

Knowing the Rabbis are clear that there is room to torture or to kill for the greater good, one must ask: who gets to define that greater good? In 1995, settler and religious extremist Yigal Amir murdered

Israeli prime minister Yitzhak Rabin who, in working toward peace with the Palestinians, was exploring concessions like dismantling settlements in the West Bank that threatened Amir's way of life. To Amir, Rabin was a rodef in his willingness to risk the settlers' safety by conceding land and weakening the military presence in the West Bank; and Rabin was a moser because he was working with Palestinians.[65] When Amir shot Rabin as the prime minister walked off the dais during a peace rally, Amir was confident the killing served a greater good. In an interview with police investigator Yoram ben-Haroush after the attack, Amir proclaimed: "I don't regret it, and I would do it again right now, for God, for the nation, for the country."[66] In Amir's view, he was within his moral and legal rights to kill the prime minister and ensure one less rodef and moser walked this earth.

Thankfully the Rabbis have a hedge against using their pragmatic approach to law to countenance extremist acts like Amir's. Halakhah, done well, is a pathway toward morality. As the next chapter will illuminate, the Rabbis work hard to create a conceptual framework—broad, extra-legal ethical principles—to keep fanatics from abusing it.

Hedging Against the Misuse of Pragmatism 9

The Rabbis understand that Jewish law and ethics are inextricably linked, yet are not equivalent. As the medieval commentator Nachmanides puts it, you can be a "scoundrel within the bounds of Torah."[1] To this point, the Rabbis tell us a tale about Rabba bar bar Hanan.[2] He hires a group of porters to transport wine for him. As the group moves the merchandise, it inadvertently breaks the wine barrels, losing all the wine. Knowing he is within his legal and pragmatic right not only to withhold payment from the porters but also to take their cloaks as restitution for his lost wine, Rabba bar bar Hanan has his revenge: he leaves the porters unrecompensed and naked. But when the porters approach Rav, the leading Rabbinic authority at the time, asking for his aid, Rav forces Rabba bar bar Hanan to return the workers' clothes and pay them for their labor. Just because Rabba bar bar Hanan is within his legal rights to punish the porters doesn't mean he should.

To prove his point Rava cites a verse: "So follow the ways of the good and keep to the paths of the just" (Prov. 2:20). For Rava, *halakhah* is not fulfilled unless one pursues a morally upright course. The letter of the law must meet its spirit—one that inspires us to walk in the footsteps of the righteous who came before us.

Rabbinic stories like this provide an important hedge against ethically suspect pragmatic actions. In presenting a set of companion questions to the framing questions of pragmatism, exploring not only "what works" but "what is right and good?" the Rabbis marry the virtuous with the practical, the noble with the sensible.

This chapter will explore some of their legal principles, stories, and discussions that guide us away from pragmatic but problematic law and logic and toward a more moral path.

Going Beyond the Letter of the Law: *Lifnim Mishurat Hadin*, Do What Is Right and Good, Do Not Follow the Residents of Sodom, Do Be a Saintly Type

Jewish law makes the pragmatic concession of exempting expert money changers from liability if they err.[3] Although the Talmud rationalizes this exception by claiming that true experts will only err given factors out of their control, questions of efficiency, speed, and self-confidence may also apply.[4] If the top money changers are overly focused on the personal consequences should they miss a counterfeit coin, they are liable to slow the flow of capital, adversely affecting the economy.

Despite this clear legal protection, the Rabbis tell the story of Rabbi Hiyyah, who willingly waves his immunity:

> There was a certain woman who presented a dinar to Rabbi Ḥiyya [to assess its authenticity.] He said to her: It is a proper coin. The next day she came before him and said to him: I presented it to others, and they told me that it is a bad dinar, and I am not able to spend it. Rabbi Ḥiyya said to Rav: Go exchange it for her, and write on my tablet [*apinkasi*]: This was a bad transaction, [as I should not have assessed the coin].[5]

Rabbi Hiyyah goes out of his way to accept the counterfeit coin and right his wrong. When the anonymous voices of the Talmud asks why he would give back funds he is not required to return, the Talmud explains that Rabbi Hiyyah acts "beyond the letter of the law."[6]

LIFNIM MISHURAT HADIN

Appearing throughout Rabbinic literature, the teaching *lifnim mishurat hadin* or "beyond the letter of law" is one of the chief ways the Rabbis temper their impulse to misuse pragmatic thinking.[7] One important instance surrounds the returning of lost articles. According to Jewish law, if you find something (say, on the street) and you can surmise that the owner has relinquished hope of ever getting it back, either because it is too generic (without distinguishing marks) or it was clearly lost a while ago, you may keep it. Later, even if you figure out its owner, you still do not need to give it back, because through the very act of despairing over ever finding it, the owner has fully relinquished ownership.

However, a rabbi named Shmuel requires a person to act "beyond the letter of the law" and return it.[8] The Talmud notes that Shmuel learned this from his father, who once found donkeys in the desert and, using the same lifnim mishurat hadin rationale, returned them after twelve months—well past the time the owner would have given up hope of ever finding them.[9]

Another case concerns a man who needs money to buy oxen and sells his land to Rav Papa. Immediately after the sale, the man realizes he does not need to take such a drastic step and tries to reverse the sale. One might think that this sale should be voided; had the seller known he had the funds to purchase the oxen, he never would have sold his land, his ignorance being a kind of duress. Although the Talmud entertains this idea, it ultimately concludes that Rav Papa can keep the land. However, knowing that it is right to return it, Rav Papa "[acted in a manner that was] beyond the letter of the law" and gave it back.[10]

The Rabbis even go so far as to assert that the Temple was destroyed in part because judges at the time "established their rulings on the basis of Torah law and did not go beyond the letter of the law."[11] Although the Talmud teaches this without explanation, commentators suggest that the Rabbis believed that judges at the time of the Temple's destruction were too strict. Because another traditional explanation for the Temple's destruction is that the people were punished because of *sinat ḥinam*, senseless hatred,[12] from the Rabbis' point of view, the judges' refusal to do more than the law required fomented discord within society and incited people to hate one another.[13]

It is not clear, however, whether lifnim mishurat hadin constitutes a requirement to supersede the law or guidance meant to model ethical living. Rabbis through the ages have debated this question.[14] Yet in either case the presence of lifnim mishurat hadin speaks to how seriously the Rabbis took our need to be morally upright even if Jewish law does not explicitly demand it.

"DO WHAT IS RIGHT AND GOOD"

Even when the Rabbis do not refer specifically to lifnim mishurat hadin, its spirit is central to Rabbinic discussions of biblical passages, most importantly the Torah's teaching that we should "Do what is right and good" in the sight of God (Deut. 6:18). When quoted, this teaching implores the Rabbis to consider the overarching moral bent of a given law.

In one instance, the Rabbis explore the case of a man who ends up indebted to another and is forced to sell his land to his creditor. After settling the debt, the original owner finds the money to repurchase his land. If he informs his creditor of his wish to recover the land, Jewish law requires the creditor to sell it to him, even over other preferred buyers.[15] Although technically the original owner has no legal claim on land that has been sold in its entirety and any new owner should be able to sell it freely, the Rabbis ask the owner to do "right and good" (Deut. 6:18) and sell it to the original owner anyway. For the original debtor, having that land means more than it would to another purchaser. Beyond sentimental value, it symbolizes reaching an important level of solvency in his life. Thus one should go beyond the requirements of the law to allow him to repossess it.

A further instance of the "right and good" principle concerns the sale of adjacent land to a neighbor. Although in most cases halakha permits landowners to sell their land to whomever they wish, the Rabbis add a caveat to the law that sellers must first offer the land, at fair market price, to their next-door neighbors, a principle known as *dina d'bar metzra* (lit. the law of the adjacent).[16] The reasoning is that farm operations (then the most common application of this law) generally benefit in productivity and efficiency from extended contiguous land. If the field owners are in a financial position to expand and the opportunity arises, they should be allowed to do so.

Knowing this, the Rabbis then explore what should be done if field owners ignore dina d'bar metzra and sell their land to third parties. Must the new owners (whom the Rabbis characterize as "impudent" if they proceed with the purchase despite having known of interested neighbors) offer it to those neighbors to right the wrong?[17] Debating the issue, the Rabbis who think buyers can keep their land see dina d'bar metzra as non-actionable; although it would be "right" to offer it to neighbors first, that is not legally necessary. And is it really the buyers' problem to right the sellers' wrongdoing?

Yet the Rabbis give the final word to the Nehardeans, the Rabbis of one of the period's great rabbinical academies (in the city of Nehardea in Persia), who hold that the buyers should be forced to sell the land back to those neighbors prepared to purchase it, whether or not these buyers were aware of the owners' violation of dina d'bar metzra prior to the sale, because Jews are obligated to do what is "right and good" (Deut. 6:18).[18]

Teachings like the "right and good" principle show that the Rabbis understand that Torah could never be long enough to cover all the technicalities of ethical living. Instead God provides overarching texts and precepts that give Jewish law a filter to help us see our way through novel questions. In doing so, we have an eye toward what is right, not just what is required of us.

DON'T EMULATE THE RESIDENTS OF SODOM

A third Rabbinic principle holds that Jews should not emulate the citizens of Sodom. The Torah tells the story of Sodom, a city God destroys because of the people's iniquities[19]—sins considered "so grave" that their behavior is deemed an "outrage."[20] Yet the text is noticeably silent on exactly what the residents of Sodom do wrong.[21] Among the many accusations the Rabbis level at them to explain why the town meets an untimely end is their selfish character.[22] The Mishnah explains:

> There are four types of character in human beings: One that says: "mine is mine, and yours is yours": this is a commonplace type; and *some say this is a Sodom-type of character*. [One that says:] "mine is yours and yours is mine": is an unlearned person (*am haaretz*); [One that says:] "mine is yours is yours is yours" is a pious person. [One that says:] "mine is mine, and yours is mine" is a wicked person.[23]

In the Rabbinic imagination, the sin of the Sodom-type (in Hebrew: *midat sedom*) is being myopically self-interested, existing in one's own bubble without concern for others. Residents of Sodom are, to use the words of twentieth-century Orthodox authority Rabbi Aaron Lichtenstein, obsessed with "one's private preserve and the consequent erection of excessive legal and psychological barriers between person and person."[24]

The Rabbis then utilize this principle as well to work around pragmatic laws. They imagine a family consisting of a father and several sons, one of whom owns a field adjacent to his aging father. After the father dies, the court splits the father's land evenly between the brothers, but because of dina d'bar metzra, earmarks the land bordering the neighboring son's property for him to inherit.[25] The Talmud gives a secondary rationale: withholding the property from this son is emulating the residents of Sodom.[26]

The reason for invoking Sodom in this case is that (at least in principle) it doesn't hurt the other brothers to split the land in a way that allows the neighboring son to have two adjacent plots, but any other arrangement does hurt him. Although one could argue that the fairest and most pragmatic way to divide the father's land is to draw lots for which land each brother gets, the Rabbis acknowledge that what is the most straightforward and seemingly fair solution is not always the most ethically just one. If another brother takes the land, it not only may hurt the adjacent field owner sibling financially but also may also arouse his animosity and resentment, a concern the Rabbis take seriously (see chapter 6). Even if the father errs in not taking dina d'bar metzra into account in his will, the other brothers cannot say, "mine is mine and yours is yours." They are obligated to right that wrong.

In a similar vein, the Rabbis imagine a situation whereby two men in business hire a scribe to write a joint document, but then one changes his mind and demands the scribe pen two documents, one for each of them. His decision not to share the cost of the single document[27] will raise his business partner's own expenditure, with negative financial effect. In response, the Rabbis invoke the concept of midat sedom and allow a court to "coerce [him to prevent] conduct characteristic of Sodom."[28] Provided he isn't changing his mind for specific business reasons,[29] but is simply forcing the other to pay for his own full document out of selfishness, laziness, vindictiveness, or the like, he must split the cost.[30] Concepts like "my money" and "your money" do not apply in situations in which one person's decisions will have an adverse effect on another.

DO BE A SAINTLY TYPE

As it happens, the Rabbis also employ the inverse to midat sedom: *midat ḥasidut*, or the saintly type. Although the Rabbis are by no means unified in their attitude toward the hasid,[31] one generally recognized for piety, moral purity, and a God-fearing nature, the term midat ḥasidut is a universally positive depiction of one who is generous beyond belief and expectation. The Rabbis derive the label from the same Mishnah where we first find the Sodom type. The text reads, "'Mine is yours and yours is yours' is a saintly person (*hasid*)."[32]

The Rabbis call upon midat ḥasidut when encouraging people to do something above and beyond what is required of them. In one case, for example, they consider whether a man of means who loses or spends all his money while on a journey and requires tzedakah to return home must later reimburse the poor of the town who aided him on the road.[33] The Rabbis first acknowledge that legally he does not need to pay them: the tzedakah he took by picking up forgotten sheaves or gleaning the corners of an owner's field, both set aside for the poor, was not earmarked for anyone specific, and at the time he took it, he truly did need the aid. However, the Rabbis implore him to offer recompense anyway, as an act of midat ḥasidut, as that's what a saintly type would do.[34] Although the Talmud does not comment further, one can assume that the "hasid," who fulfills his duties toward God "beyond the line of the law," sees himself as part of the broader fabric of society. If he receives help at another's expense, he needs to replenish this tzedakah because others need it more.

In another case the Rabbis discuss what to do if your house catches on fire on Shabbat. Though technically carrying objects out of one's house is forbidden on the Sabbath, the Rabbis provide a certain degree of flexibility for items like food and clothing (see chapter 7). Although you cannot call upon your Jewish friends for help in rescuing household items, because essentially you are asking them to violate Shabbat for your sake, the Rabbis create a loophole whereby you can "give" ownership of various home goods to your companions who then have license to run in and save their newly acquired properties. Once your companions emerge from the inferno, however, they technically don't have to return your goods—ownership has now passed to them. Rather, if they return your former possessions to you, they are acting in accordance with midat ḥasidut.[35]

In a similar vein, Jewish law provides a strict statute of limitations for when vendors are expected to accept the return of an eroded coin they once gave as change but whose value is now suspect. However, those who act in the manner of midat ḥasidut will accept the coin even after significant time beyond the statute of limitations

178   Misuse of Pragmatism

has passed.[36] Midat ḥasidut invites us to look past what is obligatory and asks us to be the best versions of ourselves we can imagine, to build a more righteous world.

Using God's Watchful Gaze to Compel Morality

The Rabbis understand that humanity's laws don't always conform with God's expectations. Sometimes God will still judge us harshly for following the law:

> Rabbi Yehoshua said: There are four matters in which one who commits an offense concerning them is exempt from liability according to human laws but liable according to the laws of Heaven [and it would be proper for him to pay compensation], and the cases are as follows: One who breaches a fence that stood before another's animal, [thereby allowing the animal to escape]; and one who bends another's standing grain before a fire [so that it catches fire]; and one who hires false witnesses to testify; and one who knows testimony in support of another but does not testify on his behalf.[37]

In all four matters, perpetrators set bad things into motion without being legally liable, as they are not the ones causing the direct damage. To take the first two examples, if you breach a fence and your neighbor's animal escapes, getting injured or killed in the process, Jewish law does not hold you accountable for letting the animal out because the animal had agency to escape on its own. In the same vein, because you didn't actively light a neighbor's wheat on fire, but only made it slightly easier for the wind to carry the embers into the adjacent field by bending the crop toward the fire, you are not directly liable for its burning. The fire might have found its way into the field without you.[38]

Because a court cannot punish you, the Rabbis' only recourse is to warn you: God is watching; God knows if you fall into the category "liable to the law of Heaven."[39] The Eternal has no patience for pragmatic loopholes. Don't risk Divine retribution by taking advantage of the law's weakness to do wrong. And if your misdeeds have hurt others, avoid God's reprisal by reimbursing them promptly for the damage done.

Because for Jews in the Rabbinic world, God's anger is a salient threat, the Rabbis allow a person or court to curse a perpetrator with God's wrath for exploiting the law to personal benefit.[40] They imagine a case whereby a person pays for an item to be picked up later but then reneges on the purchase before collecting it. As discussed, an item only transfers in ownership when the new owner takes physical possession of it rather than when money changes hands (see chapter 6), so legally the purchaser may still have a change of heart and, if so, the seller must return the money.

To combat this, the Rabbis develop a curse one can utter to convince a fickle buyer to reconsider and keep the item in question:

> [May] God, who exacted payment from the people of the generation of the flood,[41] and from the generation of the dispersion [i.e., that of the Tower of Babel] ... in the future exact payment from whoever does not stand by his statement.[42]

The Rabbis imagine that upon hearing this curse, fickle buyers will be reminded that God acts in accord with justice. Just as God punished previous generations for their wrongdoings, killing the people of Noah's era for their iniquity,[43] and scattering those who in their arrogance built the Tower of Babel,[44] God will punish them too— unless they go beyond the law and accept their purchase.

Warning about Being Too Crafty through Solomon and the Con Artist

Even as the Rabbis relish the personality traits of intellectual prowess and innovative spirit, they warn of inherent perils. One might deploy one's intellect creatively for ill purposes, metaphorically making the impure pure, and the pure impure.[45] To teach the danger in being too crafty, they explore the character of King Solomon, said to be the Bible's brightest mind, who gets into trouble by trying to outsmart Jewish law:

> And Rabbi Yitzhak says: For what reason were the rationales of Torah commandments not revealed? It was because the rationales of two verses were revealed, and the greatest in the world, [King Solomon], failed in those matters. It is written with regard to a king: "He shall not add many wives for himself, that his heart should not turn away" (Deuteronomy 17:17). Solomon said: I will add many, but I will not turn away, [as he thought that it is permitted to have many wives if one is otherwise meticulous not to stray]. And later, it is written: "For it came to pass, when Solomon was old, that his wives turned away his heart after other gods" (1 Kings 11:4). And it is also written: "Only he shall not accumulate many horses for himself [nor return the people to Egypt for the sake of accumulating horses]" (Deuteronomy17:16), and Solomon said: I will accumulate many, but I will not return. And it is written: "And a chariot came up and went out of Egypt for six [hundred shekels of silver]" (1 Kings 10:29).[46]

King Solomon, renowned for his wisdom, understands the reasons behind God's proscription against an abundance of wives and horses and, craving both, devises a way around the prohibitions whereby, he rationalizes, he can maintain his loyalty to God as well. Yet despite his sagacity and craftiness, Solomon can't outsmart God. In the end, everything turns out exactly as the text warns him it would: his wives turn him toward idolatry, and his wealth leads him back to Egypt. In essence Solomon is smart enough to see what God expects of him, but he cannot control the human impulses the law is trying to offset. Had God instead given a blanket law without rationale, as God did for almost all of the 613 commandments, Solomon would not have been able to find a way around it. It would have been absolute, and he would not have sinned.

Quite possibly the Rabbis include this teaching on the jeopardy of trusting in your own acumen—even, say, if you possess the greatest mind that has ever lived—as an admonition not only to you and me but also to themselves. The Rabbis may be smart enough to swerve around a moral obligation, but that doesn't mean they should. The Rabbinic enterprise calls for leaps of imagination and pragmatic gambles, but also for upholding moral law.

For the Rabbis, Solomon isn't the only one who takes craftiness too far. The Rabbis include discussions of the *ramayin*, the trickster or (in today's lingo) con artist who exploits loopholes for personal benefit. Sharing the same root as the Rabbinic term for loophole, *ha'arama* (see chapter 7), the ramayin takes the Rabbinic penchant for creative problem-solving too far.

For example, the Rabbis say that one reason a field owner needs to specifically leave the "corner" of the field—rather than some other portion in the middle of the field—for gleaning by the poor is that a ramayin-type field owner might designate a random section, fail to publicize it and, after the crops are untouched, claim that this confirms the poor do not need help, and then take the bounty.[47]

In another case, the Rabbis stipulate that before one purchases libations in the Temple for sacrifices, one must write the day of the week on the tokens to be used for this purchase. Otherwise con artists might get their hands on a previous day's tokens and purchase wine for sacrifices without paying.

The Rabbis also caution against—and do not publicize—loopholes that are sometimes deemed acceptable but set a bad precedent about the use of craftiness to subvert Torah law. They warn not to deliberately stop up a broken barrel on Shabbat, which is prohibited, by sticking cloves of garlic into the cracks under the guise of storing them there.[48] Likewise they advise against intentionally crossing a river by boat for some prohibited action, like checking on your crops on the other side during Shabbat, by going to sleep in the ferry and finding yourself "unknowingly" transferred to the opposite shore.[49] Only the best and brightest Rabbis, those who have earned their peers' trust to use their creativity for good, are allowed to perform these actions and walk that precarious boundary between acceptable and harmful leaps of logic.

Prioritizing Intellectual Knowledge over Innovation: *Sinai* over *Oker Harim*

In like mind, when pressed to answer which archetype of scholar is more important, specifically, which of two kinds of scholars should run their institutions of learning—a *Sinai* (one who, having memorized the whole corpus of Rabbinic literature, always has the right quote at their fingertips),[50] or an *oker harim* (lit. an "uprooter of mountains," one who lifts up the mountain of Jewish teaching by finding meaning in Torah that no one has yet seen)—the Talmud prioritizes *Sinai* scholars. The quintessential exemplar of a Sinai scholar is Rabbi Yosef of third-century Babylonia, a purveyor of received knowledge whose words are said to be so accurate, they can be tied back to the very mountain (i.e., Sinai) where God first gave Divine law to the Israelites. By contrast, Rabbi Yosef's contemporary, Rabbah, an oker harim, does not always remember everything he learns, but following the dictum of Rabbi Ben Bag Bag to "turn it and turn it again, for all is in it," interweaves seemingly incompatible texts to arrive at new, valuable insights.[51] The Rabbis' selection of recall over creativity is, perhaps, a surprising choice.[52] One might think they would esteem and emulate Rabbah as the more significant scholar. As this book argues, Judaism survives because of the Rabbis' creativity, resourcefulness, and expansive thinking. Yet the Rabbis explain their selection of the *Sinai* through an enigmatic adage: "Sinai is preferable, as the Master said: Everyone requires the owner of the wheat."[53]

Scholars have been debating what the phrase means ever since. The twentieth-century scholar, Rav Abraham Isaac Kook, Israeli's first Chief Rabbi, homes in on the word "everyone," explaining that the legal gymnastics of the oker harim are inaccessible to only but the most learned scholars.[54] Leaders cannot be so inventive that only the most elite can follow. Their teachings need to feed the masses; hence the plain-spoken, learned teachings of the Sinai are preferable. Other scholars[55] observe that oker harim need material to explicate and uproot—without texts, oker harim will be brilliant without anchor, free-floating potential. Because the Sinai is the keeper of the fundamental material, the Sinai takes precedence. Others note that just as the Rabbis view grain—often used as a metaphor for knowledge[56]—as the staple of every dish, the Sinai's Torah wisdom is the base of any argument.[57]

Developing this argument, Rabbi Levy Cooper from The Pardes Institute of Jewish Studies notes that the Rabbis' favoring of the Sinai:

> reflects the need to first have an understanding of the material before beginning to analytically scrutinize and reassemble the sources. Before we begin to dissect the hallowed texts of our traditions, our foremost task is to have a firm grasp of the sources. In Talmudic terms: With no Sinai, there is no mountain to uproot; we are merely uprooting air. Only once Sinai stands firmly, can we contemplate uprooting it.[58]

One can push the creative envelope but not at the expense of grounding in Jewish tradition.

Pragmatically, the Rabbinic preference for the Sinai also serves an important hedge against knee-jerk change. To honor the keepers of tradition, we may commit to attaining a firm grasp of the sources before innovating. If we probe the language of the laws with care, we may understand why certain precepts exist and grow accustomed to the decrees. Then we may be a little less quick to discard or revamp them—and if we still desire change, we may contemplate the ramifications of any desired "uprooting" with sufficient clarity and depth before we embark upon it.

Using Aggadah to Check Human Impulses

So, too, the Rabbis recognize the danger of law running amok, divorced from the human element of the halakhic enterprise. To reground the law in the lives of the people it is intended to serve, they utilize *aggadah* (narrative) as a key mediating force.

Narrative, they realize, can both bolster and temper law. Couching a hard legal precept in a story can show how it functions in the real world, and the story can also act as an implicit critique of the law, revealing the inequities inherent in a given legal system. Where law provides the letter, the agaddah supplies its animating force, its spirit. Israeli poet Chayim Nachman Bialik majestically explains this dichotomy:

> Halacha wears a frown, Aggadah a smile. The one is pedantic, severe, unbending—all justice; the other is accommodating, lenient, pliable—all mercy. The one commands and knows no half-way house; her yea is yea, and her nay is nay. The other advises and takes account of human limitations; she admits something between yea and nay. . . . On the one side is the dryness of prose, a formal and heavy style, a gray and monochrome diction: reason is sovereign. On the other side is the sap of poetry, a style full of life and variety, a diction all ablaze with color: emotion is sovereign.[59]

The two cases that follow exemplify how the Rabbis use aggadah to keep their pragmatic impulses in check.

A NARRATIVE CRITIQUE OF *TAKKANAT HASHAVIM*

Earlier (see chapter 6) we spoke about *takkanat hashavim* (the proclamation of the penitent), the ruling that if a thief builds his house with a stolen wooden beam, he can repay the value of the wood, rather than dismantle his home, as *teshuvah*. Although the Rabbis present the law in a straightforward manner, they include a story alongside it that raises important questions about how it might be employed:

> There was a certain old woman who came before Rav Nachman. She said to him: The Exilarch and all the Sages in his house have been sitting in a stolen sukka. She screamed, but Rav Nachman did not pay attention to her. She said to him: A woman whose father, [Abraham, our forefather], had three hundred and eighteen slaves screams before you, and you do not pay attention to her? Rav Naḥman said to the Sages: This woman is a screamer, and she has rights only to the monetary value of the wood.[60]

This brief story implicitly critiques the Rabbinic pragmatic spirit. The mysterious old woman has a moral claim. The leaders around her are benefiting from stolen property—possibly the wood from her own sukkah—and she wants them to make things right. She tries any number of approaches to get Rav Nachman to listen. She raises her voice. She reminds him about their shared Jewish heritage—both he and she are descended from Abraham. She implies that while she might not be as rich as others, she is rich insofar as she too is among Abraham's progeny. Yet Rav Naḥman ignores her, disparages her to his fellow Rabbis as "a screamer," and states that recompensing her with the monetary value of the stolen wood is sufficient to redress the wrong. One leaves this interaction feeling for her and questioning the wisdom and kindness of takkanat hashavim.

Still, the text doesn't explicitly condemn Rav Nachman. Professor Moshe Simon-Shoshan of Bar-Ilan University explains why:

> The behavior of R. Nachman and the other members of the Exilach's court is indeed reprehensible. However, R. Nachman, not the woman, is qualified to rule on technical but critical halachic issues such as those raised in this case. If we completely reject R. Nachman's authority and jurisprudence in the face of the women's moral and social critique, we hazard jeopardizing the entire rabbinic project and risk anarchy.... The story presents a

conflict between two viable voices, neither of which can totally overcome the other.[61]

Nothing can be done about the elderly woman's claim. She cannot compete with generations of Rabbinic precedent. Yet one leaves this story empathizing with her powerlessness and pain at the cost of Rav Nachman's power and callousness.

The Rabbis include this narrative to remind us—and themselves—of the human cost of these laws. Even when a cold pragmatic approach seems the only option, they caution each of us against losing sight of the collateral damage strict adherence to law may inflict on others. The problem in Rav Nachman's response is twofold. First, he does not show the old woman compassion. Second, he does not look for a middle-ground solution that might make her less aggrieved. Thankfully this story is not the final word on the topic of stolen sukkah wood.

Later Rabbinic authorities do what Rav Nachman should have done. Without condemning Nachman, the anonymous voice and final strata of the Talmud (*stam*) modifies the law. Provided one hasn't made the wood unusable by securing it with mortar, one must return the wood to the original owner *after* Sukkot ends.[62]

This compromise position honors both the spirit of takkanat hashavim during the holiday and the women's claim in the long run. Even if she is not happy with it during Sukkot, the wood is rightfully hers thereafter.

There is an artistry to this agaddah. Taken as a literary unit, the woman's story first complicates a law that might otherwise be universally heralded. It makes the reader feel for her and want to find a solution. This sets up the stam to heroically solve the problem. In doing so, the agaddah makes the compromise position more memorable than it would have been had Rav Nachman proposed it. That increases the likelihood that we too may take the harder path of owning responsibility and proposing compromise solutions to problems at least partially of our own making.

A NARRATIVE CRITIQUE OF THE LAW OF THE CAPTIVE

The Rabbis speak passionately about the need to free the captive. They call the practice a *mitzvah rabbah* (great commandment), and some Rabbis even argue that redeeming prisoners is more important than feeding the hungry or clothing the naked.[63] However, the Rabbis also temper the impulse to do everything possible to free a captive with this pragmatic edict: "Captives are not redeemed for more than their actual monetary value, for the betterment of the world (*Mipnei Tikkun Ha-olam*)."[64]

Although the Rabbis don't provide a rationale for this important amendment, there are two likely reasons for it: 1) to lessen the financial strain on a community by setting limits on how much it might have to pay to free a captive; and 2) to protect against the risk that foreign nations will step up their kidnapping efforts when they realize how much additional money they can make from ransoming Jews as opposed to others. However, as soon as the Mishnah rules this way, the Rabbis relate a counternarrative: "Levi bar Darga redeemed his daughter [who was taken captive] with thirteen thousand gold dinars."[65]

While talmudic currencies are notoriously hard to translate to modern dollars, commentators agree that thirteen thousand gold dinars is a huge sum, considerably more than the maximum price allowed by law to release a captive.[66] The fact that Levi bar Darga subverts the "fair price" rule for his daughter shows how little the law matters to an anxious father. While this ruling might protect the general populace from unwanted kidnappings, it likely feels cruel and heartless to a parent in pain. Regardless of the fact that Levi bar Darga (an unknown figure; this is his only mention in the Talmud) defies the law, the Talmud does not criticize him. It relays the story and lets the issue go.

Effectively, his story, coming on the heels of the talmudic stipulation not to overpay for captives, functions as an implicit critique of the Rabbis' position on the issue. In a perfect world, paying more than a prisoner's (ostensible) worth may be forbidden, but if it's your daughter, how could you not do everything you can to free her? Levi bar Darga's story grays an otherwise black-and-white line, opening us up to upholding compassionate solutions along with the Mishnah's hard-hearted pragmatism.

Later generations would read Levi bar Darga's story and see themselves in his brokenhearted rejection of the law. His narrative, along with others like it in the Talmud, allowed rabbis in the early years of the State of Israel to exchange dozens and, later, hundreds of Arab prisoners for a single captured Israeli soldier.[67] They would quote his story as authoritative. In their minds, and likely in ours too, narrative deserves its place as a moderating force on law, even eclipsing it when necessary.[68]

Judah's Failed Gamble

The Rabbis do not venerate all pragmatic moral gambles. Some risktakers meet harsh condemnation. Take, for example, the biblical character Judah.[69] He saves his brother Joseph from death at the hands of his brothers by suggesting that the brothers sell Joseph into slavery rather than murder him:

> Then Judah said to his brothers, "What profit [*betza*] is it for us if we slay our brother and cover up his blood? Come, let us sell him to the Ishmaelites, but let us not do away with him ourselves. After all, he is our brother, our own flesh." His brothers agreed (Gen. 37:26–27).[70]

The Rabbis denounce Judah for choosing a "lesser evil" for his brother. Rather than propose selling Joseph into slavery, Judah should have marshalled all of his influence to plea for his brother's life and safety. Even if Judah believes he is doing the right thing, he is deluding himself. His so-called compromise position enriches himself as well as his brothers; he advances his own wealth at the expense of his enslaved brother. Playing on the word profit (*betza*), the Rabbis apply to Judah the label of a *botzea*, a person who gains wealth or prestige by unrighteous acts, including violence.[71] They imagine that the line in Psalms 10:3, "The wicked crow about their unbridled lusts; the grasping [botzea] revile and scorn God," refers to Judah. To the Sages, we "scorn God" when we make moral compromises not for the general good, which is God's will, but for our own benefit.

Although the Rabbis' criticism about Judah is a short aside in a wider discussion of the merits of compromise (see chapter 2), the Rabbis' critique underscores the need to bring good intention to pragmatic thinking. Had Judah acted pragmatically for the greater good, he would not have accepted money for his brother and would have fought harder to save him, even at risk to his own standing among his siblings. We are thereby enjoined to pursue pragmatism carefully, aware of its inadequacies.

Yet despite the risks, the Rabbis generally encourage us to take pragmatic gambles. Provided that we heed guardrails (such as those explored in this chapter), the world needs courageous actors who will take moral risks. Generally speaking, pragmatism allows us to get things done, to sacrifice the perfect so that the good may blossom. It is pursing the best *possible* path you can foresee even as you wish you could walk the best *imagined* one. This is what Rabban Yochanan ben Zakkai does in his famous gamble before Vespasian. Therefore, let us end where we began: with the memory of that fateful day.

Final Thoughts

Yochanan's Uncertainty

History has been kind to Yochanan. His quick thinking before Emperor Vespasian is lauded as one of the key reasons our tradition survived the Roman siege. And without him, it is said, Judaism probably never would have adapted to a life without Temple sacrifice. Yet Yochanan does not know any of this. Even as an old man readying himself for death, he remains deeply ambivalent about his life decisions, unsure if he has made the right calls.

In one of the more haunting scenes in the Talmud, as he grows mortally ill and his students gather around him, fear and self-doubt surface on his face, and he begins to cry. His students are perplexed: what can Yochanan possibly be afraid of? Has he not lived a steadfast life of righteousness? Has he not built a vibrant Rabbinic world? Will heaven not receive him with open arms?

Hearing his students wondering aloud about their mentor's tears, Yochanan bemoans: "If God is angry with me, God's anger is eternal; if God incarcerates me, God's incarceration is an eternal incarceration; and if God kills me, God's killing is for eternity."[1] Yochanan concludes: "I have two paths before me, one of the Garden of Eden (paradise) and one of Gehenna (punishment), and I do not know on which they are leading me; and will I not cry?"[2]

Though he has gained the esteem of his generation, Yochanan has no idea whether God will reward or punish him for his actions—whether he has truly forged the right path. His only sure affirmation that he has done well in this world will be found in the eternal Divine judgment that awaits him.

The Rabbis and Us

If Yochanan could not go into death free of worry, many of us may fear the same for ourselves. *Can I expect to make a smooth transition from this world? Day after day I take risk after risk. Can I be certain I am forging my own right paths?*

"If the great Rav Yochanan ben Zakkai never ceased blaming himself for that historic decision [i.e., asking for Yavneh over Jerusalem]," twentieth-century thinker Rabbi Joseph Soloveitchik observes, "assuredly the dilemma of the two paths must always be before us as well. We should not vaingloriously assume that our actions are always the right ones."[3] Throughout this volume we have seen the Rabbis take chances, innovating and experimenting often despite uncertain outcomes. In this sense, there is something deeply religious about the Rabbis' pragmatic outlook: on the whole, their decision-making involves a leap of faith. If moral living is an imperfect enterprise, one needs to act, and to be willing to admit that in acting, we might get it wrong and have to pivot.

Philosophers call this way of thinking fallibilism. Unlike its cousin, skepticism, which holds that we can never know anything for certain, fallibilism teaches that if we try our best and behave with integrity, analyzing the information available to us and acting upon it, then we may call our beliefs valid until proven otherwise. Meanwhile, even as we behave *as if* we have the answer, we simultaneously accept that future evidence might impel us to change our approach.

All the while, the Rabbis give us tools to help us try our best and behave with integrity. As conveyed in this book, they guide us to:

Learn from everyone and everything (especially if you disagree);
Weigh the received tradition;
Study people as much as texts;
Lead people, but not too far out in front;
Seek peace;

Pursue compromise whenever possible;
Embrace change as a constant of life;
Think unconventionally and creatively when times call for it;
Take pragmatic gambles to pursue what is good.

In the end, discomfort is the price we pay for taking risks. Like Yochanan, we may feel uncertain about the paths we choose. But we simply have to go on faith that we are acting correctly.

Pragmatism matches the messiness of religious living. Without clear answers in front of us, we make a beautiful leap toward action, hoping our feet land on steady ground.

NOTES

Preface

1. For a good overview of these groups and their ideologies, see Cohen, *From the Maccabees to the Mishnah*, esp. 119–57.
2. For one articulation of this, see Schwartz, *Imperialism and Jewish Society*, 103–28, 215–74.
3. Scholars debate when exactly in the Amoraic era the Babylonian Rabbis turned to academies. See Rubenstein, "The Rise of the Babylonian Rabbinic Academy," 55–68.
4. Hayes, "'In the West, They Laughed at Him,'" 137–67.
5. See M Avot 1:1 for the chain of transmission.
6. BT Menachot 29b.
7. Saiman, *Halakhah*, 71.
8. Based on Gen. 1:28, often translated as "be fruitful and multiply."
9. The most famous of these, the Bar Kokhba revolt, was fought between 132 and 136 CE. For a comprehensive study on this war, see Mor, *The Second Jewish Revolt*.
10. The most notable exception is Berkowits, *Not in Heaven*.
11. Cedar, *Footnote*.
12. James, *Will to Believe*, loc. 2582.

Prologue

1. BT Gittin 56a (Koren Talmud Bavli).
2. BT Gittin 56b. The full text reads: As if you are not a king, Jerusalem will not be handed over into your hand, as it is written: "And the Lebanon shall fall by a mighty one" (Isaiah 10:34). And "mighty one" means only a king, as it is written: "And their mighty one shall be of themselves, [and their ruler shall proceed from the midst of them]" (Jeremiah 30:21),

[indicating that "mighty one" parallels "ruler."] And "Lebanon" means only the Temple, as it is stated: "That good mountain and the Lebanon" (Deut. 3:25) (Koren Talmud Bavli).
3. BT Gittin 56b. The full quote reads: "It is I, God, ... Who turn sages back, / And make nonsense of their knowledge" (Isa. 44:25).
4. BT Gittin 56b.
5. Josephus, *The Jewish War* 4.3.2.
6. BT Gittin 56b (Koren Talmud Bavli).
7. See BT Ḥagigah 17a.
8. See esp. Neusner, *Development of a Legend*.
9. For an introduction to the Rabbis of antiquity and the works they produced, see Fonrobert and Jaffee, *The Cambridge Companion to the Talmud and Rabbinic Literature*.
10. For an extended conversation about how to light Hanukkah candles, see BT Shabbat 21b.
11. The Torah only tells one to "practice self-denial" (Lev. 16:29). It would take until the Mishnah before that phrase would be translated to mean "eating and drinking, washing, anointing, wearing shoes, and cohabitation" (M Yoma 8:1, Koren Talmud Bavli).
12. Although the Bible commands us to teach our children about the Passover story, it was not until the Rabbis that the Passover ritual began to resemble a Greek symposium. Much of that ritual is described in M Pesachim, chap. 10, with accompanying Gemara.
13. See the Igeret of Rav Sherira Gaon.
14. M Eduyot 7:7.
15. Gratz, *History of the Jews*, 109.
16. BT Gittin 56b.
17. T Yoma 1:12.
18. For a good explanation of the difference between these groups, see Cohen, *From the Macabees to the Mishnah*, 91. On Second Temple Judaism more broadly, see Simkovich, *Discovering Second Temple Literature*.
19. BT Yevamot 15b.
20. Midrash Taanim, ed. D Hoffman, 58 (translation found in Urbach, *The Sages*, 595).
21. Urbach, *The Sages*, 596.
22. Mekhilta de-Rabbi Yishmael, 20:22 (translation found in Urbach, *The Sages*, 596).

1. Recalibrating Truth

1. BT Bava Metzi'a 59b.
2. Twain, *Huckleberry Finn*, author's note.
3. Yehoshua's use of a creative misreading actually proves his first point further. If the Torah is his to interpret, then even reading the opposite intent into a verse is within his right.
4. BT Rosh Hashanah 25a.
5. BT Rosh Hashanah 25a (Koren Talmud Bavli).
6. BT Rosh Hashanah 25a (Koren Talmud Bavli).
7. See the first few chapters of Numbers for examples of this.
8. M. Rosh Hashanah 2:9 (Koren Talmud Bavli).
9. For more information about how each of the theories manifests in Jewish thought, see Rosenak, "Truth Tests," 149–82.
10. M. Sanhedrin 11:6 (Koren Talmud Bavli).
11. Lawrence A. Hoffman, "Two Theories of Truth: Correspondence and Pragmatic," theTorah.com, https://www.thetorah.com/article/torat-emet-two-theories-of-truth-correspondence-and-pragmatic.
12. James, *Pragmatism*, 34.
13. The American pragmatist tradition viewed everything through the question "does it work?" This included discussions of scientific truths, which was a radical step for early 20th century philosophers and outside of scope of Rabbinic pragmatic discussions. The Rabbis were legal pragmatists and one should be careful not to extend their pragmatic thinking into other pursuits.
14. BT Avodah Zarah 4b.
15. BT Avodah Zarah 4b (Koren Talmud Bavli).
16. As Hayes explains, "The most propitious time to come before God in judgment is not when [God] is occupied with truth (understood, we may suppose as strict or theoretically "correct" justice), but when [God] is occupied with judgment (an activity in which strict justice is balanced with other considerations). . . . Indeed we may go so far as to say that judgment proper should not be unduly obsessed with the theoretically truth or correct answer." See Hayes, *What's Divine About Divine Law?*, 187–88.
17. M. Bava Metzi'a 1:1 (Koren Talmud Bavli).
18. See M. Bava Metzi'a 3:4–5.
19. Though it would seem this particular brand of judicial discretion is a stop-gap measure until the truth might be found, the Rabbis take their

considerations one step further. They debate what would happen if Elijah does appear. Although one minority voice, Rabbi Shimon, proclaims that Elijah will settle all disputes, the majority of the Rabbis choose at least a few areas that Elijah will refrain from weighing in on. In their view, if Elijah's words will bring people back into the Jewish community, Elijah will reveal those things. If not, Elijah will keep the truth to himself. See M. Eduyot 8:7.

20. See BT Yevamot 14a.
21. See M. Eduyot 1:12–14.
22. BT Eruvin 13b (Koren Talmud Bavli).
23. As one modern Talmudic scholar, Suzanne Last Stone, writes, "Such intellectual tolerance is limited to the realm of ideas and opinions; it does not extend to action or legal practice. Behavioral pluralism, in theory, is either a sin, the disregard of a binding norm or, in the absence of a binding norm, the sad consequence of the failure to reach consensus through rational discourse—the goal of the Halachic community." See Stone, "Tolerance versus Pluralism in Judaism," 112.
24. See M. Berachot 1:3.
25. BT Menachot 41b.
26. JT Shabbat 1:4 3c; the closest parallel appears in BT Shabbat 17a.
27. M. Shabbat 1:4.
28. Hidary, *Dispute for the Sake of Heaven*, 179.
29. JT Shabbat 1:4 3c.
30. JT Shabbat 1:4 3c.
31. BT Bava Metzi'a 59b (Koren Talmud Bavli).
32. BT Bava Metzi'a 59b (Koren Talmud Bavli).
33. Bava Metzi'a 59b (Koren Talmud Bavli).
34. Wiesel, *Filled with Fire and Light*, 145.
35. Wiesel, *Filled with Fire and Light*, 147.
36. Maccoby, *The Philosophy of the Talmud*, 179.
37. JT Sanhedrin 4:2 (22a).
38. BT Erubin 13b (Koren Talmud Bavli). See similar sentiments in JT Sanhedrin 4:2 (22a) and Lev. Rabbah (Emor) 26:2, the latter of which gives the number as forty-nine.
39. BT Rosh Hashanah 21b.
40. Ps. 8:6 quoted in BT Rosh Hashanah 21b.
41. Midrash Psalms, 12:3.
42. BT Ḥagigah 3b.

2. Upholding Compromise

1. BT Ḥullin 7b.
2. Zakheim, *The Prince and the Emperors* 193.
3. BT Ḥullin 7b (Koren Talmud Bavli).
4. Margalit, *On Compromise and Rotten Compromises*, 43.
5. The Talmud includes discussions of which ideas are outside of the pale of discussion and compromise, among them advocating for idolatry or the public desecration of Shabbat. See BT Ḥullin 5a.
6. BT Berachot 10a.
7. See 1 Kings 8:12 for an example of this.
8. See 2 Kings 3:12 for this scene.
9. BT Berachot 10a (Koren Talmud Bavli).
10. His father, Ahaz, for example, turns to Assyrian practices and offers his son as a sacrifice to Moloch (2 Kings 16:3). The Talmud expands on this, vilifying him even more. See BT Sanhedrin 103b, Megillah 11a.
11. This is actually the first commandment in the Torah, when God tells humanity, "Be fertile and increase" (Gen. 1:28).
12. See Isa. 38:5 for this scene, where God tells Isaiah, "Go and tell Hezekiah: Thus said GOD, the God of your forefather David: I have heard your prayer, I have seen your tears. I hereby add fifteen years to your life."
13. See 2 Kings 20:12–19 for a depiction of this scene.
14. See Judg. 11:35–40 for the full text of their conversation.
15. The text is sufficiently ambiguous. It reads: "And he did to her as he had vowed" (Judg. 11:39). This could mean he sacrificed her, but some scholars say it could also mean that he gave her over for a lifetime of service to the Temple.
16. BT Nedarim 22b.
17. Gen. Rabbah 60:3.
18. 1 Kings 3:16–28 tell the story of two women who come to King Solomon, both claiming to be the mother of the same child. When he offers to cut the baby in two and split it among the mothers, only one objects. Knowing that a compassionate mother would never allow her own baby to be killed, Solomon gives the baby to her.
19. BT Yevamot 14b (Koren Talmud Bavli).
20. Deut. 23:3 reads: "No one misbegotten (lit. mamzer) shall be admitted into the congregation of God; no descendant of such, even in the tenth generation, shall be admitted into the congregation of God."

21. BT Yevamot 14b (Koren Talmud Bavli).
22. BT Yevamot 14b.
23. For the most famous cases, see Tosafot to Sukkah 3a, sv. *d'amar lach mani*.
24. BT Ḥagigah 2b, BT Gittin 41b, BT Pesachim 88b, and BT Arachin 2b.
25. As with many conversations throughout the Talmud, these arguments were meant to be hypothetical. Hillel and Shammai did not own slaves in the biblical sense. For this reason—since the discussion could remain abstract and philosophical—slavery was often used to explore the boundaries of status (free vs. slave, owner vs. worker). We see something similar in Rabbinic discussion of the death penalty, which scholar Beth Berkowitz argues is concerned less with real historical cases of capital punishment, and more with broader questions of Rabbinic authority. See Berkowitz, *Execution and Invention*. For an explanation of slavery in the Jewish world during the era of this teaching, see Hezser, "What Was Jewish about Jewish Slavery?" 129–48.
26. See also BT Pesachim 88a.
27. BT Ḥagigah 2b (Koren Talmud Bavli).
28. Based on the proof text "The world was created only for procreation, as it is stated: 'He did not create it to be a waste; He formed it to be inhabited'" (Isa. 45:18).
29. See M Eduyot 1:12–14.
30. M Eduyot 5:6–7.
31. M Eduyot 5:6 (Koren Talmud Bavli).
32. M Eduyot 5:6 (Koren Talmud Bavli).
33. M Eduyot 5:7 (Koren Talmud Bavli).
34. For an example of this disagreement, see T Pesachim 8:3. For an example of his innovations: Our Sages taught a *baraita*: Rabbi Ḥananya ben Akavya permitted three activities to the inhabitants of Tiberias: They may draw water from the sea through a hole cut out of a balcony on Shabbat, they may insulate produce in the pods of legumes, and they may dry themselves on Shabbat with a towel (*aluntit*) (Eruvin 87b). All of these innovations made the lives of the citizens of Tiberias easier in their own way.
35. BT Brachot 19a.
36. For more on Williams's thinking, including the many potential critiques of it, see "Integrity" in *Stanford Encyclopedia of Philosophy*, https://plato.stanford.edu/entries/integrity/.
37. Williams and Smart, *Utilitarianism*, 248.

38. BT Sanhedrin 6b.
39. Translation follows Koren Talmud Bavli.
40. This view is consistent with his opinion during the Oven of Ahknai story.
41. Avot de-Rabbi Natan, 12:3.
42. BT Sanhedrin 6b.
43. BT Sanhedrin 6b (Koren Talmud Bavli).
44. BT Sanhedrin 6b (Koren Talmud Bavli).
45. BT Sanhedrin 6b (Koren Talmud Bavli).
46. Later the Talmud will do the same thing with the virtues of judgment and charity (*tzedakah*). Here tzedakah connotes kindness. Since strict adherence to the law does not take that into account, the virtues are often at odds. Compromise once again bridges the gap.
47. BT Sanhedrin 6b (Koren Talmud Bavli).
48. BT Sanhedrin 7a (Koren Talmud Bavli).
49. An ancient measure. This is a small measure, akin to calling it something like a dollar.
50. T Bava Metzi'a 3:5.
51. BT Sanhedrin 7a (Koren Talmud Bavli).
52. BT Sanhedrin 7a.

3. Too Far Out in Front

1. BT Shabbat 54b.
2. The word *arevim*, which is often translated as "responsible for" in the famous dictum "All of Israel is responsible for one another" (BT Shevuot 39a), shares the same root as the word guarantor.
3. Gen. Rabbah 54:3.
4. BT Shabbat 54b (Koren Talmud Bavi).
5. See Schwartz, *Imperialism and Jewish Society* for one such view on the minor role of Rabbinic leadership in general Jewish society. Nevertheless, it is the author's contention that the Rabbis legislate as if they have a great deal of power, even if this is not historically accurate, for pragmatic reasons: acting as if they have power increases their standing in the eyes of their audience.
6. BT Shabbat 55a (Koren Talmud Bavi).
7. BT Yevamot 56b (Koren Talmud Bavi).
8. See Sifra Kedoshim 2:14.
9. BT Pesachim 22b.
10. BT Moed Katan 5a.

11. BT Beitzah 30a, BT Bava Batra 60b, BT Shabbat 148b.
12. BT Bava Batra 60b. See also T Sotah 15:10.
13. "There is no joy without wine, since 'wine gladdens the heart of humanity'" (BT Pesachim 109a).
14. BT Baba Batra 60b (Koren Talmud Bavi).
15. This is a reference to *pidyon ha-ben*, a ritual whereby a firstborn son is redeemed from Temple service thirty days after his birth. According to tradition, God owns all "firsts." These include first fruits, first animals born in a season, and firstborn sons. However, a father can pay someone from the priestly line to exempt his son from the Temple service that he would be otherwise obligated to perform. This ritual has endured even past the Temple's destruction.
16. BT Bava Batra 60b (Koren Talmud Bavi).
17. BT Bava Batra 60b (Koren Talmud Bavi).
18. For examples of this, see M. Yevamot 6:6, which speaks about the need to have at least two children; BT Yevamot 62b, which compels a person to marry at any age to have children; and BT Gittin 41b, which teaches that the world was created specifically so that we can procreate. This is not to say that the Rabbis necessarily understood life as arising only from sexual relations between "male" and "female" individuals; see Neis, *When a Human Gives Birth to a Raven*.
19. This is opposed to a famous midrash about Miriam. Pharoah has decreed that all male children born to Israelites must be thrown into the Nile to drown. When Miriam learns that her father Amram has convinced the Jewish men in Egypt to stop having children in order to avoid the decree, she responds emphatically, telling him that his recklessness will mean the end of the Jewish people. His decision will cause assured ruin, and therefore it is worse than Pharoah's potential destruction, as female children are unaffected by Pharoah's edict and some male children thrown into the Nile might survive. "Your decree is harsher than that of Pharoah. Pharoah only decreed against the males, but you have decreed against both the males and the females.... It is doubtful whether the decree of the wicked Pharoah will be fulfilled, but you are righteous, and your decree will undoubtedly be fulfilled" (BT Sotah 12b, Koren Talmud Bavli). Here the argument Miriam raises is equally pragmatic, though it is less about whether people will have the capacity to follow Amram's decree and more about the effect of remaining celibate on the future of the Israelite nation.

20. BT Betizah 30a.
21. See Rashi BT Betizah 30a s.v M'rakdin.
22. BT Beitzvah 30a.
23. BT Beitzvah 30a (Koren Talmud Bavi).
24. Shulḥan Arukh, Oraḥ Hayyim 339.3.
25. Shulḥan Arukh, Oraḥ Hayyim 339.3.
26. For examples, see BT Bava Kamma 30b, BT Shabbat 12b, BT Beitzah 28a, and BT Menachot 36b.
27. Author's translation. The RJPS translation reads: "You shall keep this institution at its set time from year to year," but the Rabbinic reading of the phrase in Menachot 36b reads the word years (*yamim*) literally as "days."
28. BT Sukkah 26a.
29. For example, if you take them off and leave them next to you, a person might step on them or spill something on them.
30. BT Menachot 36b.
31. BT Menachot 36b (Koren Talmud Bavi).
32. BT Berachot 63a.
33. BT Berachot 63a (Koren Talmud Bavi).
34. BT Berachot 63a (Koren Talmud Bavi).
35. See Sifrei Deut. 34:4: "to *your sons*": "These are your disciples. And thus do you find in all places, that disciples are called 'sons,' viz. (2 Kings 2:3) 'And the sons of the prophets came forth.' Now were they the sons of the prophets? Were they not disciples? This shows that disciples were called 'sons.'"
36. In other cases of the precept one is allowed to write down the words of the Rabbis so they will not be forgotten, even though technically it is "Oral Torah" and must remain so. See BT Gittin 60a. In another instance, the Rabbis imagine that Shimon HaTzadik donned his priestly garments, which traditionally a priest could only wear during sacrificial services, to impress Alexander the Great, knowing that the king was preparing to destroy the Temple. His appearance moved the king so much that he backed down from the attack. See BT Yoma 69a.
37. For another articulation of this sentiment, see BT Ta'anit 7a. "Rabbi Hanina Bar Papa contrasted: It is written 'toward the thirsty bring water (Isa. 21:14),' and it is also written 'woe, all that are thirsty go to water (Isa. 55:1).' If a student is worthy 'toward the thirsty bring water' and if not 'woe, all that are thirsty go to water.' Rabbi Hanina Bar Hama contrasted:

It is written 'let your wellsprings spread forth (Prov. 5:16),' and it is also written 'let them be yours alone (Prov. 5:17).' If a student is worthy, 'let your wellsprings spread forth (Prov. 5:16),' and if not, 'let them be yours alone (Prov. 5:17).'"

38. For the Rabbis, imagining their edicts as situated in the context of a no-longer viable world—the Temple service—gives them a testing ground on which to consider the many broad principles of leadership, ethics, and faith in their own day at lower, more academic, and not immediately applicable stakes. There is a certain irony in the fact that the Rabbis dedicate almost half of the Talmud to legislating the sacrifices, tithes, and purity laws of the Temple, even though, living in a post-Temple era, they did not benefit from its existence. Among the many explanations offered as to why the Rabbis spill so much ink in the service of the Temple are these: having a say in how the Temple should function in the generations after its destruction proved that the Rabbis, rather than the priests of old, were in charge; historical rewriting enabled the Rabbis to change history, placing themselves in rooms they likely were not in before 70 CE since they were not important enough to be there; the Rabbis are expecting the Temple to be rebuilt one day, and they want to preserve their best understanding of what sacrificial service looked like. Yet, in this author's view, the Rabbinic approach to the Temple was predominantly pragmatic, and these explanations belie this fact.
39. BT Yoma 39a.
40. BT Yoma 44b.
41. BT Rosh Hashanah 27a.
42. BT Menachot 76b.
43. See BT Menachot 86b and BT Ḥullin 46b.
44. BT Rosh Hashanah 27a, BT Menachot 76b, BT Yoma 44b, and BT Yoma 39a (Koren Talmud Bavi).
45. One could argue, too, that giving the animals water to drink is humane, as it relieves their suffering and as such also precludes violating *tza'ar ba'alei ḥayim* the prohibition against hurting God's creatures. Interestingly, the Rabbis do not raise these points in their discussion.
46. BT Menachot 76b.
47. Meiri on BT Ḥullin 49b.
48. See BT Berachot 12b.
49. BT Berachot 30b codified in Shulḥan Arukh, Oraḥ Hayyim 126:4.
50. As per Maimondies, Mishneh Torah, Hilkhot Tefillah 12:23.

51. BT Yoma 70a. In classical legal literature this example is also termed *kevod hatzibur*, which means honoring the community. It is a form of honoring to avoid undue burdens, and thus the two terms can be employed in parallel with one another.
52. BT Yoma 52b.
53. BT Yoma 53b (Koren Talmud Bavi).
54. M Bava Metzi'a 2:3.
55. BT Bava Metzi'a 25b.
56. The reason the acquisition is valid requires background on the laws of acquisition. A thief never technically owns the items he steals. He possesses them but does not acquire ownership over them since they remain the property of the original owner. In this talmudic case, the person who unknowingly takes the chicks has not "stolen" them per se, because his actions do not fit into the Rabbinic legal definition of stealing, which includes either foreknowledge or intent. Because he didn't mean to steal them or know they belonged to someone, his possessing them includes ownership. They are his, like any random property one finds that does not belong to another. Should he wish to return the chicks, which Jewish law does not require, he would need to retransfer ownership to the original person.
57. Shulḥan Arukh, Oraḥ Hayyim 586:1.
58. Shulḥan Arukh, Oraḥ Hayyim 451:21.
59. Shulḥan Aruch, Yoreh De'ah 196:1.
60. Based on Exod. 21:15, "One who strikes their father or mother shall be put to death," which the Rabbis broaden to prohibit giving medical care to a parent. See BT Sanhedrin 84b.
61. Mishneh Torah, Hilkhot Mamrim 5:7.
62. That is not to say that the Rabbis are always understanding. The Rabbis are often impatient, stubborn, and demeaning. The system has a lot of compassion, but they don't always practice it.
63. Quote found in Ysoschar Katz, "Ode to Bediewed," *Times of Israel*, August 14, 2018, https://blogs.timesofisrael.com/ode-to-bedieved-done-just-well-enough-to-fulfill-a-duty-when-appropriate/.

4. Wisdom of the Masses

1. Indeed, even after the Rabbinic period, it may have taken some time for Rabbinic texts to acquire the type of authority we often see them possess today. See Fishman, *Becoming the People of the Talmud*.

2. Tzipuri, for example, is known as one of the most important centers of early Rabbinic innovation after the Temple was destroyed. Even there, archeologists have found a zodiac on the floor of the surviving synagogue. Scholars see this as proof of a non-Rabbinic population since the Rabbis would not have allowed the practice. For a great summary of the many differences between Rabbinic culture and the general population vis a vis synagogue life in Babylonia see Pomeranz, "Ordinary Jews in the Babylonian Talmud."
3. BT Berachot 47b.
4. For discussion of the attitude of the *Am Haaretz* on the frequency of Torah study, see BT Menachot 99b.
5. When the Rabbis speak about the general citizenry around them, it can be stomach-turning. Rabbi Judah the Prince says, "It is the unlearned who bring misfortune to the world" (BT Bava Batra 8a) and that since the laws of kashrut can be technical, only Rabbis can eat meat; those without real Torah knowledge should become relegated to vegetarianism (BT Pesachim 49b). Other Rabbis chastise the people for not upholding their own level of purity or tithing or performing substandard prayer and study (BT Berachot 47b). One talmudic account goes so far as to condone the killing of an ignoramus: "Rabbi Elazar said: It is permitted to stab an ignoramus to death on Yom Kippur that occurs on Shabbat. His students said to him: Master, [at least] say that it is permitted to slaughter him. He said to them: [I intentionally used the word stab], as this [term, slaughtering], requires a blessing [when one slaughters an animal], and that [term, stabbing], does not require a blessing in any context. Rabbi Elazar said: It is prohibited to accompany an ignoramus while traveling on the road [due to concern that the ignoramus might try to harm his traveling partner], as it is stated with regard to Torah: 'For it is your life and the length of your days' (Deut. 30:20). [An ignoramus has not studied any Torah, indicating that] he is not concerned about his own life; with regard to another's life, all the more so. Rabbi Shmuel bar Naḥmani said that Rabbi Yoḥanan said: It is permitted to tear open an ignoramus like a fish. Rabbi Shmuel bar Yitzḥak said: And one may cut him open from his back and thereby cause his immediate death by piercing his spinal cord rather than his stomach." (BT Pesachim 49b–Koren Talmud Bavli). At least these extreme machinations are rhetorical. No evidence exists that any of these Rabbis who countenance violence actually engage in it. Most likely these teachings were meant to scare

the Sage's followers away from defecting and to affirm the Sages' place of superiority in a world in which they felt challenged to assert their authority. The Rabbis did not uniformly hate the *am haartez*. Earlier stata of Rabbis as well as those based in Israel rather than Babylonia tended to be more accepting of the people (see T Avodah Zarah 3:10). Yet, except for one instance (later recounted in this chapter), one is hard-pressed to find instances in which the Rabbis praise the people outright.

6. In the Tannaitic era (pre-third century) Jews were more integrated. Then in the early Amoraic era (early third century) these interactions took a dip, recovering a little over a century later with many fruitful encounters and shared learnings. Pomeranz, "Ordinary Jews in the Babylonian Talmud," 15.

7. Neusner, *A History of the Jews in Babylonia*, 3:238.

8. For illustrations on the communal response to draughts see M. Ta'anit 1:5–6. The Rabbis' main approach is to declare a communal fast; the more people who partake in it, the more effective it will be.

9. Since the Rabbis and the masses lived in the same locales, all were responsible for the maintenance of walls and fences around their towns to exclude invaders and wild beasts. See BT Bava Batra 7b.

10. BT Pesachim 66a (Koren Talmud Bavli).

11. BT Pesachim 66a (Koren Talmud Bavli).

12. BT Pesachim 66b (Koren Talmud Bavli).

13. BT Pesachim 66b.

14. Elsewhere, too, Deborah does not credit other contemporaneous leaders. When she governs alongside a leader named Barak, for example, she seems to only acknowledge his existence after she loses and then regains her sense of prophecy, saying, "Arise, O Barak; Take your captives, O son of Abinoam!" (Judg. 5:12).

15. Author's translation. RJPS reads: "Do not deal basely with members of your people."

16. For examples see M Sanhedrin 3:7 and BT Sanhedrin 30b.

17. BT Arachin 15b (Koren Talmud Bavli).

18. BT Sanhedrin 37a (Koren Talmud Bavli).

19. BT Kiddushin 66a.

20. See BT Moed Katan 18b.

21. This line is often attributed to Mark Twain or Winston Churchill, although its originator remains unknown.

22. BT Yevamot 25a.
23. BT Yevamot 25a.
24. The Rabbis are careful not to give carte blanche to rumors like this. If the subject of the rumor has enemies or if it ceases and then someone restarts it, these caveats will preclude a husband from perpetuating the rumor so he will be believed. See BT Yevamot 25a.
25. M Gittin 9:9.
26. M Gittin 9:9.
27. BT Kiddushin 81b.
28. BT Sanhedrin 31a.
29. Because traditionally, when one swears an oath one invokes God's name, one who violates an oath takes God's name in vain, transgressing the third commandment in the Decalogue ("You shall not swear falsely by the name of the ETERNAL your God; for GOD will not clear one who swears falsely by God's name"; Exod. 20:7). Here the Rabbis are working off the assumption that no one, even the most hardened thief, will misuse an oath by lying since God is slow to forgive broken oaths and may even punish a transgressor's loved ones in response (BT Shevuot 39a).
30. M Bava Kamma 10:3. This Mishnah speaks about a person who sees his "vessels and scrolls" in someone else's possession and confronts the possessor. If there is rumor that the theft occurred, the accuser is believed and the person possessing the merchandise has to take an oath stating how much he spent on the item. If there is no rumor, the accuser has no claim on the items.
31. BT Niddah 61a.
32. Interestingly, the Talmud does not even consider that these Galileans might be guilty. Taking their innocence at face value, Tarfon only seems concerned with the correct approach to dealing with rumors.
33. M Megillah 2:2 (Koren Talmud Bavli).
34. These laws can be found in M Megillah 2:1–2.
35. BT Megillah 18a (Koren Talmud Bavli).
36. BT Megillah 18a.
37. BT Megillah 18a (Koren Talmud Bavli).
38. BT Bava Batra 74b.
39. See BT Megillah 18a, "The Sages did not know what is [meant by the word *yehav* in the verse]: "Cast upon the Lord your *yehav*" (Ps. 55:23). Rabba bar bar Ḥana said: One time I was traveling with a certain Arab [*Tayya'a*] and I was carrying a load, and he said to me: Take your *yehav*

and throw it on my camel, [and I understood that *yehav* means a load or burden]" (Koren Talmud Bavli).
40. BT Bava Batra 73b–74a.
41. BT Bava Batra 74a.
42. BT Sukkah 28a (Koren Talmud Bavli).
43. To get a sense of the ubiquity of these folk saying, consider that the Hebrew term *d'amrei inshei* (lit. "as the people say"), which often introduces a folk adage, appears 308 times in the Talmud alone.
44. BT Ta'anit 23a (Koren Talmud Bavli).
45. BT Berachot 5b (Koren Talmud Bavli).
46. In the form of produce owed to him.
47. BT Ketubot 63a.
48. BT Ḥagigah 10a (Koren Talmud Bavli).
49. BT Ḥullin 92b (Koren Talmud Balvi).
50. BT Ḥullin 92b.
51. BT Ḥullin 92b.

5. Keeping Peace

1. Although the prohibition against drinking non-kosher wine is a Rabbinic invention, they believed that the greatest among their ancestors, Nehemiah included, must have held by Rabbinic practices, even if those practices wouldn't be developed until centuries later. Thus, while this discussion may seem to us to be an anachronism, it did not feel this way to them.
2. JT Kiddushin 4:1:3.
3. See T Sotah 15:8.
4. BT Bava Kamma 83a.
5. BT Bava Kamma 83a. Almost a century later, Maimonides would codify the spirit of these Rabbinic exemptions into law in the *Mishneh Torah*: "A Jew who has an important position in a gentile kingdom and must sit before their kings, and would be embarrassed if he did not resemble them, is granted permission to wear clothes which resemble theirs and shave the hair on his face as they do" (MT Hilkhot Avodah Zarah 11:3.)
6. There is no actual Emperor named Antoninus. Likely he is an amalgam of a number of traits of emperors from that time, and his presence is more pedagogical than historical, meant to make a point about the way the Rabbis view an ideal relationship with a ruler.
7. Gen. Rabbah 75:5.

8. For a good example of this, see BT Avodah Zarah 10a–b.
9. There is no evidence that many of these rulers did what the Rabbis describe. For this reason, their presence in the Talmud must serve a pedagogical rather than a historical role. In this case, the fear of kings, Jewish and non-Jewish, is one of the key messages of this story.
10. A city in the region we know today as modern-day Turkey.
11. BT Moed Katan 26a.
12. The Rabbis surmise that one only tears their garments in mourning when the majority of a city is killed or an entire nation suffers defeat.
13. BT Ḥagigah 5b.
14. M Bava Batra 6:7.
15. At times, the Rabbis make important points about how to relate to the great powers around them by exploring issues related to Jewish kings. In their mind, reverence for their own monarchs provides a model for the respect and fear one must pay to non-Jewish sovereigns in their midst. In one of the most famous examples, from BT Sanhedrin 19a–b, King Yannai, a Jewish king, is called to testify in a trial, during which it becomes clear that no one stands up to him due to fear of retribution. Knowing it is a perversion of justice to call upon someone in court who cannot be held to the same standards as everyone else, the Rabbis legislate: "The king neither judges others nor do others judge him; he does not testify nor do others testify against him" (M Sanhedrin 2:2 and M Horayot 2:5, Koren Talmud Bavli). Knowing that the court must tiptoe around a Jewish king, who is ostensibly bound by Torah and shares a similar sense of justice, it becomes all the more important to make concessions when dealing with non-Jewish rulers. Yanni is to be feared, but no more that Caesar, and learning how to treat the former will aid us as we navigate the delicate relationship with the latter.
16. BT Ta'anit 18a.
17. BT Ta'anit 18a.
18. BT Ta'anit 18a.
19. BT Ta'anit 18a.
20. For an in-depth study of these dialogues, see Labendz, *Socratic Torah*.
21. Num. Rabbah 3:2.
22. Gen. Rabbah 17:7.
23. BT Kiddushin 40a.
24. Gen. Rabbah 68:4.
25. Gen. Rabbah 68:4.

26. Our tradition contains a sizable subset of texts that have complicated relationships with non-Jewish sources of wisdom. The Talmud famously warns its readers: "Cursed be the man who raises pigs, and cursed be the man who teaches his son Greek wisdom" (Bava Kamma 83a, Koren Talmud Bavli).
27. One other important area of overlap involves shared law. For two studies on this overlap, see Dohrmann, "Ad similitudinem arbitrorum," 365–85; and Hezser, "The Mishnah and Roman Law," 141–66.
28. Visotzky, *Aphrodite and the Rabbis*, 22.
29. BT Sukkah 28a.
30. Beyond Rabbinic recognition of the utility of such moves when interacting with non-Jewish neighbors, in some cases the Rabbis may be intellectually fascinated by the non-Jewish material; alternatively, their use of non-Jewish material may not be intentional and may simply reflect their being influenced by their surroundings.
31. Gen. Rabbah 78:7 (translation found in Visotzky, *Aphrodite and the Rabbis*, 24).
32. Notably, the Rabbis bring up this story as part of the discussion of Jacob and Esau's reunion in Gen. 32–33. In the Rabbinic world Esau is understood as the progenitor of Greece and Rome.
33. BT Meilah 17a.
34. Throughout Rabbinic literature, Rome consistently chooses outlawing key Jewish practices as punishment for Jewish rebellion. Although this story, and the prohibiting of circumcision, Shabbat, and family purity laws, likely are myth, the sentiment and lessons from the story provide good evidence for the Jewish worldview around engagement with Rome.
35. BT Meilah 17a.
36. BT Meilah 17a.
37. BT Meilah 17b.
38. For one example, see Exod. 23:23–24: "When My angel goes before you and brings you to the Amorites, the Hittites, the Perizzites, the Canaanites, the Hivites, and the Jebusites, and I annihilate them, you shall not bow down to their gods in worship or follow their practices, but shall tear them down and smash their pillars to bits."
39. BT Avodah Zarah 12b.
40. BT Avodah Zarah 18b.
41. M Avodah Zarah 3:4 and subsequent discussion on BT Avodah Zarah 44b.

42. He taunts him with Deut. 13:18: "Let nothing that is doomed stick to your hand."
43. BT Avodah Zarah 44b, quoting M Avodah Zarah 4:3.
44. BT Avodah Zarah 18b.
45. Although this answer is not given in the Bavli, it appears in a parallel text in Yerushalmi. See JT Avodah Zarah 1:7.
46. BT Avodah Zarah 18b.
47. BT Sanhedrin 74a. For a list of these sins, see Lev. 18 and 20.
48. The full text reads: "Father in Heaven! It is known to You that we desire to fulfill Your will and observe the Passover holiday by eating matzah and following the prohibition of chametz. But our hearts are pained that enslavement prevents us, and we are in mortal danger. We are hereby ready to fulfill Your commandment, 'And you shall live by them and not die by them,' and to observe Your caution of 'protect yourself and safeguard your soul.' Therefore our prayer to You is that You keep us alive, and sustain us, and redeem us speedily, so that we may observe Your laws and fulfill Your will and serve You with a full heart. Amen!" Although the prayer does not invoke *piku'aḥ nefesh* directly, it invokes and quotes its proof text: "The Torah said: Desecrate one Shabbat on his behalf so he will observe many *Shabbatot*. Rav Yehuda said that Shmuel said: If I would have been there [among those Sages who debated this question], I would have said that my proof is preferable to theirs, [as it states: 'You shall keep My statutes and My ordinances, which a person shall do'] and *live by them (Lev.18:5), and not that he should die by them.* [In all circumstances, one must take care not to die as a result of fulfilling the mitzvot]" (BT Yoma 85a, Koren Talmud Bavli). In quoting the "live by them" principle it calls to mind the lifesaving reason for eating traditionally forbidden foods. For background on this prayer, see "Passover Prayer from Bergen-Belsen," United States Holocaust Memorial Museum, https://perspectives.ushmm.org/item/passover-prayer-from-bergen-belsen.
49. BT Nedarim 28a, BT Gittin 10b, BT Bava Kamma 113a, and BT Bava Batra 54b–55a.
50. BT Nedarim 28a. Jewish law does allow a community to lie to tax collectors if the Jews suspect the collectors are not legitimate representatives of the king.
51. BT Gittin 10b.
52. BT Bava Kamma 113a.

53. This is based on Lev. 25:35–36, "If your kin, being in straits . . . do not exact advance or accrued interest."
54. See BT Bava Metzi'a 71a.
55. BT Bava Kamma 113b.
56. The Rabbis often use "idolators" as a generic term for adherents of religions other than Judaism, even though this represented a vast oversimplification of the complex and diverse religious landscape of the time.
57. T Gittin 3:18.
58. JT Gittin 5:9.
59. JT Gittin 5:9.
60. JT Gittin 5:9.
61. JT Gittin 59a.
62. JT Gittin 5:9.
63. For a digest of these scholarly debates see Crane, "Because . . . : Justifying Law," 56–59.
64. Wurzberger, *Ethics of Responsibility*, 48.
65. BT Bava Metzi'a 32b.
66. M Avodah Zarah 2:1.
67. BT Avodah Zarah 26a.
68. BT Avodah Zarah 26a.
69. See BT Ḥullin 5a.
70. See MT Hilkhot Avodah Zarah 9:2; Shulḥan Arukh, Yoreh De'ah 148:5.
71. BT Avodah Zarah 8a.
72. BT Avodah Zarah 6b.
73. At times the Rabbis do fight against foreign influence, even turning toward martyrdom to keep from acquiescing too much. For two examples of this, see the martyrdom of Rabbi Akiva (BT Berachot 61b) and Rabbi Haninah ben Tradiyon (BT Avodah Zarah 17b).

6. Avoiding Infighting

1. For a good summary of these points of conflict, see Cohen, *From the Maccabees to the Mishnah*, 142–58.
2. See M. Yadayim 4:6–8.
3. Avot de-Rabbi Natan 37:4 reads: "There are seven types of [false] Pharisees: the Shechemite Pharisee, the Nakfaite Pharisee, the Miktzoite Pharisee, the Machobaite Pharisee, the Pharisee for the sake of a profession, the Pharisee who was obligated by marriage, the Pharisee driven by lust, and the Pharisee driven by fear" (Koren Talmud Bavli). Although scholars

are perplexed by many of these definitions, it's clear that the Pharisees, the forebearers of the Rabbis, made an artform out of questioning the authenticity of their kinsmen.
4. The Siccari are mentioned throughout Josephus's writings. See most notably *The Jewish War*, book 7, chap. 8.
5. BT Shabbat 119b. The Talmud is vague about which "Temple" this teaching is referring to.
6. BT Shevuot 39a (Koren Talmud Bavli).
7. Sifrei Deut., *Ve-zo't ha-berakhah piska* 346:2.
8. See BT Sanhedrin 27b.
9. M Gittin 5:8 (Koren Talmud Bavli).
10. For discussions of these modes of acquisition (Heb. *kinyan*) see BT Bava Batra 86a.
11. M. Gittin 5:8. In fact, according to one minority opinion, Rabbi Yosei doesn't view the act of taking the olives as akin to robbery, but as "full fledged" robbery in its own right.
12. M Gittin 5:8.
13. BT Menachot 93a. Examples of this include the fact that they are not required to visit and offer sacrifices in Jerusalem during the three pilgrimage holidays, Sukkot, Passover, and Shavuot (Ḥagigah 2a); they may not write a *get* (BT Gittin 22b); and if they slaughter an animal, the animal is not considered kosher unless the slaughter was observed by an expert (M Ḥullin 1:1).
14. M. Gittin 5:8. As with the case of taking the olives, there is a debate about whether taking the object from the ḥeresh, shoteh, and katan is "akin" to robbery or robbery in its own right.
15. In liberal Judaism, *tikkun ha-olam* is often used synonymously with social justice. In the kabbalistic world, *tikkun ha-olam* is a mystical idea that when God created the universe, an accident led pieces of God to be trapped in the world we live in. As we perform God's commandments—hearing the shofar on Rosh Hashanah, praying three times daily, etc.—we free those parts of God and return them to the Divine.
16. Jacobs, *There Shall Be No Needy*, 33–34.
17. T Gittin 3:3.
18. For a full discussion of these five categories, see M Bava Kamma 8:1.
19. M Gittin 5:3.
20. M Shevuot 7:1.
21. M Shevuot 7:2.

22. For the root of the biblical command to return lost property see Exod. 23:4.
23. This is derived from Deut. 23:3: "No one misbegotten (lit. mamzer) shall be admitted into the congregation of GOD; no descendant of such, even in the tenth generation, shall be admitted into the congregation of GOD."
24. M Gittin 4:2.
25. As imaginative as the Rabbis are in fixing this particular flaw, traditional Jewish law has yet to conclusively solve the problem of the *agunah* (anchored one). Legally only a husband is granted the right to initiate a divorce. Additionally, Jewish law technically permits a husband to have multiple wives (whereas wives are not allowed multiple husbands), even though since the Middle Ages many Jewish communities condemn polygamy. Exploiting this discrepancy, a husband can deny a wife a *get* (Jewish divorce document) and thus keep her "anchored" in the marriage, unable to remarry. Though there have been attempts to fix this, including a clause in the Conservative (Lieberman) version of the *ketubah* (marriage document) that protects the bride should the couple decide to separate in the future, the traditional Jewish world has yet to fix this problem. We need to invoke the Rabbinic moral imagination to right this wrong.
26. This letter is undated. However, one can date this letter to the postwar period, given the expressed novelty of the problem of these refugees.
27. The full text of this letter can be found in the collected writings of the S'ridei Eish 2:11.
28. Chapter three of tractate Ḥullin addresses eighteen defects that render an animal *trefiah* or invalid. One of these defects is a punctured lung, *ha-re'ah nikveh*. An animal found to have this defect is not kosher and cannot be eaten. However, the Gemara is explicit that a priori, one does not need to check for such defects. An important principle in kashrut, *rov behemoth einan trefot* (the majority of beasts are not *treif*) holds that the majority of animals are kosher by default. Since most animals lack defects that will kill them within twelve months, one can assume that any animal killed without suspicion of a defect does not need checking. The defects that cause an animal to be non-kosher only become problematic if the slaughterer or butcher stumbles upon them. According to Breisch, the stringent community in question takes it upon itself to check the lungs of the slaughtered animal despite the fact that this is not required.

29. Interestingly, lo titgodedu is a creative misreading of our tradition. Originally the Bible employs the term when speaking about the prohibition against self-mutilation during one's mourning practice: "You are children of the Eternal your God. Do not gash yourselves (*lo titgodedu*) or shave the front of your heads because of the dead" (Deut. 14:1). Though useful as a way to separate ourselves from the pagan practices of time, our ancient Rabbis chose to understand the prohibition in a radically different way. They noticed that the term shared its root with the Akkadian verb *gudugu*, meaning military detachment. Thus, when our Rabbis read these words, they didn't imagine cuts and gashes but battalions joined together into disparate parts. For them, lo titgodedu must mean don't group off, don't pick sides, don't separate out.
30. BT Yevamot 14a.
31. In the Talmud. Abaye says no, Rava says yes. Maimonides rules in the Mishneh Torah in accordance with Abaye (MT Hilkhot Avodah Zarah v'Chukat Ha-Goyim 12:14).
32. As background, the Rabbis establish that an ancient "walled city" like Jerusalem reads the Megillah on the 15th of Adar. All of the other locales read it on the 14th. The reason is because the date of the Megillah reading corresponds to the end of the Jews' struggle against their Persian oppressors during the Purim story. In memory of the fighting lasting an extra day in Shushan, the archetypal "walled city," the Sages institute waiting a day to read the scroll. Although conversations of travels between walled and unwalled cities appear elsewhere throughout Rabbinic literature (JT Megillah 2:3), discussions pertaining to lo titgodedu can be found in BT Yevamot 13b.
33. BT Yevamot 14a.
34. M Pesachim 4:1. Lo titgodedu is not mentioned explicitly here, but later commentators often cite this discussion when describing instances of navigating factionalism.
35. MT Hilkhot Avodah Zarah 12:14.
36. Rosh, Commenting on M Yevamot 1:9.
37. Rosh, Commenting on M Yevamot 1:9.
38. For a broad discussion of this, see Shapiro, *Between the Yeshiva World*, 216–18.
39. Lev. 5:21–24 speaks about returning the stolen item plus, in many cases, a penalty of one-fifth its value.
40. BT Gittin 55a.

41. A similar case involves a stolen beam meant to build a sukkah. See BT Sukkah 31a.
42. BT Bava Kamma 94b (Koren Talmud Bavli).
43. BT Bava Kamma 94b (Koren Talmud Bavli).
44. BT Bava Kamma 115a.
45. Author's translation. RJPS reads: "Hear, O Israel! The Eternal is our God, the Eternal alone."
46. BT Berachot 6a (Koren Talmud Bavli).

7. Tools to Transform Law

1. See Kugel, *How to Read the Bible*, 14–16 (paraphrase of Kugel).
2. Lev. 23:40 reads: "On the first day you shall take the product of hadar trees, branches of palm trees, boughs of leafy trees, and willows of the brook, and you shall rejoice before the ETERNAL your God seven days." Here, there is no evidence these should be assembled and shaken. In fact, in Neh. 8:13–15, the people try to build a Sukkah with the four species of Sukkot.
3. The Rabbis derive all their laws of marriage from the laws of divorce found at the start of Deut. 24.
4. For examples of this concept in Rabbinic literature see BT Gittin 60b, M Avot 1:1, and BT Shabbat 31a.
5. Sifra Bechukotai, 8:10.
6. Gen. 26:5; Deut. 4:44.
7. Avot De-Rabbi Natan, 4:5. Regarding "creative misreadings," I am indebted to my teacher Rabbi David Ellenson, who was the first person to introduce me to the term.
8. There is no definitive list of these actions. The Talmud tends to speak about acts of *gemilut ḥasadim* (acts of lovingkindness) as if we already know what these are. However, most commentators agree they encompass any number of activities including visiting the sick, clothing the naked, and feeding the hungry. See BT Shabbat 127a–b and BT Sukkah 49b for examples.
9. For other examples, see Hos. 5:6, 8:11–13; and Isa. 58:6–11.
10. This is the age of bar mitzvah, the age of maturity when a young man is held responsible for his actions.
11. See M Sanhedrin 8:1.
12. M Sanhedrin 8:2 and BT Sanhedrin 70b.
13. M Sanhedrin 8:2.

14. See Mishneh Torah, Hilkhot Mamrim 7:2.
15. M Sanhedrin 8:3.
16. Author's translation.
17. BT Sanhedrin 71a (Koren Talmud Bavli).
18. This reading is one of two views recorded in the Talmud. Another Rabbi is quoted as affirming the text's literal meaning by saying that a rebellious son existed, and he (the Rabbi) sat on his (the rebellious son's) grave.
19. BT Sanhedrin 71a (Koren Talmud Bavli). Realizing, however, that the radical undoing of the biblical command to punish the *ben sorrer u'moreh* might do irreconcilable damage to the Torah's authority, the Rabbis pivot, explaining why, despite its practical absence, the text merits engagement: "And why, then, was the passage relating to a stubborn and rebellious son written in the Torah? So that you may expound upon new understandings of the Torah and receive reward" (BT Sanhedrin 71a, Koren Talmud Bavli). In the Rabbis' view, the Torah is divine. Thus, even if a given text is entirely theoretical and not at all applicable, reading it still matters. It is still holy. Torah study is a mitzvah, commanded by no less than God. Performing any commandment yields reward. And if one cannot fulfill it (such as make a required sacrifice at the Temple in a post-Temple age), one gets credit for performing it simply by engaging with it through text.
20. BT Sanhedrin 71a. The Talmud continues with a similar discussion limiting the cases in which a sinner's private residence may be stricken with the ancient skin disease *Tzaraat*. Commentators offer a few explanations for the punishment, including miserliness (BT Yoma 11b) or as a scare tactic to stop gossipers before God has to resort to afflicting their skin (Mishneh Torah, Hilkhot Negaim 12:5).
21. There is no single place where the death penalty is mentioned in the Torah. The Bible seems to take for granted that the reader knows how to prosecute and enact these punishments. This lack of clarity provides an opening for the Rabbis to innovate since they don't have to change very many explicit instructions. For information on the topic, see Erez and Laster, "Capital Punishment in Jewish Law," 218–30.
22. For the best discussion, see M Makkot 1:10, "A Sanhedrin that executes a transgressor once in seven years is characterized as a destructive tribunal. [Since the Sanhedrin would subject the testimony to exacting scrutiny, it was extremely rare for a defendant to be executed.] Rabbi Elazar ben Azarya says: [This categorization applies to a Sanhedrin that executes a transgressor] once in seventy years. Rabbi Tarfon and Rabbi Akiva say:

If we had been members of the Sanhedrin, [we would have conducted trials in a manner whereby] no person would have ever been executed. Rabban Shimon ben Gamliel says: [In adopting that approach], they too would increase the number of murderers among the Jewish people" (Koren Talmud Bavli).

23. For a full discussion of this see BT Sanhedrin 8b.
24. See Sanhedrin 40b: The Sages taught in a *baraita*: [In a trial for murder, the court asks the witness]: Do you recognize the accused? Did he kill a gentile? Did he kill a Jew? Did you forewarn him? Did he accept the forewarning on himself, [i.e., acknowledge the warning?] Did he release himself to death, [i.e., acknowledge that he is aware that the court imposes capital punishment for murder?] Did he kill within [the time required] for speaking [a short phrase, as if not, he could claim he forgot the warning]? (Koren Talmud Bavli).
25. BT Sanhedrin 17a.
26. Another famous tool is the *gezerah* (decree), which aims to "build a fence" around an existing precept to ensure that people don't break it. One prohibits a related act to keep people farther away from violating a primary sin. A previously discussed example of this concerns prohibiting the playing of musical instruments on Shabbat lest one's instrument breaks and you are compelled to fix it. "Fixing" is the true prohibition, but the Rabbis prohibit any use of the instrument to ensure you won't be tempted to break the actual law. While an important mechanism for legal change, a gezerah usually does the opposite of much of what this book is exploring, tightening a prohibition rather than pragmatically loosening it.
27. Previously examined examples include *takkanat ha-shavim* and *takkanat ha-shuk*.
28. Some commentators see the use of the term "Temple" as applying to all of Jerusalem.
29. This is based on the Rabbinic fear that someone will carry the shofar through the public thoroughfare, an act prohibited on Shabbat. "Rabbah said: All are obligated to sound the shofar [on Rosh Hashanah], but not all are experts in sounding the shofar. Therefore, the Sages instituted a decree [that the shofar should not be sounded on Shabbat], lest one take the shofar in his hand and go to an expert to learn [how to sound it or to have him sound it for him], and [due to his preoccupation] he might carry it four cubits in the public domain, [which is a desecration of Shabbat]" (BT Rosh Hashanah 29b, Koren Talmud Bavli).

30. M Rosh Hashanah 4:1 (Koren Talmud Bavli). Following this discussion, the Rabbis dispute what exactly Rabban Yochanan decreed: "Rabbi Elazar said: Rabban Yochanan ben Zakkai instituted this practice only in Yavne. They said to him: He instituted the practice both in Yavne and in any place where there is a court." Since the tradition that Yochanan established numerous authoritative courts is the more common interpretation, the existence of this dispute has been relegated to the notes.
31. Hayes, *What's Divine About Divine Law*, 289.
32. While the Torah speaks about setting up courts, it does not speak explicitly about their task in setting the new moon (see Exod. 18:21–22 and Deut. 1:15–18). However, in Rabbinic memory, the courts are responsible for this task. Additionally, the idea that one would blow the shofar on a new moon can be found in Num. 10:10 and Ps. 81:3. However, the discussion of what to do if those dates fall on Shabbat is found in its earliest iterations only during the Rabbinic period.
33. In a different part of the Talmud the Rabbis do imagine Yochanan consulting scripture when making *takkanot*. See BT Sukkah 41b. This only adds to the authenticity of his rulings, and in turn helps to bolster and concretize them.
34. BT Shabbat 23a.
35. See M Rosh Hashanah 4:2.
36. M Rosh Hashanah 4:2 (Koren Talmud Bavli).
37. M Rosh Hashanah 3:4.
38. M Rosh Hashanah 4:4.
39. See BT Rosh Hashanah 31b.
40. BT Shabbat 21b (Koren Talmud Bavli).
41. BT Sukkah 31b (Koren Talmud Bavli).
42. A lulav is made of four species: palm, willow, myrtle, and the etrog fruit. One assembles them together and ritually shakes them to observe the holiday of Sukkot.
43. See M Sukkah 3:1.
44. The Rabbis account for drought in numerous places. For an example of this, see BT Ḥullin 106b–7a. Normally a person must wash one's hands before each and every ritual moment. However, in times when water is scarce, one is permitted to wash one's hands once in the morning, provided one intends for that washing to count for the whole day.
45. For example, BT Sanhedrin 92b reads: "The school of Rabbi Eliezer ben Ya'akov teaches: Even during a period of danger, a person should not

deviate from his prominence and demean himself, as it is stated: 'Then these men were bound in their mantles, their tunics, and their hats, and their other garments, and they were cast into the blazing fiery furnace' (Dan. 3:21). [Even when cast into the furnace, they donned garments befitting their station]" (Koren Talmud Bavli).

46. For the best articulation of this, see Mishneh Torah, Hilkhot Mamrim 2:4.
47. See Exod. 35:3. According to Jewish law one is prohibited from "lighting" (rather than tending to) a fire, which is why one can keep the lights on during Shabbat but cannot turn them on.
48. The original source for this can be found in T Pesachim 2:6.
49. Each of these examples can be found explicated in some depth in Stein, "Rabbinic Legal Loopholes."
50. This law assumes there is no *eruv*.
51. M Shabbat 16:4.
52. PT Yevamot 4:10.
53. *Ma'aser sheni* was brought once a year to the Temple on years one, two, four, and five of a seven-year cycle known as *shemitah*.
54. For the original command to bring *ma'aser sheni*, see Deut. 14:22–26.
55. See M Ma'aser Sheni 4:3.
56. Lev. 27:31 reads: "If someone wishes to redeem any of *their* tithes, one-fifth must be added to them." The Rabbis read "their tithes" as indicating that only the original owner's tithes are subject to the one-fifth penalty. See JT Ma'aser Sheni 4:3.
57. M Ma'aser Sheni 4:4.
58. One of the more famous condemnations of these types of loopholes reads: "And Rabba bar bar Ḥana says that Rabbi Yoḥanan says in the name of Rabbi Yehuda bar Elai: Come and see that the later generations are unlike the earlier generations. The earlier generations would bring in their produce [from the field] by way of the main entranceway [teraksemon], in order to obligate the produce in tithes. By contrast, the later generations would bring in their produce by way of roofs and by way of enclosures, in order to exempt the produce from tithes" (BT Gittin 81a, Koren Talmud Bavli).
59. For an articulation of this rationale, see Sifre Deut. 113.
60. There is some scholarly debate about whether the Prosbul is actually a loophole. For an example of a contrary voice see Ancselotvits, "The *Prosbul*—A Legal Fiction?," 2–16.

61. BT Gittin 36a (Koren Talmud Bavli).
62. See Deut. 15:9-10: "Beware lest you harbor the base thought, 'The seventh year, the year of remission, is approaching,' so that you are mean and give nothing to your needy kindred—who will cry out to God against you, and you will incur guilt. Give readily and have no regrets when you do so, for in return the Eternal your God will bless you in all your efforts and in all your undertakings."
63. For the original source, see T. Shevi'it 8:1-2.
64. The Rabbis are transparent with their use of the loophole and often name it as such with the standard phrase *ha'arama* (cunning)..
65. BT Avodah Zarah 28a.
66. BT Rosh Hashanah 20a.
67. BT Rosh Hashanah 20b.
68. A great illustration of this appears in Bava Kamma 113a, "In the case of a Jew and a gentile who approach the court for judgment in a legal dispute, if you can vindicate the Jew under Jewish law, vindicate him, and say to the gentile: This is our law. If he can be vindicated under gentile law, vindicate him, and say to the gentile: This is your law. And if it is not [possible to vindicate him under either system of law], one approaches the case circuitously, [seeking a justification to vindicate the Jew]. This is the statement of Rabbi Yishmael. Rabbi Akiva disagrees and says: One does not approach the case circuitously in order to vindicate the Jew due to the sanctification of God's name, [as God's name will be desecrated if the Jewish judge employs dishonest means]" (Koren Talmud Bavli).
69. The former would be liable to punishment by God, while the latter would be required to bring an offering to the Temple.
70. For an example of this, see BT Horayot 11a.
71. BT Moed Katan 3a.
72. Called *ḥol ha-mo'ed*, these are the middle days of Passover and Sukkot. They are not festival days and do not require the same level of rest. Some everyday behaviors are still permitted.
73. For the full list of prohibited acts, see M Shabbat 7:2.
74. BT Mo'ed Katan 4a-b.
75. T Beitzah 3:4 (translation found in Stein, "Rabbinic Legal Loopholes," 154).
76. Rabbi Eliezer allows one to do this for only one animal because of the prohibition against slaughtering an animal with its young (see Lev. 22:28).

He believes a person cannot intend to slaughter both animals because it would mean intending to violate the prohibition.
77. See BT Shabbat 103a.
78. BT Shabbat 120b.
79. This mitzvah is called *onah* (set period) and can be found in the following teaching: "The set interval [defining the frequency of a husband's conjugal obligation to his wife] stated in the Torah [(see Exod. 21:10), unless the couple stipulated otherwise, varies according to the man's occupation and proximity to his home]: Men of leisure, who do not work, must engage in marital relations every day, laborers must do so twice a week, donkey drivers once a week, camel drivers once every thirty days, and sailors once every six months" (M Ketubot 5:6, Koren Talmud Bavli).
80. M Niddah 8:2 (Koren Talmud Bavli).
81. The Talmud continues with a story of Akiva questioning a woman to find a reason to allow her to return to her husband: "There was an incident involving one woman who came before Rabbi Akiva. She said to him: I saw a blood stain. Rabbi Akiva said to her: Perhaps there was a wound on your body? She said to him: Yes, there was a wound and it healed. He said to her: Was it perhaps a wound that could reopen and bleed? She said to him: Yes it was. And Rabbi Akiva deemed her ritually pure. Rabbi Akiva saw his students looking at each other, wondering why he ruled leniently in this case. Rabbi Akiva said to them: What in this matter is difficult in your eyes? The reason I ruled this way is that the Sages did not state the matter of the impurity of blood stains in order to be stringent; rather, they instituted this impurity in order to be lenient" (BT Niddah 58b, Koren Talmud Bavli).
82. One notable exception is that Jewish law only requires one witness in cases when one is trying to determine if a given act is permitted or prohibited. See BT Gittin 2a.
83. Additionally, if a woman can prove the death of her husband, she is entitled to the funds dictated by her marriage contract (*ketubah*).
84. The Rabbis qualify this with two items: (1) The husband and wife had to have been getting along at the time, so there is no reason to think she invented his death to get out of the marriage, and (2) they could not be entering a war zone, as people are often taken captive during war and thought for dead.
85. M Yevamot 15:1 (Koren Talmud Bavli).
86. BT Yevamot 116b (Koren Talmud Bavli).

87. See BT Pesachim 105a, which speaks about what to do if one forgets to recite Kiddush on Friday night. In reference to this the Talmud says, "The tanna does not teach cases of what if," meaning that forgetting to recite Kiddush is uncommon enough that one does not need to legislate around that scenario. See also BT Yoma 13a. Jewish law also requires the High Priest in Jerusalem to have a wife at the time he does Temple service on Yom Kippur. Since he cannot perform the sacrifices as a single man, Jewish law has another wife "on deck" for him in case something happens to his existing wife. When it was considered whether to have someone as a backup to that backup, the Talmud quips, "If so, [that you are concerned lest his wife die], there is no end to the matter." One does not need contingencies upon contingencies. For an additional example of this phenomenon, see BT Beitzah 2b, "for an uncommon matter the Sages did not issue a decree."
88. M Ḥagigah 1:8.
89. BT Ḥagigah 11b. Since this phrase appears at the end of the Mishnah, some have read it as commenting on the third category of law only. To correct for this, the Talmud goes out of its way to read the phrase as a postscript to the Mishnah as a whole, as if to say, "all of the above, from the most to the least innovative laws, form the essential parts of the Torah."

8. Sinning for the Greater Good

1. For the full essay see Sartre, *Existentialism Is a Humanism*, 30.
2. Sartre, *Existentialism Is a Humanism*, 31.
3. Sartre, *Existentialism Is a Humanism*, 31.
4. Sartre, *Existentialism Is a Humanism*, 33.
5. There are, of course, many differences between Sarte and the Rabbis. Nevertheless, in this manner the Talmud is at least suggestive of the French philosopher.
6. To take one example, the Rabbis imagine that after the Messiah arrives, God will interrogate the nations of the world, accusing many of subjugating the Jews. The Romans, they presume, will defend themselves: "Master of the Universe, we have established many marketplaces, we have built many bath houses, we have accumulated much gold and silver, and all this we did only for the sake of Israel, that they might [have leisure] for occupying themselves with the study of the Torah" (BT Avodah Zarah 2b, Koren Talmud Bavli). However, despite the fact that the Romans are not lying and because of them the Jewish people did enjoy better

infrastructure and smoother economics, God will not listen to their plea. Because supporting God's people was not their intention when making those worldly improvements, the Romans have no moral claim. Their actions are insufficient, because their intent is misplaced.

7. BT Nazir 23a.
8. BT Nazir 23a (Koren Talmud Bavli).
9. BT Nazir 23b (Koren Talmud Bavli).
10. BT Horayot 10b.
11. At times the Rabbis do speak disparagingly of the daughters' actions. See Num. Rabbah 20:30.
12. The Rabbis have no problem applying their norms to biblical characters, even those who lived before Sinai and who are not Jewish. Thus, they could have condemned the daughters for breaking commandments that had not yet been given.
13. Lev. 18:15 prohibits a father-in-law from sleeping with his daughter-in-law.
14. BT Nazir 23b.
15. The Torah also implies that Israelites who slept with Midianite women were engaging in idolatry. See Num. 25:1.
16. The Kenites, a nomadic tribe, had peaceful relations with the Israelites.
17. See Judg. 5:27.
18. BT Nazir 23b.
19. BT Nazir 23b.
20. Different camps of Rabbis viewed marital intimacy in divergent ways. To one camp, marital intimacy was supposed to be pleasurable and sacred in strengthening the marriage; to the other camp it was only to be performed for procreation and any enjoyment was considered sacrilegious. The worldview of this text falls into the latter camp. The fact that Yael does not enjoy sex means that it was solely done to protect the Jews and thus is a selfless act.
21. One midrash teaches the practical adage, "On the day a guest arrives, a calf is slaughtered in his honor; the next day, a sheep, the third day, a fowl, and on the fourth day, he is served just beans" (Midrash Psalms 23:3). Another text (BT Shabbat 127a) teaches that Abraham made God wait until the patriarch had served three strangers who had stopped to ask him for food and rest, so important is hospitality to the general good.
22. See Exod. Rabbah 4:4 for a discussion of this. For more on the Rabbinic approach to Yael, see Tamar Kadri, "Jael Wife of Heber the Kenite: Midrash and Aggadah," *Shalvi/Hyman Encyclopedia of Jewish Women*,

https://jwa.org/encyclopedia/article/jael-wife-of-heber-kenite-midrash-and-aggadah.
23. Urbach, *Halakhah*, 130–38.
24. Philosopher Michael Walzer is the first to name this the problem of "dirty hands." See Waltzer, "Political Action," 160–80.
25. BT Gittin 55b–56a.
26. BT Gittin 56a (Koren Talmud Bavli).
27. BT Gittin 56a (Koren Talmud Bavli).
28. BT Gittin 56a (Koren Talmud Bavli).
29. BT Bava Kamma 117a (Koren Talmud Bavli)
30. See BT Bava Kamma 117a. Unlike the story of Rav Kahana, these cases involve monetary penalties or excommunication for the *moser*, not murder.
31. BT Bava Kamma 117a (Koren Talmud Bavli)
32. BT Avodah Zarah 26a–b.
33. BT Bava Kamma 119a (Koren Talmud Bavli). Although the Talmud does not decide on this answer, later authorities do rule that it is not permitted to destroy a *moser*'s property, for the reason expressed. See Mishneh Torah, Hilkhot ḥovel u'mazik 8:11.
34. To modern commentators the ostensible distinction between daytime and nighttime thievery lies in the thieves' expectations. At night, when the inhabitants are presumably home but sleeping, thieves are prepared for possible confrontations, and so homeowners may need to kill to protect their property and family. In the daytime, when thieves expect people to be at work, school, or the market, they do not anticipate potential violence. They break in with the sole thought of stealing what they can, and when caught, they will be surprised and flee. For one articulation of this view, see Lieber, *Eitz Hayim*, 465.
35. BT Sanhedrin 72a (Koren Talmud Bavli).
36. BT Sanhedrin 72a (Koren Talmud Bavli).
37. BT Sanhedrin 72b.
38. BT Sanhedrin 72a (Koren Talmud Bavli).
39. M Sanhedrin 8:6 (Koren Talmud Bavli).
40. M Sanhedrin 8:5. This is not the only time the Talmud holds a person accountable for a sin the individual will probably commit. The present discussion of the thief follows a discussion of the rebellious son who is taken into the town square and presented to a court that will choose whether or not to stone him at his parents' behest (Deut. 21:18–21). Since

his behavior presages much worse conduct that will be liable for the death penalty, one is allowed to preclude future suffering by ending his life now (M Sanhedrin 8:5).

41. M Sanhedrin 8:7 (Koren Talmud Bavli).
42. Sifra Kedoshim 4:8.
43. Mishneh Torah, Hilkhot Rotzeach v'Shmirat Nefesh 1:7.
44. The Talmud does contain Jewish texts with values at odds with the practice of causing another physical or psychological pain, but few texts link those values directly with the issue of torture (even if the narratives of torture are not glorified). These include the prohibitions against oppressing strangers (based on Lev. 19:33); the fact that all humans are created in God's image (see Gen. 1:27); the Jewish commitment to human dignity (*kevod habriyot*, see BT Berakhot 19b; BT Shabbat 81b and 94b; BT Eruvin 41b; and BT Megillah 3b); and the principle that we sin when we stand idly by another's blood (Lev. 19:16). For a fuller discussion of these and others, see Crane, "Torture, Judaic Twists," 469–504. Even fewer texts appear to set limits on torture. Many anti-torture readings of the Talmud observe that torture is not glorified in Rabbinic anecdotes and narratives. When the Rabbis tell of the oppression they've faced at the hands of foreign legions, they often go into gory detail about their own torture. For example, BT Avodah Zarah 8b tells of the torturing of Rabbi Yehudah ben Bava by the Romans, who "inserted three hundred iron spears [*lulniot*] into his body, making his body appear like a sieve" (Koren Talmud Bavli). Jonathan Crane suggests that stories relaying the Rabbis' own experiences of torture may serve as cautionary tales aimed at turning readers off the idea of torture altogether. For more see Crane, "Torturous Ambivalence," 602. Additionally, the Rabbis do not consider modern concerns around torture, such as whether it yields usable information or whether it destroys the moral authority of those who employs it.
45. BT Sanhedrin 85a.
46. BT Sanhedrin 58b (Koren Talmud Bavli). The Rabbis base this on Eli's sons, who threaten others and are called sinners. See 1 Sam. 2:17.
47. Shaming, especially in the Rabbinic study hall, appears in numerous places in the Talmud. For a comprehensive study on shame in Rabbinic culture see Rubenstein, *The Culture of the Babylonian Talmud*, 67–80.
48. BT Bava Metzi'a 58b (Koren Talmud Bavli).
49. BT Berachot 43b (Koren Talmud Bavli)

50. M Arakhim 5:6 (Koren Talmud Bavli).
51. BT Arakhim 21b.
52. The vow involves a promise not to benefit from his property, which would make it impossible for him to adequately care for her as a husband is obligated to do.
53. These laws can be found in Deut. 25:5–10.
54. JT Yevamot 13:14.
55. BT Sanhedrin 7b tells of the people carrying Mar Zutra Hasida on their shoulders enroute to his lectures because of their profound respect for him.
56. BT Bava Metzi'a 24a (Koren Talmud Bavli). The Talmud is silent on the veracity of the student's confession.
57. See Rosh on BT Bava Metzi'a 24a.
58. See Meiri on BT Bava Batra 167a.
59. BT Bava Batra 167a.
60. BT Bava Batra 167a.
61. Since a fetus is "mere water" before forty days, a very early pregnancy is not considered a "miscarriage" to the same extent as a later pregnancy. This has implications for a women's purity status after losing the fetus and whether the couple's next child will have "firstborn" status. See BT Yevamot 69b.
62. BT Niddah 25b.
63. See the writings of J. David Bleich and Michael Broyde, esp. Bleich, "Torture and the Ticking Bomb," 89–121; and Michael Broyde, "Jewish Law and Torture," *Jewish Week* (New York), July 7, 2006, http://www.broydeblog.net/uploads/8/0/4/0/80408218/jewish_law_and_torture.pdf.
64. There are significant risks in using talmudic precedents to legislate for modern torture. For one, this ignores the more than millennia of discussion around torture that has appeared since the Talmud. For a discussion of some of this historical conversation see Crane, "Torture, Judaic Twists," 469–504.
65. For a fuller explanation of Amir's writings and philosophy, see Ephron, *Killing of King*, 85–109.
66. Ephron, *Killing a King*, 195.

9. Misuse of Pragmatism

1. Ramban, Commentary on Lev. 19:2.

2. BT Bava Metzi'a 83a.
3. BT Bava Kamma 99b.
4. The example the Talmud uses centers around a set of experts who unknowingly encounter a newly minted, novel coin. Since they have never seen it before, they have no basis to assess its value.
5. BT Bava Kamma 99b (Koren Talmud Bavli).
6. BT Bava Kamma 99b (Koren Talmud Bavli).
7. It is originally derived from Exod. 18:20. The Midrash reads: "And you shall show them" (Exod. 18:20); this is referring to the core of their existence, [i.e., Torah study, which is the source of life.] "The way"; this is referring to acts of kindness. "They must walk"; this is referring to visiting the sick. "Wherein"; this is referring to the burial of the dead. "The work"; this [is referring to conducting oneself in accordance with] the law. "That they must do"; this is referring to conducting oneself beyond the letter of the law (Bava Kamma 99b–100a Koren Talmud Bavli).
8. BT Bava Metzi'a 24b.
9. BT Bava Metzi'a 24b.
10. BT Ketubot 97a.
11. BT Bava Metzi'a 30b.
12. BT Yoma 9b.
13. See *Beit Yitzchak* 26:140.
14. For a good exploration of this question, see Lichtenstein, "Does Judaism Recognize?," 62–88. See also Barer, "Law, Ethics, and Hermeneutics," 9–30.
15. BT Bava Metzi'a 16b. Furthermore, he must sell it at the original cost, not factoring in appreciation. See BT Bava Metzi'a 35a.
16. See BT Bava Metzi'a 108a, BT Bava Kamma 114a, Ketubot 44a.
17. BT Bava Metzi'a 108a.
18. Halakhah follows the Nehardeans. According to Jewish law, a neighbor may take possession of the land from the new buyer. This underscores that *dina d'bar metzra* is a requirement. See Mishneh Torah, Hilkhot Shekhenim 12:5.
19. See Gen. 19:1–38 for the full story of Sodom.
20. Gen. 18:20 reads: "Then God said, 'The outrage of Sodom and Gomorrah is so great, and their sin so grave!'"
21. Prophets like Ezekiel credit the arrogance and avarice of Sodom's residents. See Ezek. 16:49–50, "Only this was the sin of your sister Sodom: arrogance! She and her daughters had plenty of bread and untroubled

tranquility; yet she did not support the poor and the needy. In their haughtiness, they committed abominations before Me; and so I removed them."

22. Perhaps the most famous view as to why they are killed points to their lack of hospitality. See BT Sanhedrin 109b.
23. M. Avot 5:10 (Koren Talmud Bavli).
24. Lichtenstein, "Does Judaism Recognize an Ethic?," 75.
25. This case study only concerns the man's sons since at the time, women were not allowed to inherit land when it could pass down the male line.
26. BT Bava Batra 12b.
27. BT Bava Batra 168a.
28. BT Bava Batra 168a (Koren Talmud Bavli).
29. The Talmud gives an example of a legitimate business reason: a business partner who realizes that the two partners no longer are aligned in their business goals: "It is not amenable for me that your defense, [i.e., the record of your claims], should be together with my defense, as you are to me like an ambushing lion, [i.e., our interests are in conflict]." BT Bava Batra 168a (Koran Talmud Bavli).
30. These rulings open the door for a corollary principle stating that if you have the ability to benefit someone and doing so doesn't harm you, you must allow that benefit to happen. The Rabbis employ the classic example of an owner of a domicile who discovers a squatter living there and asks the squatter to pay for the time spent in the domicile. Since the owner was not trying to rent the domicile during the period of illegal habitation, and provided the squatter has not damaged the place, there is no loss on the owner's part. Hence, the owner has no claim against the squatter, as "one benefits and the other has no loss" (BT Bava Kamma 20b).
31. Some Rabbis criticize the Hasid for being overly concerned with religious purity. See BT Sotah 21b, where the Rabbis reproach a Hasid for being hesitant to save a drowning woman because he might accidentally see her naked in the process.
32. M Avot 5:10.
33. BT Ḥullin 130b.
34. BT Ḥullin 130b.
35. BT Shabbat 120a.
36. BT Bava Metzi'a 52b.
37. BT Bava Kamma 55b. In shorthand this principle is called *Dinei Shamayim*, the judgment of heaven.

38. For an in-depth explanation of these laws see Rubenstein, "The 'Laws of Heaven,'" 80–82.
39. BT Bava Kamma 55b.
40. The Rabbis speak a great deal about the fear of angering God. See Mekhilta de-Rabbi Yishmael 22:23 and Sifrei Deut. 43:24.
41. An alternative translation would be "punishment."
42. M Bava Metzi'a 4:2.
43. God brings a flood that wipes out the entire human population except for Noah and his family. See esp. Gen. 6:9–7:22.
44. There is little consensus regarding what was wrong with building the tower. Some commentators see it as humanity's attempt to wrest power from God (Gen. Rabbah 38:6). Others see their need for punishment as stemming from the fact that the builders cared more about the building than the people who were building it, and thus took advantage of their workers (Pirke de-Rabbi Eliezer 24).
45. Lev. Rabbah (Emor) 26:2. The Rabbis use this phrase as a positive; here the inverse is used to make a different point.
46. BT Sanhedrin 21b (Koren Talmud Bavli).
47. BT Shabbat 23b.
48. BT Shabbat 39b.
49. BT Shabbat 39b.
50. BT Berachot 64a and BT Horayot 14a.
51. M. Avot 5:22.
52. Generations of scholars struggled to prioritize the two categories of thinkers before coming to this conclusion. See BT Horayot 14a: Rabbi Yoḥanan said, Rabban Shimon ben Gamliel and the Rabbis disagreed with regard to this matter. One said: Sinai, [i.e., one who is extremely knowledgeable], is preferable; and one said: One who uproots mountains, [i.e., one who is extremely incisive], is preferable (Koren Talmud Bavli).
53. BT Berachot 64a and BT Horayot 14a (Koren Talmud Bavli).
54. *Ein Ayah* on *Berakhot Ein*, found in Rav Yitzchak Blau, "Breadth, Depth and Choosing a Rosh Yeshiva," Torat Har Etzion, January 17, 2016, https://www.etzion.org.il/en/shiur-1-breadth-depth-and-choosing-rosh-yeshiva.
55. See Ramah cited by HaKoteiv in Ein Yaakov.
56. Perhaps the most notable example of this occurs in the Rabbinic discussion of which fruit Adam and Eve ate in the Garden of Eden. Some Rabbis assume the fruit was actually wheat. Just as children usually begin to speak once they can eat bread, so too were Adam and Eve introduced

to the "knowledge of good and evil" once they ate wheat. See BT Berachot 40a.
57. See Rashi to BT Berachot 64b sv. L'marei Chitah.
58. Levy Cooper, "World of the Sages: Foundations of a Mountain," *Jerusalem Post*, July 25, 2007, https://www.jpost.com/jewish-world/judaism/world-of-the-sages-foundations-of-a-mountain.
59. Bialik, "Halacha and Aggadah," 45–87.
60. BT Sukkah 31b (Koren Talmud Bavli).
61. Simon-Shoshan, "Talmud as Novel," 129.
62. BT Sukkah 31a.
63. For this discussion, see BT Bava Batra 8b.
64. M Gittin 4:6 (Koren Talmud Bavli).
65. BT Gittin 45a (Koren Talmud Bavli).
66. See Rashi on BT Gittin 45a, S.V. *b'tlisar alphei dinarei*, who acknowledges this but tries to parse the difference between an individual and a community paying more than a person is worth.
67. See BT Gittin 58a, when R. Yehoshua ben Hannania saves a child held captive in Rome for much more than he is worth, and the child grows up to become the great Rabbi Yishmael ben Elisha.
68. For one famous example, see Halevi, *Aseh Lekha Rav*, vol. 7, no. 53.
69. BT Sanhedrin 6b.
70. Author's translation. RJPS reads: "What do we gain by killing our brother and covering up his blood?"
71. BT Sanhedrin 6b. RJPS, for example, translates the word *botzea* in Prov. 1:19 to mean those who "pursue unjust gain."

Final Thoughts

1. BT Berachot 28b (Koren Talmud Bavli).
2. BT Berachot 28b (Koren Talmud Bavli).
3. Soloveitchik, *The Rav Speaks*, 52.

BIBLIOGRAPHY

Ancselovits, Elisha. "The Prosbul—A Legal Fiction?" *Jewish Law Annual* 19 (2011): 1–16.
Barer, Deborah. "Law, Ethics, and Hermeneutics: A Literary Approach to Lifnim Mi-Shurat Ha-Din." *Journal of Textual Reasoning* 10, no. 1 (2018): 9–30.
Berkowits, Eliezer. *Not in Heaven: The Nature and Function of Jewish Law (Contemporary Jewish Thought)*. Jerusalem: Shalem, 2010.
Berkowitz, Beth. *Execution and Invention: Death Penalty Discourse in Early Rabbinic and Christian Cultures*. London: Oxford University Press, 2006.
Bialik, Haim Nahman. "Halacha and Aggadah." Translated by Leon Simon. In *Revealment and Concealment: Five Essays*, edited by Leon Simon, 45–87. Jerusalem: Ibis, 2000.
Bleich, David J. "Torture and the Ticking Bomb." *Tradition: Journal of Orthodox Jewish Thought* 39, no. 4 (2006): 89–121.
Cedar, Joseph, dir. *Footnote*. United King Films, 2011.
Cohen, Shaye. *From the Maccabees to the Mishnah*. 3rd ed. Louisville KY: Westminster John Knox, 2014.
Cox, Damian, Marguerite La Caze, and Michael Levine. "Integrity." *The Stanford Encyclopedia of Philosophy*, accessed October 1, 2023. https://plato.stanford.edu/archives/fall2021/entries/integrity.
Crane, Jonathan. "Because . . . : Justifying Law/Rationalizing Ethics." *Journal of the Society of Christian Ethics* 55, no. 1 (Spring-Summer 2005): 55–77.
———. "Torture, Judaic Twists." *Journal of Law and Religion* 26, no. 2 (2010): 469–504.
———. "Torturous Ambivalence." *Journal of Religious Ethics* 39, no. 4 (2011): 598–605.
Dohrmann, Natalie B. "Ad similitudinem arbitrorum: On the Perils of Commensurability and Comparison in Roman and Rabbinic Arbitration Law."

In *Legal Engagement: The Reception of Roman Tribunals and Law by Jews and Other Provincials of the Roman Empire*, edited by Katell Berthelot, Natalie B. Dohrmann, and Capucine Nemo-Pekelman, 365–85. Rome: Publications de l'École française de Rome, 2021.

Ephron, Dan. *Killing a King: The Assassination of Yitzhak Rabin and the Remaking of Israel.* New York: Norton, 2015.

Erez, Edna, and Kathy Laster. "Capital Punishment in Jewish Law" in *Routledge Handbook on Capital Punishment*, edited by Robert M. Bohm and Gavin. M. Lee, 218–30. New York: Taylor & Francis, 2018.

Fishman, Talya. *Becoming the People of the Talmud: Oral Torah as Written Tradition in Medieval Jewish Cultures.* Philadelphia: University of Pennsylvania Press, 2013.

Fonrobert, Charlotte Elisheva, and Martin S. Jaffee, eds. *The Cambridge Companion to the Talmud and Rabbinic Literature.* Cambridge, UK: Cambridge University Press, 2007.

Gratz, Heinrich. *History of the Jews.* 3rd ed. Vol. 4. Philadelphia: JPS, 1894.

Halevi, Hayyim David. *Aseh Lekha Rav.* 9 vols. Sefaria.org.

Hayes, Christine. "'In the West, They Laughed at Him': The Mocking Realists of the Babylonian Talmud." *Journal of Law, Religion and State* 2 (2013): 137–67.

———. *What's Divine About Divine Law? Early Perspectives.* Princeton NJ: Princeton University Press, 2015.

Hezser, Catherine. "The Mishnah and Roman Law: A Rabbinic Compilation of ius civile for the Jewish civitas of the Land of Israel under Roman Rule." In *What Is the Mishnah? The State of the Question*, edited by Shaye J. D. Cohen, 141–66. Cambridge MA: Harvard University Press, 2023.

———. "What Was Jewish about Jewish Slavery in Late Antiquity?" In *Slavery, Cultural Discourses, and Identity, Part 2*, edited by Chris L. de Wet, Maijastina Kahlos, and Ville Vuolanto, 129–48. Cambridge, UK: Cambridge University Press, 2022.

Hidary, Richard. *Dispute for the Sake of Heaven: Legal Pluralism in the Talmud.* Providence RI: Brown Judaic Studies, 2010.

Jacobs, Jill. *There Shall Be No Needy: Pursuing Social Justice through Jewish Law and Tradition.* Woodstock VT: Jewish Lights: 2010.

James, William. *Pragmatism: A New Name for Some Old Ways of Thinking.* Cambridge MA: Harvard University Press, 1975.

———. *Will to Believe and Other Essays.* In *The Complete Works of William James.* London: Delphi, 2018. Kindle.

Kaniel, Ruth Kara-Ivanov. "'Gedolah Aveirah Lishmah': Mothers of the Davidic Dynasty: Feminine Seduction and the Development of Messianic Thought, from Rabbinic Literature to R. Moshe Haim Luzzatto." *Nashim: A Journal of Jewish Women's Studies & Gender Issues* 24 (Spring 2013): 27–52.

Kimelman, Reuven. "A Jewish Understanding of War and Its Limits." In *Confronting Omnicide: Jewish Reflections on Weapons of Mass Destruction*, edited by Daniel Landes, 82–99. Northvale NJ: Jason Aronson, 1991.

Kugel, James. *How to Read the Bible: A Guide to Scripture, Then and Now*. New York: Free Press, 2007.

Labendz, Jenny. *Socratic Torah: Non-Jews in Rabbinic Intellectual Culture*. Oxford, UK: Oxford University Press, 2013.

Lichtenstein, Aharon. "Does Judaism Recognize an Ethic Independent of Halakhah?" In *Modern Jewish Ethics: Theory and Practice*, edited by Marvin Fox, 62–88. Columbus: Ohio State University Press, 1975.

Lieber, David. *Etz Hayim: Torah and Commentary*. New York: Rabbinical Assembly/United Synagogue of Conservative Judaism, 2001.

Maccoby, Hyam. *The Philosophy of the Talmud*. Milton Park, UK: Routledge, 2010.

Margalit, Avishai. *On Compromise and Rotten Compromises*. Princeton NJ: Princeton University Press, 2009.

Mor, Menahem. *The Second Jewish Revolt: The Bar Kokhba War, 132–136 ce*. Leiden: Brill, 2016.

Neis, Rafael Rachel. *When a Human Gives Birth to a Raven: Rabbis and the Reproduction of Species*. Oakland: University of California Press, 2023.

Neusner, Jacob. *A History of the Jews in Babylonia*. Studia post-Biblica, 5 vols. Leiden: Brill, 1966–1969.

———. *Development of a Legend: Studies on the Traditions Concerning Yoḥanan Ben Zakkai*. Leiden: Brill, 1970.

Pomeranz, Yoni. "Ordinary Jews in the Babylonian Talmud." PhD diss., Yale University, 2016.

Rosenak, Avinoam. "Truth Tests, Educational Philosophy, and Five Models of the Philosophy of Jewish Law." *Hebrew Union College Annual* 78 (2007): 149–82.

Rubenstein, Jeffrey. *The Culture of the Babylonian Talmud*. Baltimore: Johns Hopkins University Press, 2003.

———. "The 'Laws of Heaven' in Sefer Hasidim." In *Freedom and Responsibility: Exploring the Challenges of Jewish Continuity*, edited by Rela Mintz Geffen and Marsha Bryan Edelman, 69–89. New York: Ktav, 1998.

Saiman, Chaim. *Halakhah: The Rabbinic Idea of Law*. Princeton NJ: Princeton University Press, 2020.

Sartre, Jean-Paul. *Existentialism Is a Humanism*. New Haven CT: Yale University Press, 2007.

Schwartz, Seth. *Imperialism and Jewish Society: 200 bce to 640 ce*. Princeton NJ: Princeton University Press, 2001.

Shapiro, Marc B. *Between the Yeshiva World and Modern Orthodoxy: The Life and Works of Rabbi Jehiel Jacob Weinberg, 1884–1966*. Liverpool: Littman Library of Jewish Civilization, 1999.

Simkovich, Malka Z. *Discovering Second Temple Literature: The Scriptures and Stories That Shaped Early Judaism*. Philadelphia: JPS, 2018.

Simon-Shoshan, Moshe. "Talmud as Novel." *Poetics Today* 40, no. 1 (2019): 105–34.

Soloveitchik, Joseph. *The Rav Speaks: Five Addresses on Israel, History, and the Jewish People*. Brooklyn NY: Ktav, 2002.

Stein, Elana. "Rabbinic Legal Loopholes: Formalism, Equity and Subjectivity." PhD diss., Columbia University, 2014.

Stone, Suzanne Last. "Tolerance versus Pluralism in Judaism." *Journal of Human Rights* 2, no. 1 (2003): 105–17.

Twain, Mark. *Adventures of Huckleberry Finn*. Mineola NY: Dover, 1994.

Urbach, Ephraim. *Halakhah: Its Sources and Development*. Moshav Ben Shemen Mosh, Israel: Modan, 1988.

———. *The Sages: Their Concepts and Beliefs*. Jerusalem: Hebrew University/Magnes Press, 1975.

Visotzky, Burton. *Aphrodite and the Rabbis: How the Jews Adapted Roman Culture to Create Judaism as We Know It*. New York: St. Martin's, 2016.

Waltzer, Michael. "Political Action: The Problem of Dirty Hands." *Philosophy & Public Affairs* 2, no. 2 (Winter 1973): 160–80.

Wiesel, Elie. *Filled with Fire and Light: Portraits and Legends from the Bible, Talmud, and Hasidic World*. New York: Schocken, 2021.

Williams, Bernard, and J. J. C. Smart. *Utilitarianism: For and Against*. Cambridge: Cambridge University Press, 1973.

Wurzberger, Walter. *Ethics of Responsibility: Pluralistic Approaches to Covenantal Ethics*. Philadelphia: JPS, 1994.

Zakheim, Dov S. *The Prince and the Emperors: The Life and Times of Rabbi Judah the Prince*. New Milford CT: Maggid, 2021.

SUBJECTS INDEX

Aaron, 16, 48–52
Abba Sikkara, 1–2, 8
Abraham, 59, 186
acquisition, laws of, 71, 106, 113–15
adultery, 41, 81, 104, 117–18, 158, 167
agunah, 206n25. *See also* adultery
Ahasuerus, King, 31
Akavya ben Mehalalel, 44–47
Akiva, 10, 16, 29, 86
Am ha-Aretz (Am Haaretz), 88, 206nn4–5
Amir, Yigal, 169
Ammonites, 156
Antoninus, 92–93
Aphrodite, 101–3
arevut, 112
Asher Ben Yechiel (the Rosh), 121

Babel, tower of, 180
Balaam, 68
bar Kamtza, 159–61
bedieved, 70–73
Ben Bag Bag, 183
Ben-Haroush, Yoram, 170
ben sorrer u'moreh, 132–34
Ben Temalyon, 99
Bialik, Hayim Nachman, 185

binding, 168–69
botzea, 189–90
Breisch, Mordechai Yaakov, 199

Canaanites, 78, 158
captives, law of, 188–89
Cestius Gallus, 9
charity, 106–7
childbirth, 59, 108–9
Christianity, 56, 154
compromise: and integrity, 40, 44–47, 49; in the courtroom, 47–51; messiness of, 40–43, 125; risk of avoiding, 37–40
Cooper, Levy, 184

David, King, 6, 157
death penalty, 133–34
Deborah, 77–79
debts, 141–42
dina d'bar metzra, 175–77
dina d'malkhulta dina, 105–6

Eliezer ben Hurcanus, 13–14, 18–19, 28–31, 48–49, 146
Esau, 93
Essenes, xii
Exilarch, 55, 186

fallibilism, 192
field owners, laws for, 143, 175–77
folk sayings, 186–87
fox parables, 85, 97–98

Gamliel II, 6–8, 15–18, 29, 101–3, 118
Gehenna, 159, 191
gemilut ḥasadim, 130, 217n8
get (document), 117–18, 167
Golden Calf, 27, 51–52

halakha v'ein morin ken, 62
ḥalitzah, 168
Hayes, Christine, xiii, 135, 197n16
heresh, 115, 214n14
Hezekiah, King, 37–39
Hillel, 8, 24–28, 40–44, 63–64, 76–79, 141–42
Holocaust, 105, 119
Honi the Circle Drawer, 86
Hosea, 130–31
humility, 18, 26, 32, 37, 78, 161

idolatry, 20, 38, 52, 94–95, 101–2, 106–9, 153, 165, 181
ir ha-nidaḥat, 133–34
integrity, 44–47, 82, 154. *See also* compromise
intent: as loophole, 102, 145–47, 182; God's, 24; in sin, 59, 61–62, 154–59; and sinners, 163–66
Isaiah, 37–39, 157

Jacob (Bible), 92–93
Jacobs, Jill, 116
James, William, xx, 21
Jephthah, 39–40

Jerusalem: authority of, 135–36, 142; destruction of, 1–9, 58, 100, 130–31, 160; sacrifices in, 65, 141
Judah (Bible), 156–57, 189–90
Judah the Prince, xiii, 84, 92–93, 109–10, 149
Judges, 14–18, 23–24, 133–34, 142, 173
Judges, book of, 78

kalan, 115, 214n14
killing. *See* murder
Kook, Abraham Isaac, 74, 183
kerovin l'malkhut, 92
Kugel, James, 127–28

Levi bar Darga, 188–89
l'hatḥilah, 70–73
"Liable to law of heaven," 179–80
Lichtenstein, Aaron, 176
Lifnim mishurat ha-din, 172–74
Loft of hananiah, 26
loopholes, 114, 139–47, 178, 182–83
lo titgodedu, 119–22, 216n29, 216n32, 216n34
Lot's daughters, 155–56
lulav, 128, 137, 139

ma'arit ayin, 110
ma'aser sheni, 141
Maimonides, 72, 121, 165–66
mamzer, 41, 118. *See also* adultery
Margalit, Avishai, 37
Marta bat Baitos, 1
menstrual purity, 72, 98–100, 147–48, 169
Messiah, 157

Midianite, 157
midat ḥasidut, 177–79
midat sedom, 176–77
mipnei darkhei shalom, 106–8, 113–14
mipnei tikkun ha-olam, 116–18, 188
mishum eivah, 108–10
moserim, 159–63, 169–70
Moses, xiii, 16–17, 33, 67, 121, 129, 136
murder, xii, 2, 29, 52, 94, 105, 158, 161–70, 189

Nachmanides, 171
Nazarites, 57
Nehardeans, 175
Nehemiah, 91–92
Neusner, Jacob, 75
new moon, 15, 137, 144

otzar beit din, 141–45
Oven of Akhnai, 33

Passover, 6, 71–72, 105, 120, 140, 154
pesik reisha, 146–47
piku'aḥ nefesh, 105
Pharisees, 7, 111
pragmatism (defined), xii, 21
Proclus ben Prospus, 101–2
proof texts, 127–30
Prozbul, 141–42

Rabin, Yitzhak, 169–70
ramayin, 182
rape, 80, 156, 165
Rava Bar Bar Hana, 85, 171
rebuke, 4, 39, 54–56, 61, 86, 166
Reuven ben Isterobeli, 98–100

"Right and good" principle, 174–75
robbers: permission to kill, 163–64; returning stolen property, 51, 86, 123–25
rodef, 165–66, 169–70
Rome, 1–5, 7, 9, 59, 93, 95, 98–100, 159–60
Rosh Hashanah, 15, 66, 71, 135
rumors, 79–83

Sadducees, xii, 7, 111
Saimen, Chaim, xiv
Sanhedrin, 6, 135
Sartre, Jean-Paul, 153–54
Second Temple, xii, 1, 6, 100, 111, 159–60
sha'at ha-deḥak, 138–39
sha'at ha-sakanah, 138–39
Shabbat: carrying on, 61, 77, 135, 139, 140, 178; dancing and singing during, 60–61; loopholes for, 77, 139–40, 145, 178; and mishuh eivah, 108–9; roman prohibitions against, 98–99
Shammai, 8–9, 25–27, 36, 40–44, 111
Shapur, King, 93–94
shemitah, 143
Shimon-Shoshan, Moshe, 186–87
shofar, shofarot, 15, 66, 71, 73, 135–37
shoteh, 115, 214n14
Sinai vs. *oker harim*, 183–84
sinat ḥinam, 173–74
sinning: for the sake of heaven, 154–59; unwitting vs. intentional, 58–62
Sisera, 78, 158

Sodom, 155–56, 175–77
Solomon, King, 40, 180–83
Soloveitchik, Joseph, 192
Sons of B'terah, 76–77
stam, 4, 187
stumbling blocks, 57–58
subterfuge, 98–100, 110, 144–45
Sukkot, 128, 137, 139, 187

Takkanot: analysis of, 134–38; and takkanat ha-shavim, 122–24; and takkanat ha-shuk, 124–25
Tamar, 156–57
tefillin, 62–63, 125–26
terumah, 140
teshuvah, 122–25, 165, 185–87
thieves. *See* robbers
tirḥa d'tzibbura, 68–70
torture, 166–69
truth: and compromise, 41, 48; narrative as, xix–xx, 5; theories of, 18–21, 31–33
tza'ar ba'alei ḥayim, 36, 204n45
Tzadok, Rabbi, 4–5

Urbach, Ephraim, 9, 159

Vespasian, 2–6, 191
Visotzky, Burton, 97

Weinberg, Yechiel Yaakov, 119–22
Wiesel, Elie, 30–31
Williams, Bernard, 47

Yael, 158
Yannai, King, 80–81
Yavne, 3–7, 17, 135–37, 192
Yehoshua ben Levi, 13–18, 21
Yehudah HaNasi. *See* Judah the Prince
yibbum, 167–68
Yochanan ben Zakkai, 1–5, 8–10, 85–86, 97, 130–31, 135–37, 191–92
Yom Kippur, 52; establishing the date of, 15–17, 144; frugality on, 66; and *tircha d'tzibura*, 69

Zakheim, Dov, 35
zealots, xii, 1–5, 7–9, 111

BIBLICAL SOURCES INDEX

Bible
  Genesis
    1:27
    1:28
    6:9–7:22
    19:30, 32
    26:5
    32:5
    37:26–27
    38:25
  Exodus
    13:10
    18:20, 21–22
    20:7
    21:10, 15
    22:1–2
    23:2, 4, 23–24
    24:9
    35:3
  Leviticus
    5:21–24
    16:29
    18:15
    19:14, 16, 17, 33
    22:28
    23:4
    24:40
    25:35–36
    26:36–38, 46
    27:31
  Numbers
    9:2
    10:10
    20:8, 20
    25:1
  Deuteronomy
    1:15–18
    3:25
    4:44
    6:4, 7, 18
    13:2–4, 8, 13–19
    14:1, 22–26
    15:1–2, 3, 9–10
    17:11, 17
    21:18–21
    23:3
    25:5–10
    30:12, 20
    32:7
  Judges
    4:17–22
    5:6–7, 12, 27
    11:35–40
  1 Samuel
    2:17
  2 Samuel
    7:23
  1 Kings
    3:16–28
    8:12
    10:29
    11:4
  2 Kings
    2:3
    3:12
    16:3
    20:12–19
  Isaiah
    10:34
    21:14
    38:1, 5
    44:25
    45:18
    55:1
    58:6–11
  Jeremiah
    30:21
  Ezekiel
    16:49–50
  Hosea
    5:6
    6:4, 6
    8:11–13
    14:10

Zechariah
8:19
Malachi
2:6
Psalms
8:6
10:3
55:23
81:3
Proverbs
1:19
2:20
3:17
4:8
5:16, 17
9:8
11:24
23:23
Nehemiah
1:11–2:1
8:13–15
Daniel
3:21
Mishnah
Berachot
1:3
Ma'aser Sheni
4:3, 4
Shabbat
1:4
15:4
Pesachim
4:1
Yoma
8:1
Sukkah
3:1
Rosh Hashanah

2:9
3:4
4:1, 2, 4
Ta'anit
1:5–6
Megillah
2:1, 2
Ḥagigah
1:8
Yevamot
6:6
15:1, 4
Ketubbot
5:6
Gittin
4:2, 6
5:8
9:9
Bava Kamma
8:1
10:3
Bava Metzi'a
1:1
2:3
3:4–5
4:2
Bava Batra
6:7
Sanhedrin
2:2
3:7
8:2, 3, 5, 6, 7
11:6
Makkot
1:10
Shevuot
7:1, 2
Eduyot

1:12–14
5:6, 7,
7:7
8:7
Avodah Zarah
3:4
4:3
Avot
1:1
5:10, 22
Horayot
2:5
Ḥullin
1:1
Yadayim
6:6–8
Niddah
8:2
Tosefta
Shevi'it
8:1–12
Shabbat
7:2
Pesachim
2:6
8:3
Yoma
1:12
Beitzah
3:4
Sotah
15:8, 10
Gittin
3:3, 18
Bava Metzi'a
3:5
Avodah Zarah
3:10

Arachin
  5:6

Jerusalem Talmud
Ma'aser Sheni
  4:3
Shabbat
  1:4
  2:4
Megillah
  2:3
Kiddushin
  4:1
Yevamot
  4:10
  13:14
Gittin
  3:3
  5:8, 9
Sanhedrin
  4:2
Avodah Zarah
  1:7

Babylonian Talmud
Berachot
  5b
  6a
  10a
  12b
  19a, 19b
  28b
  30b
  40a
  43b
  47b
  61b
  63a

  64a
Shabbat
  12b
  17a
  21b
  23a, 23b
  31a
  39b
  54b
  55a
  81b
  94b
  102b
  103a
  119b
  120b
  127a–b
  148b
Eruvin
  13b
  41b
Pesachim
  22b
  49b
  66a, 66b
  88a, 88b
  105a
  109a
Yoma
  9b
  11b
  13a
  39a
  44b
  52b
  53b
  69a
  70a

  85a
Sukkah
  26a
  28a
  31a, 31b
  41b
  49b
Beitzah
  2b
  28a
  30a
Rosh Hashanah
  20a, 20b
  21b
  25a
  27a
  29b
  31b
Ta'anit
  7a
  18a
  23a
Megillah
  3b
  11a
  18a
Moed Katan
  3a
  5a
  18b
  26a
Ḥagigah
  2a, 2b
  5b
  10a
  11b
  17a

Yevamot
14a, 14b
15b
25a
56b
62b
69b
116b

Ketubot
63a
97a
44a

Nedarim
22b
28a

Nazir
23a, 23b

Sotah
12b
21b

Gittin
2a
10b
22b
36a
41b
45a
55a
55b–56a
58a
60a, 60b
81a

Kiddushin
40a
66a
81b

Bava Kamma
20b
30b
55b
83a
94b
99b
113a, 113b
114a
117a
119a

Bava Metzi'a
24a, 24b
25b
30b
32b
35a
58b
59b
71a
83a
108a

Bava Batra
7b
8a, 8b
12b
54b–55a
60b
73b–74a
74b
86a
167a
168a

Sanhedrin
6b
7a, 7b
8b
17a
19a–b
21b
27b
30b
31a
37a
40b
58b
70b
71a
72a, 72b
74a
85a
92b
103b
109b

Shevuot
39a

Avodah Zarah
2b
4b
6b
8a, 8b
10a–b
12b
17b
18b
26a–b
28a
44b

Horayot
10b
11a
14a

Menachot
29b
36b
41b
76b
86b

93a	**Midrash**	68:4
99b	Mekhilta de-Rabbi	75:5
Hullin	Yishmael	87:7
5a	20:22	Leviticus Rabbah
7b	22:23	26:2
46b	Sifra	Numbers Rabbah
92b	Kedoshim, 2:14	3:2
106b–107a	Bechukotai 8:10	20:30
130b	Kedoshim 4:8	Avot de-Rabbi
Arachin	Sifrei Deuteronomy	Natan
2b	34:4	4:5
15b	43:24	12:3
21b	113:3	37:4
Meilah	346:2	Midrash Psalms
17a, 17b	Genesis Rabbah	12:3
Niddah	4:4	23:3
25b	17:7	Pirkei de-Rabbi
58b	38:26	Eliezer
61a	60:3	Chapter 24